INTRUDERS FROM THE UNSEEN WORLD

INTRUDERS FROM THE UNSEEN WORLD

Mary's Story

To Pat Robertson ~

Lexie Fry

Lexie Anderson Fry

Library of Congress Control Number: 2020910387

ISBN-13: 978-1-7352425-0-7

Publisher, L. J. Anderson, Milpitas, CA

www.LexieAndersonFry.com

In Honor and Memory of Mary

A woman of amazing courage, optimism, and fortitude under extraordinary circumstances and adversity. Through five years of suffering, battling demons, she remained strong, even while friends failed to believe.

Not understanding what this was or why it was happening, she wanted others to avoid the suffering she endured.

Hoping others will be set free, she wanted her story told.

PREFACE

For many of us, it's easy to believe God creates us humans for eternity. We grow up thinking one day when we die we will go to heaven. Whether we go to heaven or to the other place, we will live there forever.

God created angels for eternity too. Those of us who have read the Holy Bible, the Word of God, understand that Satan disobeyed God and God cast him from heaven. He took a third of the angels with him, whom we call fallen angels or evil spirits or demons. Demons are intelligent beings with interesting personalities who have been around for thousands of years.

In Jesus' days on earth, demons bothered people just as they bother people today. Jesus cast demons out of people's lives. Someday, Satan and his demons will be confined, but that hasn't happened yet [Revelation 20:1-3]. Because we sometimes label demonic manifestations "illnesses," people may erroneously think demons no longer exist. We attempt to treat these conditions with pills, and fail to acknowledge the actual cause. Although demons are real, they can be defeated.

Andrew Wommack, in *One Year with Jesus in the Gospels* writes, "Satan would like you to think he is tougher than he really is ... but he has been defeated .... Now he can only roar as a lion seeking to devour uninformed souls who don't know their authority in Christ (1 Pet.5:8). Today, realize that whatever Satan is fighting you with is only temporary. Don't quit. In due season you will reap, if you faint not (Gal.6:8)." He recommends we put on the armor of God. Good advice.

When Mary's experience began (Mary is my mom) it didn't take long for me to recognize her symptoms as demonic, because twenty years earlier I had a similar experience. I inadvertently attracted demons into my life by being unaware of God's protections regarding sin. I hadn't yet read the Bible, and a woman I saw on television who talked about automatic writing influenced me. She used it to contact the dead. In my naiveté I didn't give thought to the possibility of consequences. You will read about my experience in this book.

When in His grace the Lord released me from demonic torment I still had the typed material I accumulated while listening to the voice of a demon spirit. Afterward, through the Holy Spirit, I was told I had been born again and that I must burn those pages. Immediately I placed them in our fireplace, lit a match, and destroyed them. In the Book of Acts (Chapter nineteen, verse nineteen) we're told the people of Ephesus who had been practicing sorcery burned their incantation books (scrolls) at a public bonfire.

Even though I had an experience similar to Mary's, I knew little about these matters and nothing about spiritual warfare. *Mary's Story* was written from a journal I kept during her experience, and you will see as you read her story how we both learned to use Scripture to combat demonic forces. If someone you know has unresolved problems, physical, mental, or spiritual, demons may be at work. This Bible-based book can help. Come with us on Mary's journey as we learn about spiritual beings in the unseen realm.

TABLE OF
CONTENTS

CHAPTER 1
UNWELCOME COMPANY

For God hath not given us the spirit of fear; but of
power, and of love, and of a sound mind.
2 Timothy 1:7 KJV

NEITHER MARY NOR I recall if the kitchen remodel was complete
or not when strange things began happening. The downstairs
neighbors were out of town, and their two Shiatsu dogs were being cared
for by someone staying in their unit. Mary telephoned me complaining
about cigarette smoke coming upstairs. I don't recall her saying when the
music began. Had the neighbors returned home, or was their live-in
puppy-care person still there? Mary called me several times, saying she
hadn't slept very well because the music awakened her.

"What music?" I asked.

"I don't know," she said. "There's music coming from downstairs. It's
not too bad, old tunes, and some songs have a male singer with quite a
good voice."

When I asked, Mary couldn't name any of the music, but said it
sounded like music from perhaps the 1930s or the 1940s, music she had
enjoyed in her earlier years. She continued to hear the music, which she
believed was coming from the downstairs unit. It became a regular thing.
One night the music became louder and kept her from sleeping. The
neighbors were home from their trip, so she telephoned them. It wasn't
too late to call, she reasoned, about 9:30 p.m.

"We don't have any music on," Barbara, the downstairs neighbor, said.
"We're in our bed."

Immediately that got my attention! Where was this music coming
from that Mary heard? Weeks became months, and Mary complained
more and more. And then she told me she heard voices! The singer with
the good voice spoke to her! She talked to me about some things she

heard, all along confirming to me, "I'm not crazy; I'm not!" The voices and the music were most active during the night, which kept her from sleeping. That's not good for anyone, certainly not a ninety-two-year-old. Suddenly I realized demons were tormenting Mary!

Rolling hills surround beautifully landscaped grounds in the senior community where Mary lives. She has a lovely view of hills, trees, and a glimpse of Mt. Diablo through the leaves of a nearby tall redwood. Deer are seen, sometimes walking along paved roads, while wild turkeys stroll the golf course. Amenities include shuttle services, the golf course, tennis courts, pools, a gymnasium, and classrooms where various clubs meet.

After living in the Oakland hills forty-three years, Mary sold her home and came to live with me, her only child. I sell residential real estate and don't always keep regular hours. Sometimes we ate late. I guess regular mealtimes become important as we age. Mary and I had been living together in my home for about two years when she decided—then at the age of 91—to go back to independent living. (Mary isn't a stereotypical ninety-one-year-old. She's spunky, healthy, energetic, and quite independent.) The reason she gave for moving from my home was she didn't want to be "stuck at home," when the day came she could no longer drive.

Mary now lives upstairs in an eight unit building. When she purchased her unit in September 2004, the newer carpeting in the living room didn't match the old stretched carpeting in the hallways and bedrooms. The forty-year-old kitchen remained original. The stovetop was six inches below the countertops, architects possibly expecting residents to be cooking from wheelchairs. Previous owners enclosed the original balcony with glass windows, which increased the home's square footage. "I can use it for an extra sleeping area when the cousins come to visit, and I can have my coffee out here in the mornings," Mary said.

After taking possession of her new home, she wanted to remodel the kitchen. "I've always wanted a blue and white kitchen," she said. We interviewed contractors, shopped for cabinets and appliances, and got the job rolling. The kitchen remodel was stressful for Mary; the job took longer than the estimated completion date given her by the contractor. Mary is a good cook who likes good food. For months she had only her microwave with which to prepare her meals, and she carried her dishes and utensils to the hall bathroom, the closest running water, to wash them.

When mentioning Mary's experience of hearing music and voices to a few friends and relatives, we heard, "Don't be absurd! How do you know? Those things don't exist! It's in her head! She's losing it! She's old; her brain's not right!" In April I talked with one of our Italian cousins who lives in London, and told him about Mary's problem. He said his partner "had called her last week, and she was crying. It's got to be in her head. We're so sorry." He was right about one thing. It was in her head. Demons invaded her soul—the part of us that is our mind and our emotions.

Later that day I spoke with Mary on the telephone. She told me she went grocery shopping, to the gym, and had lunch.

"I'm sick of that noise I hear all day long," she said. "I'm sick of it; it's pounding my ear. It's always sex, sex, sex.

"When I got into the car, I heard, 'Mary, where are you?' I just want to disconnect his voice!"

Mary's sleep has been interrupted for some time now. She is tired and feels helpless. We continued our conversation, and she talked about the lot she owns in Sonora, that she and Russell (her second husband) had purchased in the 1960s. They had planned to build a home and retire there, but he passed away in 1976.

"That lot cost under $3,000 when we bought it," she told me. "I'm having a beer in case you don't know it ... I think this guy's an alcoholic," she said, referring to the voice of the demon.

It's not Mary's custom to drink much alcohol. She might have a glass of wine or a bourbon with lots of ice and a little water when we celebrate birthdays in restaurants, but she doesn't drink often.

The next day I arranged a conference call with Mary and my cousin Sally, Mary's niece. With her Catholic background, Sally might know where to find an exorcist.

Mary was the first child born to Italian immigrants, Antonio and Giulia, in San Francisco. Though named Maria, she went by Mary, just as her younger sister Celestina was called Sally—and later named her own daughter Sally. Maria's and Celestina's mother died during the Spanish flu pandemic of 1918-1920, when Mary was five years old and Aunt Sally was four. Two years later, their father remarried.

"His paesani [friends, countrymen] told him about a widow who would take care of us kids," Mary told us.

Most Italians are Catholic. Mary's step-mother, Maria, made sure both Mary and her sister (my Aunt Sally) participated in the studies necessary to take their first communion. Although Mary doesn't recall attending church after that, Aunt Sally maintained her Catholic beginning. She attended mass regularly, and sent her two children to Catholic schools. Something must have happened to harden Mary's heart. During my growing-up years we didn't attend church, and I remember her saying she had no use for and no interest in going to any church—period.

"I feel like someone's living with me," Mary explained to Sally and me on the telephone. "There's three of them, and they share me. He seems so secure in what he's doing, and he puts these little chips in my house."

"Mom," I said, "There are no chips in your house. He's lying. Demons are of the devil, and the devil is the father of lies [John 8:44]."

(We don't know what "chips" are; we think the evil spirit made it up.)

Neither Sally nor I knew know what to do for Mary. Sally agreed we should find an exorcist, but as she hasn't attended church for many years, she suggested I contact her brother, Bob, who plays in the band at his church. Bob said there are exorcists within the Catholic Church, but they are few and far between, and certainly there were none at his church. He gave me the telephone number of the Diocese of Oakland, the Chancery Office, and suggested I call them. It took several calls before someone answered the phone. I attempted to explain Mary's problem, but no one offered a solution, or even a willingness to help.

Next I talked with Paul, director of the prayer ministry at the Protestant church I attend. He agreed to come out to Mary's home with his wife to see what they could do. On April 7, 2005, I drove Paul and Anita to Mary's home at Walnut Creek. We agreed with him as he prayed, and he anointed the doorways of the rooms of her home with oil. We dedicated her home to the Lord. Paul asked if Mary had anything inappropriate in her home, but after a brief glance, pointed nothing out to us.

I have since learned many things are inappropriate in a Christian home, foreign gods, false religions, occult objects, things that diminish the glory of God. But at the time I didn't understand and failed to pursue it.

The following day I received an email from my neighbor, Donna. We attend the same church and often walk around the neighborhood together. "I've been praying for you and especially your mom. How did it go yesterday?"

I thanked her for her prayers and told her it seemed to go okay yesterday, but Mary heard *them* while we were there. And after I returned home, Mary called me to say she still heard them, but they were quieter. She related to me that one of them asked the main one, "What are you doing? You're supposed to leave; you'll get in trouble." But they haven't left. She still hears them in her mind. No one can hear them but Mary.

†

One morning Mary called and said, "I'm so scared ... " When she called again in the afternoon she seemed more puzzled than scared. I gave her three phrases to tell them if they annoyed her: (1) "I belong to Jesus;" (2) "Jesus has forgiven my sins;" and (3) "In the name of Jesus Christ, go away now." I don't know if this will help, but she wrote them down.

With Paul and Anita we prayed all around Mary's house, and all around Mary. What else can we do? When I told Jack, my former husband, he suggested I call a Christian counselor referral center, which I did. I was told I should write a letter to Mary's doctor and go with her to the doctor to rule out if it's physical before we say it's demonic. Mary said she had already told her doctor, and he said he just wants to know how it comes out. She insists she's not "nuts," and I don't think her doctor thinks she's nuts either. The counselor said our brains are fragile, and it could be medications. But Mary takes minimal meds, only one for blood pressure, and insists it is not altered brain chemistry.

I brought Mary to my house for a few days, but the evil demonic spirits came with her. There is an uncomfortable presence in my home. There is a pressure in my bedroom and in my body, a tingling, shaky sensation. I am making notes of these strange things, and today my computer would not turn on. The lights just blinked every few seconds. I had to unplug and restart my computer.

Mary was here with me when a kind, godly man came over to the house with Anita, Paul's wife. David is an elder at the church I attend. He has read about demons, and he brought a few pages of a book called *The Adversary*. He also brought scriptural references and additional written material he felt might be helpful. David told us, "We have authority over the devil. We have more authority than fallen angels. You [Mary] believe in God, and they cannot have you." Repeating Scripture, we said phrases like:

"He who the Son sets free is free indeed." [John 8:36]

"The enemy comes only to steal and kill and destroy." [John 10:10]

"Submit to God, resist the devil, and he will flee from you." [James 4:7]

"All have sinned and fall short of the glory of God." [Romans 3:23]

"Because he loves us ... by grace you have been saved." [Ephesians 2:4 & 2:8-9]

David led Mary in prayer to invite Jesus into her life and to be her Savior. Paul had done this same thing in Walnut Creek, and both times Mary stumbled on the name Jesus. I mentally noted Paul had overlooked it, but this time I spoke up. It was important for her to get it right. I can suggest two possible reasons for her stumbling on words, and particularly on the name of Jesus. One reason is demons hate Jesus. They know He is the all-powerful Son of God. They know Jesus' crucifixion, resurrection, and ascension into heaven defeated Satan, and one day he and his demons will be thrown into the lake of fire. But they don't want to give Mary up; they want to keep her from the Lord's salvation. Another reason may be because Mary is hard of hearing and David speaks softly.

As noted earlier, Mary has never been a churchgoer. Mary believed in God, but she wasn't sure about Jesus. I knew she was not saved. About five years earlier, I had given her a gift of the *Quiet Time Bible*. It contains the New Testament, the Psalms, and some commentary. But it remained unopened on her bookshelf. I have prayed for her for years. Whenever I tried to talk with her about her need for a Savior, before all this trouble began, she always said, "I pray to *my* God. He knows how I am." Like many, she wanted God her way, instead of submitting herself to the one true living God, and accepting His Son Jesus and the work He did for each of us on the cross.

Years ago, when I experienced a problem with demons, they deprived me of sleep. Now Mary has this problem, and they deprive her of precious sleep. Mary is staying with me again for a few days, and neither of us is getting much sleep. One reason I bring her here to stay at my house is so she will get more sleep and have less interference in her life from these evil spirits. But when Mary comes here, the demons come with her. Last night I didn't get to sleep until after 4:00 a.m. At that time I tried to turn on the light beside my bed to pray for the protection of the armor of the Lord [Ephesians 6:10-18]. The bulb burned out at just that moment. Coincidence?

A heaviness clings to me. Sometimes I feel a burning sensation on my upper back. In my home office I sensed the same heavy dark oppressive presence I experienced when I entered my bedroom yesterday after returning home about 5:30 p.m.

I spoke on the telephone with David. He agrees it is a mental battle. "But is this solely mental, or demonic, or both?" he wondered. He has prayed for clear direction. When he was here praying about religious spirits the other night, Mary said they started getting mad, and he had discerned confirmation, "... truly a demonic presence. A feeling of oppressiveness jives with demonic activity," he said. "The stuff about them being able to read her mind doesn't jive."

He doesn't believe demons can read her mind, although she says they do. She thinks something, and they comment on her thought. This makes sense to me. These spirit beings are *in* her mind. They are there, where she thinks. This is identical to the experience I had, which I will share with you later.

David said, "The devil can put thoughts into your mind. Demons can pick up on your body language. Some activities they engage in with Mary, like singing and talking, are not typical of my experience. One possibility is that they were in her apartment and 'glommed on' to her. I have to be honest ... cases in the past with similar experience, when they finally got on medication the problems went away. There might be a physical component. Be aware of the possibility that it may be physical. If her doctor puts her on medications, take it."

Mary and I also wondered if demons were residing in her home when she moved there. We inquired of the neighbors, and learned that in 1987 a man had died in Mary's unit, and his wife continued to live there until her family moved her away, incapacitated, and they sold the place to Mary. We were told they found the woman one day sleeping in her car. Mary has gone to her car too, attempting to get away from the noises the demons were making.

†

Mary visited her primary care physician. On a prior visit she mentioned hearing voices in her mind, and on this visit she told him she was still hearing voices. He ordered a series of lab tests.

She called me when she returned home and said, "I'm still living with three people. The head demon got mad at me, and said a bad word. He's so angry!" She said he told her he was going to "break glass and smash it in her house."

A few days later, I drove again to Walnut Creek and brought Mary back to my home. David came to the house on Saturday to pray with us in our effort to help Mary get rid of the intrusive spirits. He brought Karen with him, also from church, who has training in spiritual warfare.

David said, "You have to give demons permission to get to you."

I told him Mary gave them permission. When this first started, and I realized from my own experience these were demonic forces, I told her right away she had to oppose the music she was hearing. But she responded to me she liked the music, saying "It's from the old days, and the singer has such a good voice." She wasn't yet a believer, she knew nothing of the unseen world, and she didn't realize the looming danger.

Karen said, "What you need to know when they come at you, is to pray in the name of Jesus, and tell them to go!"

David said, "If you see an image, pray that God will take it away if it's not from Him, or intensify it if it is from God."

David drew from his knowledge of the spirit world. However Mary had not yet seen images; she was only hearing voices. He led us in prayer, then asked Mary if they were still with her.

"I still hear their voices."

David said, "From the spiritual perspective, they think they have some right to be there. We need to find out what that right is so we can ask them to leave."

David again led us in prayer. Mary's practice of reading horoscopes came to mind. She cuts them out of the newspaper and sends them to people on their birthdays. This is an occult activity, grievous to the Lord, and must be avoided. Just as Satan lied to Eve in the Garden of Eden by twisting the truth, horoscopes are partial truth and total deception. Mary understood and renounced those past activities.

Mary told us the names the spirits called each other, in order from least to most dominant. "Abraham, Porgi, and Walter ... they have beautiful voices," she said.

Karen addressed Walter directly, "I bind you spirits ... confusion ... destruction. God has given Mary a spirit of power, love, and a sound mind."

That evening after David and Karen left, Mary and I went out for Chinese food. It would be quicker than cooking. When we got home, together we prayed the warfare prayers Mary says aloud every night, which were posted online by a Canadian Presbyterian church.

Mary came into my room in the middle of the night, afraid.

She said, "He's very faint; where is he?" referring to the demon. "I thought he was in here."

Why did she wonder where he was? Perhaps it's normal to want to know where one's enemy is.

"No," I said, "he's not in here," but I too felt discomfort. How do you fight something you can't see?

We discovered we each had been praying constantly in our own rooms, from the time we said goodnight to each other and gone to bed. I prayed for ministering angels to watch over us and for warrior angels to combat any demons that were here. I know the Lord has not given us a spirit of fear, but I told the Lord that night I was scared, and I prayed until I literally, physically, felt the Holy Spirit (or something!) enter me. It felt like something had pressed right through the entire front of my body. Initially I wondered, "What was that?!" But within a few minutes a calmness come over me. I didn't understand it, but I know He is always with me, and I sincerely welcome His presence. Hours lapsed before I could relax enough to sleep. How many nights has it been now, without sleep?

†

Mary went to church with me today, her first time in church in many years. I prayed the service would have particular relevance for her, but unfortunately the air conditioning made it way too cold and the music was much too loud for her elderly ears. As we walked out following the service, Mary said it surprised her the devil had found her there, at the church. And I had that oppressive burning on my back.

Later in the afternoon I heard Mary talking with JoAnn on the telephone (JoAnn is my step-mom Ann's niece, who lives in Montana). "He's still with me as much as ever, but not as loud. It's from midnight that I got the works .... "

Mary asked me about the Ten Commandments, so I found them for her in the Old Testament [Exodus 20:1-17] and also in the New Testament where Jesus explained the greatest commandment [Matthew 22:36-40]. We looked up Paul the Apostle of Jesus and read his bio from *Everyone in the Bible*. And as has become our habit, we put on the whole armor of God. Suddenly Mary has developed an interest in the Bible! She has experienced the effect the Word of God has on her enemies!

†

This afternoon Mary told me *he* said *he* wanted us to say or do something. While she was still talking I immediately said aloud, "The Lord rebuke you Satan; you must flee from here! Go where the Lord Jesus sends you!" Mary has been telling me she doesn't listen to them as much, which is progress. Sometimes they speak to her directly and sometimes they just talk among themselves and she hears their conversation. Whatever their method, it's all torment. Everything they say or do is their attempt to destroy her.

This remains a trying time. We both have had only one good night's sleep, and we need to gain strength. I still feel a little "creeped" when she relates what Walter has said to her, but I am stronger now, thanks to God and His Word.

Mary and I both love being out in the garden. It seems everything is blooming. The cherry trees, though in leaf, still have some blossoms. The apple is growing into a beautiful tree, and it too is blossoming. I picked oranges today from some higher branches. The orange also has blossoms, and although its fruit keeps well on the tree, it's time to harvest the remaining oranges so the tree can nourish its next crop. The Swiss chard still looks good; I'll pick a bunch for tonight's dinner. Primarily a cool weather crop, it does less well when the days begin to warm.

I hunger for the Word, and would like to spend more time reading the Bible with Mary. I'm eager to share with her some fabulous stories of the Old Testament. Together we read the story of David and Goliath

[1Samuel 17], as it seemed relevant to show her who David was, who wrote so many Psalms we read, enjoy, and find helpful. We also read the story of Adam and Eve in Genesis, which gave Mary an idea of how wily our adversary is, and has always been.

Another bad night. Satan was relentless. Before bed both Mary and I felt his ominous presence. A flying insect dive-bombed me in my room last night. It came right toward me, fast and direct. I saw a small flying insect, and questioned in my mind if the bug that flew at me was a real insect or a fake bug made up by Satan. We have been reading that we are to "cast down imaginations" [2 Corinthians 10:5].

This wasn't the first time I had insects come at me, only to slap my hands together directly on them, and find nothing there. I have seen unreal flying insects with odd, zig-zag flight patterns since this trial began. Mary and I felt so oppressed last night. We prayed together before we went to bed, and then I continued to pray silently in my room, lest the evil one hear. I asked God to cast him out, even though I—as a believer in Jesus Christ—have the authority to cast him out. He is so wicked; he has not fled.

I worry about Mary, her age and her declining health from lack of sleep, as she goes through this ordeal. She was sleeping when I glanced into her room before coming downstairs this morning. I asked the Lord God to keep her strong and alive during this trial. I hope He doesn't bring her home to Him during this time—before the demons are cast out—that Satan doesn't win, but that He and Mary have the victory.

> And the God of all grace, who called you to his eternal glory in Christ, after you have suffered a little while, will himself restore you and make you strong, firm and steadfast. 1Peter 5:10 NIV

I heard the bathroom door shut. Thanks be to God—Mary is up! Satan continues to step up his attacks. He has not left me alone either. I felt that uncomfortable pressure against my back, although I prayed the glory of the Lord be my rear guard [Isaiah 58:8]. Daily, sometimes more than once, Mary and I put on the armor of God. Sometimes the Lord gives me a burst of strength, and I resolve to fight Satan and not to fear him. Faith casts out fear.

CHAPTER 2
THE BATTLE BEGINS

> The LORD said to Satan, "Where have you come
> from?" Satan answered the LORD, "From roaming
> through the earth and going back and forth in it."
> Job 1:7 NIV

I T'S APRIL, AND Mary has been hearing music, noises, and voices since November. She believes her house is haunted, as she has no other explanation for what is happening. Intermittently, she stays with me, in an ineffective attempt to get away from the sounds she hears.

I am certain Mary's trouble is demonic activity, but I don't know why she is targeted. She is of sound mind and she enjoys good health. Her eating habits are good; she prepares her own meals and avoids processed foods. She eats lots of fruits and vegetables, not a lot of meat, and uses mostly olive oil to cook. Before moving to Walnut Creek she enjoyed a garden with fresh, delicious, organic produce and herbs to use in her cooking. She has exercised moderately throughout her life, primarily from maintaining a garden, and after retirement by playing golf. She smoked cigarettes for many years, but gave them up over thirty-five years ago.

As her friends urge her to see a doctor, late one morning the two of us walked into her doctor's office in Oakland. Mary shared the fact with him she has been involuntarily listening to strange voices and sounds. He looked thoughtful, but didn't comment. He heard this before—on her last two visits. Her blood pressure was 116 over 54. He gave us results of her recent lab tests, within normal ranges. I watched him write on her chart. He stayed with what he knew; he didn't comment on Mary hearing voices.

†

When Mary stays with me, the demons come with her and attempt to bother me too. It's 12:52 a.m., and I have not slept. The maniac shoots his darts at me all night. I pray. I verbally resist him—again and again. He assaults me physically by touching nerves, and I need to touch or rub that area on my skin. I asked the Lord to be my rear guard, yet Satan causes my back to feel prickly hot with his flaming arrows. I have "shod my feet with the equipment of the gospel of peace [Ephesians 6:15]," yet my feet tingle. In order to shut him out of my mind I pray, sometimes silently, sometimes aloud. Silently, I sing praise songs to the Lord to prevent evil thoughts from invading my mind. It seems as if he is flying back and forth around me, like an insect. And a dull roar sounds far away. It comes closer ... and then with relief I realize it's an airplane, breaking the silence of the night.

From my room I hear her breathing and know Mary is asleep; I'm thankful for that. There's such a pressure about my head and ears. "Lord," I pray, "please send warrior angels to combat these evil unwelcome guests. The battle is yours, Lord, please help us."

Lying in bed, I wonder what the relentless low roar is that's outside or beyond. I live on the perimeter of the city at the foothills. Sometimes I hear sounds in the night, a car, occasionally a train. But this is a low, oppressive roar. The pressure squeezing my head over the past days is worse tonight. When he battles us, our knees become weak, almost shaky. And we each get a bad taste in our mouth. I have it now. It seems like I should brush my teeth—but I already did that.

My light is on as I sit in bed writing this. There is no sound from Mary's room. The doctor gave her a light sleeping pill, which she said helps, but only for about four hours. The voices wake her around 4:00 a.m. I hope this morning will be different; I hope we both will sleep.

April 23

We each recounted the events of the previous night. Mary was up twice.

"They were so loud!" she said. "They started after midnight. They said, 'Lexie should leave you alone and keep you from reading all this stuff about God.' Then early this morning he said, 'When are you coming back home?' and that's usually when he says what he wants to do to me. I won't go into details.

"This morning they were talking, and another demon told them 'Mary is with Jesus,' but Walter went on anyway. He said, 'I'm his long lost love, and I want Mary. I want to f— her. I want to love Mary,' and the other guy said, 'Mary is with Jesus, Mary is with Jesus.' It might have been Abraham; he doesn't talk much.

"I think he's sex crazy. All he talks about is sex. They just go on and on about me and Jesus, and him determining I am his and he wants me and he's going to get me. I heard more talk, but it wasn't clear.

"I thought they were tormenting you! What I heard sounded like it was coming from your room, but it came from downstairs. Before this all started there was a lot of singing, and they called me Maria and they called me Mary and they gave me the hot seat. And then he goes on about when am I coming back to Walnut Creek. He's mad, and he will punish me when I come back home."

I said, "They can't do that, Mom!"

Mary replied, "I know he *can* do it because he can with the music—he makes it loud!"

I talked with her about increasing her faith, to which she replied, "I kept saying prayers all night, 'God will protect me, God will protect me.'"

Satan hates us. He's trying to thwart my efforts to increase Mary's faith and to cast him out of her life.

†

Jack, my former husband, drove down from his home in Quincy for business in our area and stayed with us last night. He will stay tonight as well. After clearing the table following dinner, we asked Jack to join us in our warfare prayer.

About 7:30 the next morning I awoke to the sound of Jack's travel alarm, a low irritating buzzzz coming from the den downstairs, where he had slept. Because Mary is under siege and may need me, she and I have been sleeping with our bedroom doors open. I don't know if Jack left the double doors to the den open or not, but the dull monotonous sound of the alarm cut through the quiet house. I lay in bed, waiting for him to turn it off. Where is he? In the bathroom? I didn't hear the shower. Ah, finally! It stopped. I lay in bed for a few more minutes before getting up.

I had promised him eggs and Canadian style bacon for breakfast, so I got up, threw on my robe, and went downstairs.

Jack was sitting on the sofa in the family room, open to the kitchen. He already had a cup of yogurt, and when I inquired how he wanted his eggs, he said he didn't want the eggs. I made coffee. I mentioned his alarm. He didn't even look up at me as he replied, "I don't have an alarm." Incredulously I said, "Are you sure?" Well of course he was sure.

Although we pray day after day, night after night, the devil is still with us. As I write these words, I feel my upper back burning again. He doesn't want me to spread the word of Jesus' love for us. He doesn't want souls saved to spend eternity in heaven with the Lord. He wants to draw people down into the pit with him.

I told Mary about hearing the alarm earlier today, and she related to me some things the demon called Walter said to her.

"He said I did it to him again. He said I did something terrible to him, and he will get me for this. He will get me for breach of promise. Oh God, I can't believe what I'm saying! I couldn't catch all the words he was using. He said, 'All my treasures are in your house—the wiring in the house, in the closet, in your bathroom.' He thinks I've got stuff in all his treasures! And then you know what he does? He was very mad. And then he becomes mellow. I was the one he loved, his childhood sweetheart. He went to Sheridan School."

The demon tells Mary she's his long lost love. But how does the demon know Mary went to Sheridan Elementary School in San Francisco? I didn't even know which elementary school my mom attended.

†

We've been searching for people with knowledge of supernatural things so we can figure it out and get Mary free. Most people with whom I speak believe only God has access to our minds. We have been told demons are everywhere, like germs, and they get information about us from our body language. Mary claims they read along with her while she's reading her Bible. She hears them say the words she is silently reading. That fits; they could read over her shoulder. The written material we received so far on this subject strongly suggests one must verbalize orders to Satan and his demons, not just think them, as they can't respond to thoughts. But Mary insists they do reply to her thoughts. They engage in conversation with her mentally.

We know there are three sources of our thoughts. Some come from our own mind and will, some can come from the Holy Spirit, and thoughts can also come to us from the evil one. Now I understand what Paul means when in Ephesians [6:16] he talks about Satan's fiery darts.

Mary continued telling me what she heard the demon say to her during the night.

"He said to me, 'You love Porgi, who is only 22.' He goes on telling me I love Porgi, who is younger! I think he's crazy! I try not to listen, but I can't help but listen. I can't stop them! He said I was his first love, and we made love. That was a damn lie; your father was my first!

"When you guys were talking downstairs, he kind of laid off the talk. He says he still loves me though."

I responded, "He doesn't love you Mom; he wants to steal your soul!"

"He needs me to keep him out of Hell," she countered. "I know I'm important to him in that way. I don't know any way he figures that, but otherwise I had a pretty good night."

"We're getting there, Mom." I saw no point in telling her she could not keep him from Hell, but that he, along with the rest of the demons and the devil himself, are destined for the lake of fire.

"I think so," she replied. "I heard it last night, but it wasn't loud enough to disturb me, and I finally went to sleep."

Mary takes a driving test tomorrow morning in Walnut Creek. The Department of Motor Vehicles requires her to take not only a written test but an on-the-road test, as she has visual impairment. They require a signed document from her eye doctor. Jack drove her home to Walnut Creek this afternoon as he headed north, back to Quincy. He planned to stay overnight at her place and then head out in the morning.

Jack called me from Mary's place and said I should "go easy on the spiritual warfare stuff," as she is a new Christian. I told him we turned to spiritual warfare because she was so scared. I said I recognized from my past experience her trouble was demonic activity, and that is exactly how and why she became a Christian. Along with prayer, spiritual warfare (verbally quoting applicable Scriptures) is the only way we know to help her deal with and eliminate the problem. She hears their voices, feels them touch her body, and generally torment her, especially at night when she needs her sleep. Reading the Bible, I told him, is helping her change old erroneous thought patterns.

†

On a break the next morning, I called Mary from a title company. She said the spirits were quieter last night, but because of their constant chatter she didn't get to sleep until after 2:00 a.m.

"Abraham told Walter to let me go, but Walter said he would *not* give up," she said.

I assured Mary he *will* give up and leave, and she believes that.

Mary's macular degeneration is a non-aggressive type. She sees well enough to drive, but she doesn't take chances. Voluntarily she remains off freeways, and seldom drives where she's not familiar. She enjoys using her car to shop nearby and do her errands, but to do that, the Department of Motor Vehicles must be assured she's capable of driving in all situations, freeways included. I talked with Mary again at 10:00 p.m.

"I'll see you in two years," the DMV officer had said to her, smiling.

"I hope so!" she said to him in response.

Yes! At ninety-two, my mom retains the privilege to drive for two more years!

April 26

Mary says warfare prayers morning and evening. Paul's New Testament letter to the Ephesians is the spiritual warfare letter. Paul begins in chapter six, verse ten, by telling us to be strong in the Lord, and in the power of his might. Verse eleven instructs us to put on the whole armor of God so we can stand against the wiles of the devil. He tells us we do not wrestle against flesh and blood, but against principalities, powers, and rulers of the darkness. We wrestle against spiritual wickedness in high places. He describes the equipment we need to defend ourselves: the belt of truth, the breastplate of righteousness, the sandals of the gospel of peace, and the shield of faith, with which we can quench all the fiery darts of the wicked. We put on the helmet of salvation and take the sword of the Spirit. The only piece of armor used for offense is the sword of the Spirit, which is the Word of God, the Scriptures.

We read in the book of Genesis [1:3] that God created everything with the Word of his mouth, "And God *said*, Let there be light, and there was light." And we read in Revelation, referring to Jesus [19:13-16], " ... and his name is called The Word of God .... And out of his mouth came a sharp sword, and with it he struck down the nations." Warfare prayers that include Scripture wound demons.

Mary said, "I didn't have a bad night last night; it was mild. I woke up a little; he was talking to me. His friends were telling him he should leave me. He pleaded with them, said he had a foot in the door, and please don't take him off this assignment."

I told Mary I was happy she had some sleep last night, and I reminded her she must give up her curiosity about the demons. I asserted they could use her wonderful natural curiosity as a hook, continuing to influence and torment her, and stay with her. When I asked if she was going to Bible study tomorrow, she said she was. This is her church time, as she doesn't yet attend a church. A retired pastor who lives in the community leads the Bible study classes. Mary enjoys going, she's met some nice people there, and it helps her learn and understand the Bible. She continued to tell me about her day.

"I was talking to this neighbor of mine. I learned today that he and his wife are Catholic; they believe in spirits and things. He asked if I had a crucifix. I told him I didn't. I told him someone had died in the house. I used to think that was superstitious stuff, but now I know these demons latch on to you, and I'm convinced they are out there because the Bible mentions it. Jesus was knocking them out all the time."

Mary is right. (For Bible references regarding Jesus' interactions with demons, see Appendix A.)

April 28

I came downstairs this morning and turned on the Today Show while I waited for water to heat for my coffee. Suddenly the picture changed, and the screen had the word "Live" in the corner. The commentator was discussing the Michael Jackson trial. As programming switched to a live broadcast, I believed there was some breaking news, and I continued to watch. When the video returned to the studio, I saw Ross McGowan discussing the Jackson case. This surprised me, as McGowan was on the Fox network, and I had been watching the local NBC affiliate. The channels changed. How did it happen? The TV remote was several feet from me—I had not touched it.

They're back! I felt that burning sensation, and my vision seems a little blurry again. I have to concentrate. I try to ignore it as I empty the dishwasher, and when physical symptoms come, I cast them out: "The Lord rebuke you Satan! In the name of our Lord Christ Jesus, flee from me!" I directed in a loud voice. I also shot up a quick nonverbal prayer to God to get them out of here. Mary isn't here this week, but we continue our study of Acts that we began reading together.

In the evening Mary called to report, "They were quiet in the night, just low music, and I could sleep. But this morning I woke up to hear him saying, 'It's 7:00 o'clock! Get up! Time to get up!'"

She got up and went to her Bible study class. Earlier, cautiously, she had shared her story with a few people there whom she trusted. Those kind people said they prayed for her. Only two more sessions before they break until Fall.

Mary and I learned early on you can't talk about the spiritual realm with many people, Christian or non-Christian, and mentioning demons often ends a conversation. Even pastors have turned away from us. Do they not have expertise in spiritual warfare? Maybe they don't believe those parts of the Bible. Perhaps some are fearful. We have not been given a spirit of fear, and it is necessary for us to discern the dangers lurking in the unseen world. Not only do we need to know how to fight, but we need to learn what *not* to do, in order not to open doors to evil.

April 29

Today I received a disappointing phone call from our friend Loren, one of Mary's neighbors. He said he had good news. He had talked with Mary who told him the demon voice she's hearing told her he—the demon—is a particular neighbor which he named. Loren thought this was good news for Mary because he learned that neighbor is dying of cancer. Loren believed the voices would stop when the neighbor dies.

Doesn't he get it yet? I explained it to him. Doesn't he know that a neighbor, a mere human male temporarily residing on this earth, as we all are, does *not* have the capability of talking to another person's mind? Sixteen homes share Mary's driveway, and the poor dear neighbor sick with cancer probably has no idea Mary even exists.

I find this discouraging. We have spent much time getting Mary to understand that demons, spirit beings, are invisible to us but can exist in our physical environment. Residents in her community have signs with their names near their front doors. Demons can read the neighbors names. It's all lies!

> Be sober, be vigilant; because your adversary the devil, as a roaring lion, walketh about, seeking whom he may devour. 1 Peter 5:8 KJV

I called Mary to remind her to read the sheet of paper that discusses how falling into the old rut of erroneous thought patterns can give Satan a foothold. I emailed words she could use to rebuke Satan and cast him out, and I told her this was all she was to say to him. She must say it out loud, not just think it, even though they respond to her thoughts.

I feel it's important for Mary to come back to my house for another week. The demon voices disturbed her last night. The strongman—or head demon—Walter, told her he is "going to Hawaii for a week," but he would leave someone else in charge. He said, "The others will do things to you." He continues to feed her lies, and she believes some of them. She says most things they say are lies, but sometimes they actually do some things they say they will do. I hate this so much! When I asked if she resisted him verbally, she said, "No. I didn't talk to him." While it is not appropriate to converse with them, remaining silent won't drive them out either.

When David first came to my house to pray with us, he brought a couple pages from a Bubeck book which includes a prayer about putting on the Armor of God. Following the prayer, Bubeck writes:

> "The important thing is to put on your armor. See its vital importance and appropriate what our Lord offers to you for your victory and protection. How tragic and heartbreaking it is to see believers reeling and staggering under Satan's assault with little hope of victory. The victory is already provided. It

remains for us only to aggressively use it and not passively assume it."

Starving for answers, I ordered two copies of three of his books, *The Adversary, Overcoming the Adversary,* and *Preparing for Battle; a Spiritual Warfare Workbook,* the latter of which is so very helpful.

You must understand. Mary had never picked up a Bible, had little knowledge of Jesus Christ, and had not attended a church service since early childhood. Knowing nothing about the Kingdom of Heaven, or angels, or fallen angels, i.e. demons, she was not equipped. And she knew nothing about Satan, everyone's enemy.

By reading Bubeck's teachings, Mary can better understand the world in which we live and also the heavenly realm. She knows more is going on than what we see and touch.

> While we look not at the things which are seen, but at the things which are not seen: for the things which are seen are temporal; but the things which are not seen are eternal. 2 Corinthians 4:18 KJV

Why do we want to believe only good things and ignore bad things? Some people say they believe in heaven, but they don't believe in hell. One day the pastor at the church I attend quoted C. S. Lewis saying, "Every inch of earth is claimed by God and counter-claimed by Satan." How insightful.

Why doubt things one can't see? We believe in electricity. How about cell phones? They send and receive video—with nothing plugged in. Most of us don't know how they work, but we accept them. When we pick up and read the Holy Bible, we see the truth about the heavens and the earth with our spiritual eyes. The Bible is a history of mankind, prophecy of the future, and a guidebook for us human beings while we're on this earth. This book changes lives. Once we have accepted Jesus Christ as Lord, He sends the Holy Spirit to dwell within us. In prayer we can ask the Holy Spirit for help to understand as we continue reading God's word.

Mary spent several weeks with me. We studied the spiritual warfare workbook *Preparing for Battle.* We learned about angels, about using the Sword of the Spirit to defeat evil forces, and how footholds become strongholds.

April 30

Last night when she called, Mary sounded meek and frightened. She has not resisted Satan's efforts effectively. She *thought* the resistance, and he repeated it back to her. I told her to say it out loud. We prayed together, then Mary read aloud spiritual warfare as I followed along. If we don't fight, we lose.

†

As Loren brought Mary to Milpitas today, the three of us had dinner together. Then Loren went home, and Mary and I prayed together. The books we're reading confirm to us we must verbally resist the devil. The authors reason there is no evidence the evil one has access to our minds; only God has full access to our minds and our hearts. The devil can shoot fiery darts, or thoughts, into our minds, but so far I've found no one who agrees he can read our minds. Mary says when she reads her Bible she hears them follow along and read it with her. And when she *thinks* a question, they answer it.

Mary has told me repeatedly she's curious about what the voices say. I told her the demons may use her natural curiosity as a temptation, and this may be his stronghold. I cautioned her to quickly, verbally, rebuke and resist.

May 2

After church yesterday, Mary and I read the Bible, and in the evening prayed warfare prayers. Mary hadn't mentioned demons all day. But after our Bible reading—which we both think makes Walter angry—Mary was upstairs getting ready for bed, when she heard the loud "thump, thump, thump," sounds he makes.

"How are you?" I asked when Mary came downstairs the next morning.

"Like a ragged old lady," she said. "We don't get up enthusiastically like we once did."

"How did you sleep last night?" I inquired.

"I slept good," she replied. "He talked to me even after I read him that thing. He ignores it. Very peculiar. He bathes only once a week, he told me, and I just couldn't help saying, 'It would be better if you washed three times a week.'"

Is he attempting to use humor and amuse her to keep his foothold, I wondered? Or does she forget he's a spirit without a body to wash?

"But he's getting weaker," Mary continued. "I didn't get the hot seat, but I got the same old talk."

May 4

I'm bringing Mary home today so she can go to her Bible study tomorrow morning. I'm glad she enjoys it; it helps familiarize her with the Bible, and it's an opportunity for fellowship with other Christians.

When Mary came downstairs this morning, she reported to me what the demons said to her:

"Mary's going home. Mary's going home. Mary's putting something in her little eyes. Oh, Mary's putting nail polish on.

"I have no privacy, Lexie," she agonized. "He knows everything that's going on. And all he talks about is f—ing, f—ing, f—ing, and thrust, thrust, thrust!"

He told her he would bring in another spirit. We know he lies, but nonetheless it's disconcerting. Mary is responding exactly correctly now. In the night I heard her saying, "The Lord rebuke you Satan ... " This morning she told me he rebelliously tells her he resists her when she says that to him.

I received a telephone call from David this afternoon. He asked how Mary was doing and told me he talked with Karen. She told him she has never seen a situation where spirits have not submitted to the name of Jesus Christ, and have not done what they were told to do. She said to David, "If these spirits have such a strong presence there, they must have grounds. We might want to focus and pray that God will reveal to us what it is, that God allows these guys to stay there."

David suggested it may be a repentance issue. "There are a lot of things that can give the enemy 'rights' to interfere in a person's life ... unconfessed sin, especially sexual sin." He mentioned the Scripture about "two being joined as one." David recommended taking Mary through her history and then asking for forgiveness. "Soul ties," he said. "There is a spiritual connection; there is a joining at the spiritual level when you have sex."

For this cause shall a man leave his father and mother, and shall be joined unto his wife, and they two shall be one flesh. Ephesians 5:31 KJV

He continued, "It could be a transference that occurs. Go through the boyfriends. Renounce the relationship, confess the sin, and ask for forgiveness. Pray that the Lord will bring things to her mind that help her.

"It could also be ancestral ties. It could be in the bloodline, spirits that have been passed down from generation to generation. It may be an ancestral avenue to explore and pray through. The only way is to pray. If you get a sense there was a sin, you can ask God to protect you and cut off any rights the enemy has to be there. Ask for forgiveness. Pray and ask God to reveal if there are any curses. That can be another avenue allowing the enemy to bother people."

Once while David was at the house, he suggested we get people with a well-developed gift of discernment. "But," he said, "Most people that have that gift have left our church." He had already talked with Paul, one of our church leaders, about it.

He mentioned the program Cleansing Streams saying, "Anyone can profit from it. It's a systematic approach when you get out of whack." He recommended the class, periodically offered at our church.

Following my conversation with David, I called Mary to convey what he said. The Bible teaches us sex outside of marriage is sin [1 Corinthians 7]. We discussed going through her memory, recalling past boyfriends, considering those relationships, confessing sexual sins, and renouncing them. She said she would do that.

CHAPTER 3
USING SCRIPTURE TO RESIST

For the word of God is quick, and powerful, and
sharper than any two-edged sword, piercing even to
the dividing asunder of soul and spirit, and of the joints
and marrow, and is a discerner of the thoughts and
intents of the heart. Hebrews 4:12 KJV

M Y MOM AND dad, Mary and Lee, married nine years before I was
born and remained together until I was six years old, when they
divorced. Single again, Mary dated for about ten years, then married our
next-door neighbor, Russell, in December 1956. Before that Mary had
always rented, and for various reasons we moved often. When she married
Russell, we moved from Oakland to a newly constructed home in San
Lorenzo. This was Mary's first experience with home ownership, and a
dream-come-true for her.

Mary's father had been a farmer. Growing up, they always had fresh,
delicious food, and now she had a garden of her own where she could
plant whatever she wanted. We lived in the San Lorenzo house about
three years before moving to another new home in the Oakland hills. I
left that home at age twenty.

May 5

"Mary cheated on Lee Grant Anderson. Mary cheated on Russell Her-
leman. Mary is a whore." Mary reiterated to me the words she heard the
demons saying in her mind as they mocked her, citing her two husbands.

"He's a liar!" Mary cried out to me on the phone, referring to one
demon, "Your father was my first!

"But Walter says he loves me, he wants me," she continued. "I took a pill and fell asleep. But I woke up to the words, 'I want you; I want to marry you.'

"I confessed," she said to me, "but I can't remember all of them. You know who they are," she said as she named the boyfriends she dated during her single years.

"Clark and Paul ... , I didn't realize I had so many boyfriends in my ten years of singledom! I spent a long time talking to Him," she said, holding back tears.

"Lexie, I have no privacy; he says he'll be with me forever," meaning the demons listen to everything she says, even her prayers.

I called Mary the next day.

She said, "He says he doesn't sleep and they don't want me to sleep, so they go into their repertoire. Sometimes it's a buzzing sound, and the volume and intensity varies. I call it 'the hisser.' It sounds to me like it's coming from different areas of the house. Sometimes it's a gang of demons, having a party. I endure other strange sounds from Walter, Porgi, and Abraham too, including listening to them talking among themselves. It's all too loud for me to sleep.

"He talks nice in the daytime, but he torments me at night."

†

Last evening I prayed about the possibility of Mary's problem being caused by ancestral demons. I brought to the Lord something David told me about—the possibility that demons believe their "right to be there" could be due to an ancestral tie. Demons can remain in families for generations. Three suicides have occurred in our family in this generation, and also a still-born death and the death of a month-old child.

Mary has been talking to our cousin Teresa, who lives in Italy in a small town south of Milan. She is a widow with two unmarried sons.* The older son, Matteo, became shy and withdrawn. The family didn't talk about it, but we American cousins wondered if he had some mental illness. His brother said he's "difficult."

Teresa and her husband owned an antique shop and bought and resold furniture and art objects. Teresa retired after her husband died, and Mat-

*(Their names have been changed to preserve their privacy.)

teo became more withdrawn. Mary, Sally, and I visited the cousins in 1998. Although we shared several meals with Teresa and her younger son Luca in their home—and Matteo was home at the time—we did not see him at all. He remained in his room while we were there.

A few years later we heard the appalling news. Matteo had dressed in nice clothes, saying he was going out. He went to the train station in a nearby town and threw himself onto the tracks in front of an oncoming train, ending his life.

Now that Mary is suffering from demonic oppression, she and I have a different opinion about the cause of Matteo's reclusive behavior; demonic forces may possibly have troubled him too. Matteo had done beautiful work restoring and refinishing various furniture pieces that his parents purchased for resale. He could have worked on a piece of previously-owned furniture that had a demonic attachment.

How naïve I had been to think doctors or psychiatrists could have helped Matteo. What could they have done? They prescribe drugs, which may mask a problem by suppressing a symptom, but do they unmask the cause of the problem? If pills don't fix the problem, people continue to suffer or go to live in institutions—with more pills. There is no secular answer to demons. The answers are in the Holy Bible. The only effective weapons against demons are prayer and the sword of the Spirit, which is the Word of God.

†

Mary continued telling me about her night. She awakened when they gave her what she calls the "hot seat," a buzzing sound and heat all around her.

"This morning they started in around 5:00 a.m.," she said, "but didn't bother me. Abraham told Walter, 'Stop; Mary is with Jesus.'"

About 7:00 a.m. Walter began telling her more lies. He said he had been married. I told her spirits don't marry.

Mary replied, "He's pretty smart. He said he was a prisoner of war, but he loves his grandchildren. The youngest one is 33. Now he's 86! Before he told me he was 83! He said he was a war prisoner for 22 years. No war has lasted that long!"

It may not seem like it, but little by little Mary is getting it. She understands this is Satanic, and his demons are telling her lies. The concept of demons remains difficult for her as she just began reading the Bible at age ninety-two. She asked me if dead people can become demons, and I said no, they cannot. I again explained that demons and angels are not humans; they are spirits. I explained that God made angels to be spirit beings and He made people to have physical bodies. There are messenger angels and ministering angels led by God to help us throughout our lives, but there are also evil angels who went with Satan when he disobeyed God. We call them fallen angels, and these fallen angels are the demons bothering Mary.

Mary was talking with her neighbor, Loren, about going somewhere, when the spirit told her how to get there.

"He gave me directions!" she told me on the phone. "I thought, 'my God, he knows everything!' And he's always asking me if I love him because he says he loves me. I hate him! I just wonder what will happen tonight, because I need a good night's sleep every night."

We talked about finding and purchasing a little bistro set, a table and two chairs she could put on her front porch.

Saturday Evening

"That little speech didn't help one bit," Mary declared to me around 6:00 p.m. over the telephone.

"They say they're here to stay. They say they like me. But I don't like them. It's goofy. It's like living with somebody. Gee, you can't even go to the bathroom without knowing someone is staring at you."

Mary's first golf lesson is scheduled for Tuesday morning. One reason for moving to the retirement community was to play golf, another skill Mary developed after retiring. She played often when she lived in Oakland, and occasionally while she lived with me. One day, playing the Tony Lema course in San Leandro, she got a hole in one. A proud day for Mary, to be sure!

†

Tomorrow is Mother's Day and we plan to get together at Walnut Creek. Mary is fussy about food, and often critical of restaurant food. In her opinion, Mother's Day is not the day to dine out. She believes with so many folks taking their moms to brunch or dinner, restaurant staffs are stressed and can't do their best. She claims the food is an effort of mass production, so we stay home Mother's Day, and eat out in her honor on another day.

I drove to Walnut Creek, where Loren joined us for dinner at Mary's house. After our meal we prayed together and asked the Lord for a hedge of protection from Satan's attacks and for protection for others who are praying for us. We asked for discernment to see what rights the demons claim, allowing them to bother Mary. After Loren went home, Mary and I continued reading the book of Acts.

Alone in the car on my way home, I thought and prayed. I asked God what might displease him about my life or, particularly in this case, in Mary's life. The thing that keeps coming to mind is the little carved wooden Buddha Mary has on top of the television set in her living room. A few inches tall, it shares space with a small carved elephant and a tiny ceramic teddy bear wearing a dress, a pink hat, and a necklace, all gifts to her. Remembering the commandment, "You shall have no other Gods before me [Exodus 20:3]," I mentioned the Buddha to Mary when placing the flowers I brought her on the television set. She replied saying, "God knows how I am."

Her comment might come from someone who doesn't know the Lord—someone who makes up their own god. I pondered the fact that Mary, a believer in Christ, keeps a foreign god, an idol, on her television set. She meant He knows that to her it's just a figurine, a remembrance of a friend, and not a god, but God mentions idols throughout the Bible. He hates them. He tells us He is a jealous God [Exodus 20:5]. And why not? He did wondrous things; he created the earth, man and woman, and everything else in, on, above, and below the earth. He deserves credit and respect. When Old Testament people made and worshipped idols, he got angry. It's still a battle.

May 9

Mary is reading *The Adversary*. I spoke with her this afternoon and she acknowledged to me, "I have a demon." She said she verbally resisted when she heard the demon's voice, but he responded that he resisted her. She said she took a short nap, but while resting she was aware of them talking. He continues to talk about "f-ing" her, and says he won't leave, even though the others say they want to leave.

It's all lies! Demons try to get their victim to believe their lies, and then they lead that person to destruction. The demons who tell her they want to leave are lying. They may get some kind of relief from their own suffering when they invade and torment a living person with a physical body. From the gospels we learn Jesus spent a good part of his ministry on earth casting out demons from people. Demons bother people in different ways, and most people suffering from demonic influence don't hear voices and have no idea what's causing their problem. "Oh, it's hereditary," I hear some people say. Many people accept their problem and don't fight. People need to fight, and our offensive weapon is the sword of the Spirit. Demons fear disclosure. They feel they have a home in the person in which they dwell. They want to remain, not be cast out.

The book, *Pigs in the Parlor,* suggests various demon groupings, each with a ruling spirit or strongman. There is seldom a single demon. Examples of groupings can be bitterness, rebellion, jealousy, depression, addictive and compulsive, sexual impurity, occult, among dozens more. Each grouping can have several subgroups. For example, a spirit of jealousy could include spirits of envy, suspicion, distrust, or selfishness.

Mary enjoys reading her Bible. It's pleasant and comforting to her, and she says she's learning from it. She said to me, "I asked God to stop my sexual desires and to take away the urges that come when he [Walter the demon] goes into all this."

†

I'm trying to work. I've read my Bible, put on the full armor of God, and cast out evil. Yet he persists. When I returned home this afternoon, the house didn't feel right. Sitting at my desk in front of my computer, I noticed a flying insect hovering between me and my monitor. It looked like a small bee, but instead of the body being horizontal, it was vertical. It appeared to be about three-eighths of an inch long. I debated for a moment before attempting to smack it between my hands. When I clapped, skin hit skin, and no insect lay dead. It didn't fly away; it disappeared, just as it had appeared.

> "For we are not contending against flesh and blood, but
> against the principalities, against the powers, against
> the world rulers of this present darkness, against the
> spiritual hosts of wickedness in the heavenly places."
> Ephesians 6:12

One day last year our pastor preached on overcoming Satan. "The devil is a splitter," he said. "Satan wants to separate us from God. The devil is nasty and merciless; he hits people when they're down. The devil knows the Bible, but when he quotes it, he misapplies it."

After being in the wilderness forty days without food, Jesus was hungry. The devil, knowing Jesus was hungry, tempted him to change rocks into bread, but Jesus responded by quoting the Bible. He said, "It is written, man does not live by bread alone, but by every word that comes from the mouth of God [Matthew 4:4]." Jesus quoted that passage from Scripture available in his day, Deuteronomy 8:3.

Late this afternoon I spoke with Mary, who said the demons are getting worse.

"They're going to chain me to the floor tonight," she said.

"Mom! Don't believe those lies! Don't even listen to them," I almost shouted.

This gets me so upset; I have to remind myself that self-control is a fruit of the spirit [Galatians 5:22]. Apparently she hasn't been resisting quickly or assertively enough. I reminded her to use the sword of the Spirit.

"Oh yes, I do that every morning," she said, referring to putting on the armor of God, found in Ephesians 6.

I asked her to tell me what the sword of the Spirit *is*, and she said it was a sword.

"But what *is* the sword of the Spirit?" I repeated.

"It's the word of God," I said. "It's your Bible! The only thing demons flee from is the sword of the Spirit, or Scripture from the Bible."

She has sheets of paper with various scriptural references that have helped others battle in spiritual warfare. I asked her to take an hour and look them up, and verbally tell Satan she resists him, and read those Scrip-tures out loud when the demons speak to her.

I have been blessed with my mom being in good physical and mental health for so long, that I may not always realize she is ninety-two years old, and has impaired vision. I'll look up those references, type them for her in a large font, and email them to her. Then she can print it.

I have considered various ideas regarding rights the evil ones may claim they have to torment Mary. Could it be the small wooden Buddha on her television set? Could it be some sin of our ancestors that attracted the demons which descended upon Mary? Could it be a generational curse? The easiest idea to test would be the little Buddha. "Just get rid of it!" I have implored her. Yet it remains. Mary went to her bible study yesterday and talked with two women there. She mentioned the Buddha, and the women said they didn't know about those things, but they would get rid of the Buddha.

> "You shall not bow down to them or serve them; for I the Lord your God am a jealous God, visiting the iniquity of the fathers upon the children to the third and the fourth generation of those who hate me, but showing steadfast love to thousands of those who love me and keep my commandments." Exodus 20:5-6

I read this Scripture to Mary, and we tried to discuss it, but until she fully understands she can be stubborn. She insists it's not *her* god, and she doesn't want to give it up. I asked her to pray about it. Satan can put blind-ers on people, and she seems blind to the fact that Buddha is something people bow down to—and that it has no place in a Christian home.

May 16 Milpitas

When Mary came downstairs I said, "Good morning Mom, how are you doing?"

"Okay," she responded. "I had a hard time sleeping. They were so noisy last night. I had a session with them this morning; I told them to stop all their excuses, all their lying. Sometimes they say things that are funny. They said they need an eviction notice. I told him he didn't need an evic-tion notice.

"They use me for their fantasies, and that gives them their jollies, and they want to do that fantasy morning, noon, and night, so they keep waking me up, saying 'it's now time for another session,' so I lost control. I even said, 'Get the Hell out!'"

I reminded her we've learned they don't respond to conversation, but only to Scripture. She told me she knows that, but she just lost control. She continued telling her story.

"Every morning I get this plaintive sound ... sort of 'Oh Mary ... sleep ... sleep ....' I don't know what he's saying when he talks quietly. He's different in the morning, but at night he kicks up his heels."

The demon was talking to her while I was talking with her, and she told me he wanted to give her a message for me. I stopped her immediately, and we said a warfare prayer together. She told me he doesn't like me.

May 17

When Mary's at my house we pray together, we put on the whole armor of God; we do spiritual warfare together, and demonic activities diminish, even though we haven't yet been successful in casting them out. When she returns home she may not be as diligent, or she may not remember to use the sword of the Spirit to rebuke them. They absolutely do not respond to emotional pleas, or to kindness. One can't say, "Please go away." Only Scripture rebukes them. When she's home, the demons gather steam.

She has written instructions to help with spiritual warfare. She knows what to do, and she has scriptural references. Looking up each reference is time consuming, but when an evil thought enters one's mind, we must deal with it directly and quickly, verbally, with confident authority.

> Behold, I have given you authority to tread upon serpents and scorpions and over all the power of the enemy; and nothing shall hurt you. Luke 10:19

I awakened abruptly in the middle of the night by a loud crash-bang sound. I shouted, "Mom!" as I swung my legs out of bed and onto the floor.

"Lexie?" she said, as I walked into her room. "Did you hear that?"

"Yes," I said.

"That was in my ear!" she said. "Can I come into your room? They won't leave me alone."

"Of course." I said.

Only once before has Mary come into my room to finish the night in my bed—which at king size is plenty big for two small women. I prayed silent prayers to God for a hedge of protection around us and to gag the demons so Mary wouldn't hear their chatter. But they followed her into my room. After several minutes it was evident she was restless, so I told her to close her eyes, and I turned on the light. My Bible was by my bed, as were several sheets of warfare specific Scriptures and notes. I spoke aloud from the notes I typed yesterday, personalizing the Scriptures:

"We have authority to loose the Angels of the Lord to battle demons, and we have authority to bind demons, for it is written ... "

> Truly, I say to you, whatever you bind on earth shall be bound in heaven, and whatever you loose on earth shall be loosed in heaven. Matthew 18:18

We loosed warrior angels upon the demons, and thankfully Mary told me a few minutes later the demons had quieted down. It took a while for me to get back to sleep. Even though God has not given us a spirit of fear, but one of courage, I feel somewhat anxious about diligently knocking out any wrong thought that might surface to my consciousness. I fell asleep mentally repeating Scripture I had memorized. I have done this before when feeling threatened, and have entreated Mary to do the same. "Either quote Scripture or sing a praise song to the Lord," I said. It can be aloud or silent—although silent seems better if one really wants to go to sleep. The point is to keep our mind filled with good stuff so the bad stuff can't get in.

> "Finally, brethren, whatever is true, whatever is honorable, whatever is lovely, whatever is gracious, if there is any excellence, if there is anything worthy of praise, think about these things." Philippians 4:8

†

Mary reiterated some of their latest speech, which she has no choice but to listen to.

She said, "At first he was so mad, he was furious, he sounded like a madman. He was counting all my sins; he counted up to forty-something. 'You won't make it through the gate to Heaven,' he said. He went on telling me I'm unfit for Heaven. He said 'I'm going to kill you Mary,' because I would live and he didn't want me to live, and all that crap. He's so dramatic with all this terrible stuff he will do to me. It seemed like it went on endlessly ... and then finally he mellowed.

"As I was thinking about all my sins, he tells me he loves me. He said Lee told him I was good; he talked to him and he talked to Russell and they both said I was good, and he wants me. [Both Lee and Russell are deceased.] Then he brings you into it, saying you need a grandson and he can do it. He and I can give you a grandson. Can you imagine? Stupid talk like that. He thinks he has a foot in the door, but he hasn't. They get worse after midnight. How he was carrying on. I think it's a performance.

"It must be sexual. He's determined to get me to give in. 'Save me, save me,' he says. Sex seems to be something to do with saving him. Maybe because two people become one, he thinks he'll get to Heaven that way. I don't know."

"Could there be a more disgusting thought than sex with the devil?" I said.

"I don't want *any* sex," Mary replied. "All I know is, he's making me sick! He's wrecking my system! No sleep! I don't know what he will do. I know he can't hurt me, but it's stressful having something pounded into you that you don't want to hear. And then, in another vein, he'll say something sensible like 'read the Scriptures Mary,' and then he prays for me. You don't know what you'll hear. It's not good stuff. It makes me kind of nervous because my body will jolt from time to time. I don't know how much longer I can endure it."

CHAPTER 4
RESCUED FROM DARKNESS

Jesus said, "No, go home to your friends, and tell them what wonderful things the Lord has done for you and how merciful he has been." Mark 5:19 NLT

THE REASON I recognize Mary's problem as demonic is because something similarly strange happened to me in 1983. Demons invaded my mind, just as they have invaded Mary's mind. Before I tell you about that horrific experience and how it occurred, allow me to tell you how I came to know who Jesus is.

When I was about six years old, my mom and dad divorced and my dad moved from our house in Oakland to San Francisco, where he worked. My mom now had to get a job, and about that same time my aunt and uncle (my father's sister) moved in with Mary and me. After Mom left for work each morning, Aunt Sigrid made tea and toast, put them on a tray, propped up pillows, and climbed back into bed to read her Bible. She invited me to join her. She fixed tea and toast for me too, but my tea was mostly milk. I told her I would prefer more tea than milk, but that didn't change the situation. I continued to receive weak tea.

Sigrid read the gospels to me. I had never heard such captivating stories before! I was awestruck by the stories Jesus told and the miracles He performed. Although Mom and I did not attend church, I learned that Jesus is the Son of God. When I walked home from school, my Aunt Sigrid was there for me. My aunt and uncle were not with us very long however, before moving to their own place, at which time my Bible studies ended.

†

I was close to my dad and divorce separated him from my daily life. He came to our house to see me on Friday nights. Mary took that opportunity to go out with her friends. Frequently, she went dancing at the Ali Baba ballroom. Dad and I stayed home, popped deliciously fragrant buttered popcorn in a large pot on the stovetop, and played games. When daylight lingered and days were warm, Dad took me to play miniature golf. He always won, but it was great fun for me nonetheless. Afterward we went to Guy's Drugstore, where we sat at the counter on upholstered stools and ordered ice cream sundaes. Drugstores operating in the 1940s often had fountains.

I looked forward to seeing my dad each week. During the summer when school was out, and when he had vacation time, he liked to go to the ranch, his childhood home, and he often took me with him. The ranch comprised one hundred sixty acres of unspoiled beauty in Sonoma County. Dad left metal drinking cups at springs flowing with icy mountain water. When we walked in the summer heat, we stopped and refreshed ourselves with cold, delicious spring water. He loved to hunt and fish, and he taught me about the outdoors. I had a collection of rattles cut from rattlesnakes he killed. In contrast, Mary was not at all an outdoor person. She was afraid of mice and bats, and both got in the house at the ranch built by my paternal grandfather in 1896. He died when I was two; I have no memory of him.

†

After high school I went to work at the local telephone company in downtown Oakland, where I met Linda. She invited me to her church, which I soon joined, although at that time the youth group was more of a draw for me than seeking the Lord. I had confessed my faith; I considered myself a Christian, but I was neither learning nor following the principles of the faith. And before long I moved away from home, and no longer attended church.

Without fellowship with other Christians, it never occurred to me to read the Bible. I lived in the world; I didn't intentionally sin, but I did things unaware they might displease God. I didn't realize that without wisdom from the Bible I could not discern truth from error. Many years later, when the following experience occurred, I could probably have recited a few of the Ten Commandments, but because I hadn't read His

Word—and learned what sin is according to the Almighty—I did not realize occult activity was not only sin, but dangerous. So, in the most difficult way, I learned that when we sin we step away from God's protection.

†

Years went by, I had daily schedules of my own, and I saw my dad much less frequently. He died in November 1969. On July 31ST that year, he and my step-mom Ann—whom he married when I was eleven—watched our astronauts land and walk on the moon. I'm glad he got to see that. In the middle of that night Ann heard something; she saw that Dad was not in bed, and found him lying on the bathroom floor.

Every night after working in San Leandro I drove to San Francisco, where he lay in a hospital bed at U.C. Medical Center. They had diagnosed him with a malignant brain tumor. He couldn't speak. One night before he died, I held his hand, and I asked him to squeeze my hand if he could hear me. I felt a weak tug. My heart broke. My dad lay trapped inside his body. Maybe that's why a television program got my attention one day in early 1983. Maybe that's why I began doing automatic writing.

†

In October 1982, I learned my job was being transferred to Los Angeles. I declined to relocate and, therefore, became out of work. While between jobs, one day I turned on daytime television and watched an interview with a woman who wrote a book about contacting relatives who had died. She told us how to do it. Without hesitation, I did it. I wanted to contact my dad. Every day at the same time I sat down at my typewriter, spoke some words, and soon typed words began flowing onto the paper. I didn't know what I wrote until I pulled the paper out of the typewriter and read it. In ignorance, I believed I was communicating with or about my dad.

I hadn't been involved in the daily writing activity very long before hearing audible voices in my head. They talked to me and told me things. They promised things. They kept me from sleeping. It was not good. I could not get them to stop talking, or to leave. Weeks passed. While lying awake one night, listening to them talking—sometimes to each other and sometimes to me—I suddenly realized I had been taking dictation from the devil! A demon actually, who called himself Lily. This was a sickening thought, and I immediately stopped the automatic writing. But the torment continued, week after week, with no sleep.

Exhausted, with no appetite, I lost weight. Being married at that time, I prepared dinner for the two of us, but I couldn't eat. The voices of the demons were in my head all the time. As with Mary's experience, it wasn't as bad in the daytime. I thought my own thoughts and did my own things. I ignored them to an extent. But at night they increased their activity and conversation, and they were too noisy for me to sleep. That was their intent—to deprive me of sleep. My husband, Jack, slept peacefully beside me. Their voices were audible only to me. And in the beginning I believed the things I heard them say.

They said they would give me powers and clairvoyant vision. To do this, they said they had to operate on my eyes. Although I felt nothing, they told me I now had the ability to predict things. My husband was a fan of major league football, and playoffs were about to begin. On television, commentators were giving their opinions. Immediately, the name of the winning team of a not-yet-played game came to my mind. I occasionally watched games with Jack, but at that time I was not yet a football fan. I didn't have a clue who would win. But that day I told my husband the name of the winning team in the upcoming game. And when the game was played, the team the demons predicted won. They gave me many predictions; some proved true, and some did not.

I told Jack about the voices I heard day and night, and he listened. But I glanced over at him, sitting next to me on the sofa; his eyes were closed. He said nothing, but this talk made him uncomfortable. Jack grew up in a Christian family, going to church during childhood, but neither of us went now. When his grandmother from Oregon visited with us, we went to church on Sunday and we thanked the Lord for each meal. But she didn't visit often, and we didn't keep in close touch with her. In those days long-distance telephone calls were costly.

One startling incident that took place during this time of torment had to do with my cat, Serena. Before my job was transferred, I had worked for a trucking company in an industrial area. No one was around at night, and our neighbors were two horses. While I had the job, I sometimes picked a handful of greens from our side of the fence and passed them over to the horses. There was also a hungry cat who seemed to want to be friends with me. I brought her food during the week, but as no one was there to feed her on weekends, one day I brought her home.

Serena readily adapted to having a family, and we allowed her both inside and outside our home. One day the voices in my head were frantic! "Your cat is dead!" they told me. "She's down on Warm Springs Boulevard." It shocked me! How could she have wandered over five blocks away? I told Jack, who was home at the time, that Serena was dead. I wanted to find her body so I could bury her in our backyard. I asked him to come with me to find her. Reluctantly he followed me as I went into the garage, after picking up gloves and a large plastic garbage bag. As I stepped down the two steps into the garage, the cat walked in front of my legs! I screamed! My dead cat! Serena! Obviously, she wasn't dead at all. I felt relieved she was alive, but I was very upset that those demon creeps had lied to me. I still didn't know the devil is the father of lies.

> For you are the children of your father the devil, and you love to do the evil things he does. He was a murderer from the beginning. He has always hated the truth, because there is no truth in him. When he lies, it is consistent with his character; for he is a liar and the father of lies. John 8:44 NLT

That night, totally exhausted, they continued to deprive me of sleep. I was so angry with them; they lied to me! I listened to them talk, and I responded to them with a thought. The demons and I conversed inaudibly. When I confronted them with the lie, and asked why they told me Serena was dead when she was not dead, they said, "Oh, we're sorry; we had to startle you to make the transition complete." It scared me when he mentioned a "transition," and I inquired about it. Although I could hear several voices, Lily, the main one, spoke to me. He said something about one of them entering me. This was very scary stuff!

I remembered the little Presbyterian Church in Fremont we had gone to a few times when Jack's grandmother visited. I called and set up a time to meet with their Pastor, Paul. He brought me into his office, and I told him my story. He reached into the top drawer of a four-drawer vertical file, labeled Top Sacred, and pulled out a couple of lists of Scriptures for me. We both got down on our knees, and he prayed for me. I took the Scriptures home and found them a comfort to read. At Pastor Paul's direction, I read them out loud. The following day I continued to be tormented, and I called Pastor Paul to tell him the activity of the demons continued.

"We have prayed about this. Wait on the Lord," he said to me.

Helpless, I hung up the phone.

During this period of torment I mentioned what happened to me to a few close friends, including my mom. No one wanted to believe me, and no one wanted to talk about it. A day or two after I called Pastor Paul, I felt uncomfortable and weak, and spent the afternoon lying on the sofa. It felt like I was in a battle—and the battle was raging around me. I didn't hear specific voices I can recall, but I knew there was a lot of activity in that unseen realm, and it went on for several hours.

And then suddenly they were gone. My mind was quiet. I had peace. I fell to my knees and thanked and praised the Lord. Our Lord Jesus had sent his angels to fight for my soul. And they won. Hallelujah to my Lord! I was born again that year, a fact the Holy Spirit confirmed to me. I began reading the Bible, which has made a great impact on my life, teaching me truth and giving me discernment and wisdom. God, through his Word, has shown me how he would like me to live my life, and how to protect myself from the devil and his demons.

I confessed my Christian faith around 1960, long before this 1983 experience. But my faith was academic, not a saving faith, and the difference was I lacked a relationship with the Lord Jesus Christ. In ignorance I became involved in dangerous occult activity which led to demonic torment. Had I read the Bible, I would have discovered in Leviticus [20:27] the Lord forbids communication with the dead. I had no idea that God, in his goodness and wisdom, would allow and use this experience to prepare me to help my mother twenty-two years later.

CHAPTER 5
SATAN'S STRONGHOLD

Be sober, be vigilant; because your adversary the devil walks about like a roaring lion, seeking whom he may devour." 1 Peter 5:8 NKJV

YESTERDAY AFTERNOON DAVID again came to the house, this time with Joanne and Natalie, to see if they could help Mary. While praying that morning, David said Psalm 18 came to mind, and he led us in prayer.

"I will love thee, O Lord, my strength. The Lord is my rock, and my fortress, and my deliverer; my God, my strength, in whom I will trust; my buckler, and the horn of my salvation, and my high tower. I call upon the Lord, who is worthy to be praised: so shall I be saved from mine enemies." Psalm 18:1-3 KJV

As we prayed through verses David saw as applicable, he tailored his words for Mary's situation ... "submit to Jesus" ... "cover Mary with the blood of Jesus." We prayed over ancestral ties, curses, and Mary's family, including her step-mom. Joanne shared some of her favorite Scriptures regarding sleep.

"I will both lie down in peace, and sleep; For You alone, O Lord, make me dwell in safety." Psalm 4:8 NKJV

"When you lie down, you will not be afraid; Yes, you will lie down and your sleep will be sweet.
Proverbs 3:24 NKJV

"Casting down arguments and every high thing that exalts itself against the knowledge of God, bringing

every thought into captivity to the obedience of Christ."
2 Corinthians 10:5 NKJV

Even now, years later, I say 2 Corinthians 10:5 each night before I go to sleep. When I haven't recited Scripture, I have sometimes seen grotesque, supernatural beings in my mind, while drifting off to sleep. I believe I am targeted because I am helping Mary. Just because we don't see them doesn't mean they are not around. In his first letter Peter tells us to be sober and vigilant, because our adversary the devil walks about like a roaring lion, seeking whom he may devour [1 Peter 5:8].

†

When Mary came downstairs, she said she slept well the night after our friends left, but last night there was no sleep before 3:00 a.m. The demon is talking to her today. He said he is leaving, but he has not left. He told her she "may meet lady angels—which are worse than the men."

Our search for answers led us to Bubeck's book, *Overcoming the Adversary*. As we read, I noticed where Mary was to read the word "Savior" she said "favorite." I repeated it to her several times before she said it correctly. I noted this substitution of key words before—beginning when Mary accepted Jesus as Savior—and even when David prayed with her. Is Satan responsible for these errors?

†

Back home in Walnut Creek, Mary called me Saturday morning.

"I had a good night's sleep. They sneaked into my room but they didn't disturb me. I have no action here this morning except that hissing."

She said the day before he had provoked her to anger.

"They were active, singing and ranting on, with a 'one-two-three thump.'"

She told him to get out of her house, it was her house, and they were too noisy. He said he would never leave. When she confronts him, she must do it in the name of our Lord, as there is power in the name of Jesus.

Mary continues progress in reading the Bible and *The Adversary*. She verbally combats demonic forces daily with spiritual warfare. I believe we have a grip on this now, and it will soon be over. Mary must be careful not to sin, not swear at the devil, actually not converse with him at all. When he knows there is no hope for him with Mary, that she does in fact belong to the Lord, that she has confessed her past sins and has been forgiven, he must flee.

As her knowledge increases, her fear diminishes, although the demons continually annoy her and still disrupt her sleep. She got up three times during the night to move somewhere less noisy. Each time she read selected Scriptures to those evil ones, which she said quieted them down for a little while.

Loren came by and put together the little bistro table Mary had ordered online for her front porch, the area serving as a small patio.

"It's cute," she said, "but it's not worth the money. It's sturdy, but very heavy."

†

The next time I talked with Mary she was rushing about, planning for her niece Evelyn's visit. Over the past weeks I have gathered that sometimes the noise level with which the demons torment her is decreased. She told me that after prayers and after warfare they're somewhat quieter. Their talk continues to be sexual. What can she do? I recommended surrendering her whole self to the Lord. I suggested she talk with Him about "putting off the old man," and "putting on the new man." I asked her to get her Bible and told her I would call again in a few minutes when I had my Bible in my hand.

Before touching redial I knelt by my bedside, and asked the Lord to show us—especially Mary—what right the evil ones claim to intrude upon her life. I asked what He, Lord of all, needed from her before he would cast out the evil ones. I called Mary back and reminded her God is sovereign and in control of all things. I asked her to turn to Ephesians, a letter of Paul's written from Rome, to the Christians at Ephesus.

> "Put off your old nature which belongs to your former manner of life and is corrupt through deceitful lusts, and be renewed in the spirit of your minds, and put on the new nature, created after the likeness of God in true righteousness and holiness." Ephesians 4:22-24 RSV

I asked her to mark those Scriptures and take time before Evelyn arrived to go over them with the Lord in prayer. I hung up the telephone, ever hopeful we may have found the key to ending this trial.

†

"This morning I heard that fast, fast music," Mary whispered into the phone, as Evelyn was not yet up.

"They had it on so loud! I thought, 'when is it going to end?' but thank God it dimmed and didn't bother me too much."

After Evelyn went home, Mary was exhausted. But as soon as she fell asleep, *they* woke her up. She doesn't feel comfortable driving when she hasn't slept, so she went to church with neighbors. She told me she dozed off a couple times, "just for a few seconds."

June 4

Another awful night. Walter threatened her. He said he would win, he hated her, and he didn't let her sleep. Later she heard him saying to Abraham, "Jean's coming over; she'll move in. Wait till Mary sees her; the Chicago fire scarred her."

"They come on for an hour or two, I hear them talking, and then they drop off. These two seem to converse about me," Mary told me. "He was so mad at me, so distraught. The spiritual warfare got to him, and he was acting like it had done him a great disservice. Around 3:00 a.m. I fell asleep. But he came back after 4:00 a.m. and they lingered and sang and talked. He talked about how he hated me, and Porgi said he still loves me. Then the mean one said he loves me—Walter said he 'just can't help himself, he just loves me.'"

All three demons tell her they like her. She knows it's lies. It's torment.

Mary continued, "I didn't get up until 10:00 o'clock, but as I was lying there resting in the early hours, I heard him say 'Mary's still sleeping.' When daylight came he said to me, 'Change your hairdo.' That struck me so funny, but I didn't like it either." She laughed. "I'll tell Nick.

"But Walter was so mad—he was in a rage! The way they would get to me. When he was talking to the other guy—I couldn't hear everything—

they'll have a band of a hundred other people. 'Wait till she gets this,' he said, 'it will drive her crazy. It will drive her out.'"

Mary said, "I don't want to hear someone saying, 'Mary's going to the toilet, Mary's going to pee now.' I want my freedom. I feel like I'm bound, like a slave here. I don't like having to take something to go to sleep. I've had people living with me for many months. Nothing eventful went on last night, but my room was too noisy, so I slept in the guest room. I bumped my calf on the futon; it's still pulled out from when Evelyn was here. The corner's not pointed, but when you bump it ... it's bruised me in the past. I hit it kind of hard last night in the dark, and I felt blood, so I had to get back to my room and get a bandage. You should see my leg; it's full of purple marks.

"Anyhow, I finally got to sleep, but I woke up and heard them talking. Interesting things. But the one I think is my guardian, he's always taking my part ... "

I interrupted and told her no one is taking her part; this is their hook to remain with her.

"I'm just telling you what it's like. I'm not haywire yet. I can't do much talking; they're listening to me. The one with the good voice that tortures me, the other one was telling him how great I am. There's someone in the group in sympathy with how I'm feeling. He said 'it isn't right that you don't let Mary sleep.'"

She continued telling me the strange beings with her are sexual. She resists them and she leaves her bedroom and puts a pillow over her head.

"He saw me with the pillow over my head, and he talked with Abraham, who told him he had no business to get me to leave my bed. Abraham was indignant that Walter forced me to leave my bed, and Abraham was giving him heck.

"Anyhow," she continued, "he's got an obsession. It's got to end. I feel I'm getting close because they know there will not be anything for them. Nothing. I'm not doing what he wants me to do. So what are they here for? He keeps me in a jittery state. I'm not getting proper sleep, let alone getting out of my bed, going elsewhere to get some sleep where it's a little less loud. I heard all this very serious talk. They said such terrible things! I was in shock! I thought, 'What's he doing to me? What are these people?'"

I talked with her, pleaded with her, and encouraged her to pray to

God for help in consistently resisting the evil one by using relevant Scriptures. I reminded her that the sword of the Spirit is the Word of God; the only effective weapon we have against the devil is the Bible with its truth. When she addresses the evil one, she must command him, using the authority the Holy Spirit has given to her.

Again, I told her not to listen to them. I understand she has no choice, but when they are talking, she can fill her mind with something good, such as singing a song of praise to the Lord. She can sing out loud, I said, or sing silently in her mind. But fill her consciousness so she doesn't hear what they're saying. I told her I was certain that if they didn't want her to know what they were saying, she would not hear it. Hearing them is their effort to get to her. She believed they were speaking to themselves, but it may be an act put on for her. It's just more deceit. They want her to think they are talking to one another; that's their game. I told her she must *never* believe them, even though we know the devil may tell nine truths to get us to believe one lie.

She must resist by reading her Bible, praying, trying *not* to listen, but filling her mind with song or Scripture when they speak. And when she must address them to stop harassment, she must not converse or plead with them, but only say or read relevant Scripture passages. The Word (the sword of the Spirit) is our weapon for offense. I said if she did this consistently, they would leave. She admits not entirely resisting. We prayed together on the phone, but she had to go. She had a hair appointment with Nick. I told her I would drive to Walnut Creek in the afternoon to pick her up. The apricots are ripe, and I know she wants some.

June 19

In Milpitas we continued studying, and I realized we kept coming back to, "You shall have no other Gods before me ... no idols." We discussed this and talked to the Lord about it too.

When I brought her home, she picked up the tiny statue of the Buddha and we walked out to the dumpster area. I closed the door behind us to pray. Mary surrendered herself to God, and she tossed the Buddha into the trash. We should burn these things, but there is nowhere to burn safely at Mary's place. At least we got it out of the house.

Mary called the next morning.

"They awakened me early, but not as early as before, about 5:00 o'clock," she said. "The stuff I heard that kept me awake was kind of interesting, so I had a pretty good night. Anyhow, it's a beautiful day. I wanted to hit some golf balls, but it will take time to make soup. I gave some apricots to Pat; she lives above Loren."

June 22

"I've got a very big problem," Mary began when she called Wednesday morning. "They haven't left yet, and I don't know what to think. They started in at 3:00 a.m. and went on to 8:00 a.m. I can tell you something you don't think is true, but I do. The hissing sound does something; it gives them a look at me. I have more to say, but I won't say it now. It's very disheartening. I can't get away from it. This problem is unnerving me; I'm not much good at anything."

She went outside onto the porch to talk, hoping they wouldn't hear her.

"This hissing sound does something to my body; I get jolted. I can hear sizzling. I can only believe what's happening. He's just toying with me, and he will not give me up. He says he can see me. I had to take my shower, and I had to step out ... "

Mary has a translucent glass shower door.

"He can read my mind," she continued. "I don't know if anything's in my hair. He said he put something in my hair. Something is going on, and I'm not dreaming it. Every room in the house has that buzzing sound. He can see everything. It feels real to me. This is a pretty old guy, and he's pretty sharp—grammatically correct. In a way, he's quite interesting. But I'm being tortured. And he has the other two. They're saying terrible things to me. It's got me scared. I feel like a slave in my own house."

I hung up the phone feeling disheartened. Mary's report depresses me. The demons seem to be stepping up their game. I immediately began praying and continued praying in my car on my way to a downtown meeting.

June 29

Both Mary and I need a break, a change of environment, and as Ann's niece, JoAnn, flew in from Montana for a visit, the three of us drove to the Monterey peninsula. When we three prayed together, Mary had a good night, although they still harass her. We did warfare last night and again this morning. She will win this battle. She needs to become more positive. Aren't Christians hopeful and joyful? As she is new in the faith, she needs to learn more about God, to depend on him, and not worry. She is making progress, and it does takes time. We continue to pray that God will say "Enough!" to Satan and make him leave. Mary and I are confident that day will come.

When she's with me, I can give her a little guidance, which seems to help, but she is older and needs repetition to learn new skills. It's when she goes back to Walnut Creek that the evil ones seem to gather strength. She needs support from Christian people who understand demonic oppression to hold tight to God and not believe Satan's lies. It seems I am all she has now, but she is learning to understand the unseen world.

We crammed a lot into our brief visit to the Monterey peninsula, including visiting the Mission at Carmel and riding the carousel on the Boardwalk at Santa Cruz. Mary needed help to get her leg over the wooden horse, but enjoyed the ride. She did say the saddle was hard on her butt. We also went to the beach where I was the only one to take off my shoes and socks and frolic in the surf, which was fabulous! They would have loved it. Who cares if you have to wipe a little sand off your feet?

†

Lately it seems Mary has been staying with me more than she has been home. She prefers being home, but the demons bother her more there. Perhaps when she's home alone, she's slower to resist. When she's here, we spend hours reading the Bible and studying a spiritual warfare workbook, *Preparing for Battle*, written by a Baptist pastor, an expert in this area.

I want to book a flight to Europe to see my cousins, but hesitate to be away from Mary for a week. Last Saturday she called in total desperation. She had seen images of four of the demons, in human form, on the window of her microwave oven. It frightened her, so I drove to Walnut Creek at 9:00 p.m. to bring her home with me. She was afraid to be alone at her place.

I have done little income-producing work this summer, spending time with Mary, but on the other hand, if I was busy, I wouldn't be able to get away.

July 28, 2005

Mary slept okay last night. But said she moved the bed because the hissing sound was all over the house and seemed to her it was "getting into her hair." I know. That makes little sense to me either. How can a sound get into one's hair? But that's how she described it. I do believe physics laws on this earth differ from those existing in the spiritual realm.

We are almost through the workbook, and Mary and I have learned a lot. Can she retain it? I underlined several critical passages and suggested that when she's home, she reread this book.

Last night was also the first night she took the sleeping pill her doctor prescribed for her. Months ago he prescribed a lighter dosage, but she said that only helped her get to sleep. It didn't hold through the night, nor did it alleviate the troubles of the night. When prescribing a stronger dose, he told us she would sleep without hearing voices. However, there was activity last night. Sleeping pills do *not* block out sounds or intrusions made by demons. From my room I heard Mary speaking warfare Scriptures in her battle with them.

CHAPTER 6
TESTS, THERAPY, AND FALSE GODS

Wherefore take unto you the whole armor of God, that
ye may be able to withstand in the evil day, and
having done all, to stand. Ephesians 6:13 KJV

I PICKED UP Mary in Walnut Creek yesterday afternoon, and we drove
to the Pill Hill district in Oakland for a CT scan of her brain. We want
to be sure there is no physical cause to her problem. The doctor had faxed
the lab request and a campus map to me. We maneuvered through various
hallways to radiology, stepped up to the counter, and presented our document.

"Do you have an appointment?" the woman behind the counter asked.

"An appointment? No, we don't have an appointment. We've never
needed an appointment for lab tests before," we both told her.

Well, not only did we need an appointment, but it could not be today.
They were closing, and we were at the wrong building anyway. The clock
showed 4:00 p.m. I pointed to our instructions showing they were open
to 5:30 p.m. and I pointed to the map, clearly showing the North Pavil-
ion.

"This is the old form," she replied casually.

"Where do these forms come from?" I asked.

"The doctors order them," she replied.

I left my conference early to bring Mary in for the scan. In Friday
afternoon Bay Area traffic I drove from San Jose to Walnut Creek, then
to Oakland. Now we had to maneuver through even more traffic to go
from downtown Oakland back to San Jose. As we inched our way along
Broadway, Mary and I reminisced about the old buildings. We recognized
many—although they were no longer used in the manner they once had
been.

"Capwell's used to be here," Mary said.

"Yes, I remember, and this is the building that housed Kahn's, where Dad used to work," I chimed in.

"And that corner store, that was Roos Bros.," Mary reminded me.

We both worked downtown for years. It was Oakland's main shopping area before suburban malls began emerging in outlying areas.

Many old buildings are gone; in their place grand tall buildings house hotels and offices. A few brick buildings with small windows remain, attempting to stand proudly amid larger newer buildings fashionably dressed in flashy glass siding. Trees still line the street, dappling the pavement with shade. We had time to enjoy the view, as traffic inched along toward the freeway.

†

On Monday I joined friends at the movies. As I was leaving, one of them stopped me.

"I talked to Dean Edell," [a medical doctor with a call-in radio show] she said. "He said your mom could have a small tumor or a neurological dysfunction."

Some of my friends are concerned about Mary. Unfortunately, they will not consider the possibility that there is a supernatural, or spiritual, cause to her problem. Like many people these days, they don't believe demons exist. Although it's disappointing to me when people don't believe Mary's story, I can understand. It might be difficult for me to believe too, if I had not experienced demonic activity personally.

Mary's symptoms fit descriptions of demonic interference, but we want to rule out any possible physical cause. Mary had many tests recently, and all results were normal.

Some friends think Mary has dementia or another brain problem, but she doesn't. Mentally, she is perfectly fine. I worry about her because she's frail and now weighs only eighty-seven pounds. We have covered all the medical bases, and we want others to know the true cause of this situation.

"I haven't lost my mind!" Mary insists. Indeed she has not.

Although this is a horrific experience for Mary to bear, good also has come from this trial. She has accepted Jesus as Lord and has almost completed reading the entire Bible. Mary used to call me fanatic, but now she loves reading her Bible, and spends more time than I do with it. We hope that, "after she has suffered a little while, God, who has called her by Christ, will perfect her, establish her and strengthen her" [1 Peter 5:10].

August 26

We rushed through breakfast, and this time with appointment in hand, once again drove to Oakland for Mary's CT scan. They placed her in a room with a large donut-shaped computer. The "donut" appeared to stand on edge, with the head of a narrow cot in front of the hole in the donut. Mary was told to lie down and not move. I planned to remain with her, as this was new and she was a bit apprehensive, but the technician asked me to leave with him to avoid radiation. The room had a window, on the other side of which was a smaller room with desks and some computer equipment. He and I went into that room, where he told me it would take a couple of minutes for him to prepare the paperwork, and then the scan would begin. The computer takes data from x-ray images and converts them into pictures on a monitor.

As the scan began, the cot Mary was resting on moved into the middle of the machine, then moved slightly forward every second or so. I closed my eyes for a brief silent prayer. When I opened my eyes, I looked through the window at Mary, then looked down at the monitor where images were changing too fast to see. And then it was finished. An attendant helped Mary to sit up, and then to stand, and we were done. (We received the scan results the following week, and everything was normal.)

After today's appointment we drove down Telegraph, which runs parallel to and converges with Broadway.

"The street lights are nice, aren't they," Mary said.

"Yes," I replied, "they're lovely."

Tall decorative poles each held two lights with torch-shaped diffusers, giving them an old-time look.

"I remember when the lights were gas, and a man used to come by each night and light them," Mary told me.

†

Almost a year has gone by and we continue to seek help. I am proud of my mom. She keeps a positive outlook under the worst of adverse circumstances. She tells me daily she knows this trial will end, that these demons will leave her, and she looks forward to the day when this experience dims to a memory.

†

I host a small group of people from church, and one woman in the group, Olivia, said she too once had a demon problem and heard voices. She and her husband empathized with Mary, who was staying with me, and they prayed with her.

Olivia brought Christian praise music to our next meeting for me to pass along to Mary, who was back in Walnut Creek. Olivia suggested Mary always have music in the house to praise the Lord. Demons cannot stand against the truth of God. As Mary has no way to play the music, she decided to buy a CD player and some appropriate music CDs that will play continuously throughout the night.

†

I arrived at the endodontist's office in Walnut Creek at 10:00 a.m., and following a root canal, drove to Mary's. It was lunchtime when I arrived, and I was still experiencing effects of the Novocaine. I brought some big red seedless grapes with me. One by one I slipped them into the left side of my mouth, trying not to bite the right side of my still-numb lip. Cottage cheese and cantaloupe were in Mary's refrigerator, so I helped myself, piling some onto a plate. Mary told me Bill [not his real name] was coming over again to help her. She called me one afternoon the previous week, feeling down after Bill had been there.

Mary hasn't been shy about sharing what she's going through, so some neighbors know she's having a problem with interference from the supernatural realm. Barbara, who lives downstairs from Mary, gave her the name of "a psychologist who knows about these things." As I was pouring a glass of cold water to go with my lunch, the doorbell rang. Mary answered the door, and I introduced myself to Bill. He had brought with him a framed eight by ten inch picture for Mary, of a bearded, turbaned man with dark hair and a gray beard.

Bill said, "Doesn't he look a little like Jesus?"

"We don't know what Jesus looks like," I responded. (The man in the picture looked to me like he could be related to Osama bin Laden.)

Bill said the problem was that the spirit bothering Mary didn't have a place to go. I thought he was planning to have the spirit go to the individual in the picture. I didn't quite understand. Mary has been paying Bill for his services, and as he told me he preferred to be alone with her, I said I would go to a neighbor's place. Bill said he planned to use the kitchen area, where I was at the moment, as Walter [the demon spirit] either liked that area, or could be heard better there. I made a quick call to the neighbor, took my lunch with me, and left.

Gingerly I ate my lunch at Loren's place, after which he suggested we go for a walk. Their senior community is beautiful, full of pines and oaks and liquid amber. Seasonal color is plentiful. The liquid ambers had the spotlight, their reds, oranges and yellows contrasting against the ubiquitous greenery and vast blue sky, accented by a few white puffy clouds. We plodded uphill toward one of my favorite trees, a small pomegranate. "It should have fruit on it," I commented, as we hiked closer in anticipation. The last time we walked this route there were blossoms on the tree. Yes! Pomegranates! Not too big, about tennis ball size, and not too many, but enough to decorate the tree nicely. As we traveled onward, we saw three deer feeding, a doe and a couple of yearlings.

Although Bill has an office about three miles away, he prefers to come to Mary's home. At her neighbor's suggestion, Mary had called Bill, hoping he could cast out the demons. We learned later Bill's theory is to treat the demons with love. This is contrary to what Mark Bubeck teaches in his publications on this subject. And so far, Bubeck is the only authority we have found with positive results—i.e. demons leave the victim. Bubeck, a former pastor, operates an institute to teach his methods to others. We have been relying on his teaching, which is scriptural, and backed up with Bible verse. We have had some success with his teaching, but when demonic activity decreases, Mary always wants to go home. But at home she may not always react appropriately, such as reacting immediately to an intrusion.

Living with demons is difficult. Others can teach, lead, or influence

Mary a small part of the time, but most of the time she is alone ... with *them*. They lie to her day and night, and I'm sure sometimes it's difficult for her to discern truth from falsehood.

As Loren and I returned to our buildings following our walk, I saw Bill's car parked near Mary's place; he was still there. I left my plate, fork, and glass on Mary's front porch, and drove home. Today is Election Day. I had been home long enough to walk down the street to cast my vote before Mary called. My poor little mom ... she was almost in tears.

"I am hearing a lot of noises," she said. "Hissing, like steam coming out. He [Walter] was turning on a thunder noise, and I just sat there and that sneak couldn't find me, and then he found me. I was sitting in the chair, not moving. 'Oh, she's under a chair' he said. They wanted me to go back to my room, but I couldn't because they touch me with what feels like wires on my private parts.

"In a couple weeks it'll be a year I've been tormented and harassed, and you can't fight back. I feel like a little mouse with a cat picking me up and tossing me back—abusing me. I'm in an emotional state, and I'm not an emotional person, but I get teary."

I told her it's a good thing to cry. Crying releases harmful chemicals from our bodies.

"When you've had a life of oppression, you learn not to do it. My step-mother had no sympathy, so I know I'm inhibited. I can't go and have a good cry ... I choke up though. I think, 'what have I done to deserve this?' Maybe my suffering might knock out some of my other bad things. It might reduce some of them."

I told her Jesus Christ loves her with unconditional love, and that by His suffering on the cross He paid our sin debt in full. I said that by our suffering through trials, God conforms us to be more like his son, Jesus. I reiterated that she should not hesitate to call me, even in the middle of the night.

Her strength came back.

"I'll be okay; I know they can't hurt me."

Mary told me they keep saying they will free her, but they don't.

"My defense is my vacuum cleaner; they don't like it. And I play the CD in the night; I turned it on three times last night."

I feel bad for Mary. She hasn't grasped how to play the CD player continuously. The buttons are small, the labels smaller, and she has trouble seeing them. She would have to push the mode button three times, through other menu items, to get a CD to play repeatedly. I got down on my knees to pray. I asked the Lord to send the demons far away from my mom, to release her, and to give her His peace. And I talked with Mary about Bill. I think his methods are impeding any progress we have made.

November 20

When I talked with Mary Sunday afternoon, I asked if she went to church. She told me she did not, that she had a terrible night. The demons kept her from getting any sleep, and she stayed in bed this morning until 11:00 o'clock. She amazes me. Her demeanor was strong. I mentioned to her she seemed to be growing stronger, and she agreed. I asked if she read the "armor" [Ephesians 6:13] today, and she said she certainly had, that she reads it—prays it—twice a day.

Mary told me the demons attempt to rape her. They touch her private places with what seems to her like wires, and to avoid that she puts pillows up against herself. Today she told me she has been using a large metal spoon to divert the rays they use. We spoke about casting down imaginations [2 Corinthians 10:5], and she is aware of this intellectually. But she says the demons have power, and she feels the things they do to her. They have told her, "If she gives in to them ... ," but we won't even go there; it is just not an option. Mary stands firm against them, as she should.

On the phone together we prayed a prayer from the book, *Preparing for Battle*.

> "Lord Jesus Christ, in You I have success, sustenance, and security. I am seated with You in heavenly realms. You clothe me with righteousness. All that I am and have You have provided. Your promises and faithfulness surround me like a shield. There is nothing or no one who can come between You and me. Thank you that I am a winner as long as I persevere in the grace and strength You give me. Amen."

Mary said she could hear their hissing sound, something they turn on or off at will. She was playing CDs, praising the Lord as she prepared a spaghetti sauce for the lasagna she planned to bring to my place on Thanksgiving.

"They don't like my music," she said.

"Good! Keep playing it!" I replied.

"They have turned it off," she said. "Then I have to turn it back on."

We bought the CD player the last time Mary stayed with me. Olivia lent music to us for her to play to ward off these evil beings, and I gave her a few of my Christian teaching CDs. She feels like she should play Christian music at night, while she tries to sleep. She has learned to operate her CD player continuously and to use the remote control that came with it so she can control it from her bed. We don't know how they stop it from playing, but she can simply begin it again with the remote.

November 26

I telephoned and spoke with Edwin [not his real name] about the voices Mary is hearing. Edwin is the retired pastor who directs the Bible study group Mary attends. He said the condition probably is not schizophrenia and mentioned that his daughter-in-law is a psychologist. He ignored my mention of the word "demon."

"She needs to see a psychiatrist," he said.

He gave me his daughter-in-law's name, Lilah [not her real name], saying, "She has experience with demonic problems. If she can't help, you must go to a psychiatrist."

December 5

Mary called. The problem persists. She said she would call Lilah again.

"Isn't she away all this month?" I asked.

"Yes, that's what Edwin said, but *they* [the demons] say they know her. They said she knows a lot of Italians."

"Mom," I said, "they don't know her; they're lying!"

"They were telling me she wasn't around. Now they say she's back, and they want to free me before she gets to me, and he's listening to everything I'm saying now, on the phone. They know her, and she gets money from them."

"Mom," I said, "this is not possible …. "

"This is what I'm hearing," Mary continued. "They admit they're spirits, but they say they're businessmen, and they have lots of money. They're great story tellers. He's thinking of what he will do to me next."

I told her to use the authority she has in Christ over them. She says she does, and they pay no attention to her.

Mary said, "I know they're liars, but I'm just telling you this is what I hear! They torment me in a lot of ways, and it's getting on my nerves— very badly! They do more than tormenting. Well anyhow, I'll try to call her again and see what happens."

Mary talked to Lilah the psychologist, but nothing came of the conversation. "How close are you to Jesus?" she had asked Mary.

I explained our triune God to Mary, the Trinity, and again she accepted Jesus as her Savior. It's notable that *they* disconnected our phone conversation three times while Mary asked Jesus to be her Savior.

I asked Mary, "Can I call Dr. Hege [her primary care physician], and get a couple of names of psychiatrists, anyway?"

Mary said, "No, I'd rather wait. I'm not ready for that kind of expense. I've already spent hundreds of dollars for someone who's supposed to be knowledgeable. He was analyzing my adversaries, not getting them out! He said he has to go through each one of them. Well, that would cost me a fortune. Why should I pay for him to analyze *them*? I don't know if they're real or lousy rotten spoiled angels, or whatever you call them. We can't prove it, and they know it, these adversaries. When are you coming out to finish my paint job?"

I told her I was planning to come by tomorrow, and I would paint her bedroom wall.

December 6

I talked with Mary on the telephone twice today, as she had a terrible night. She wasn't able to stay in her bed because they were too active there. She brought her covers and pillows into the living room and stayed there, in an upholstered chair, until they bothered her too much at that location, and then she got down on the floor, all to avoid their molestation and abuse.

"You don't know how I protect my private parts. It's awful, but I have to do it," she disclosed to me. She said she didn't get to sleep until after 3:00 a.m.

Mary said, "I will fight to the end! It's a battle! Today I'm not in good shape. If you only knew what I take ... you couldn't take it."

CHAPTER 7
READING, LEARNING, AND SPEAKING WITH JESUS

Draw near to God, and he will draw near to you.
James 4:8

OVER THE TELEPHONE for the past two nights, I read and Mary repeated Anderson's list of Scriptures included in his book, *The Bondage Breaker*. He helps us understand that in Christ we are accepted, secure, and significant. He comments on the armor of God, the protective power of prayer, on binding the strongman, and demon personality traits. Even though Satan's power has been broken by Jesus' crucifixion, Satan holds on to those he has imprisoned until we demand release based upon our authority in Christ.

Last night Mary was too tired to go over Anderson's list. She had not yet said her prayers, and it was almost ten o'clock. However, when we repeat those Scriptures before bedtime, she has better success during the night. The demons are quieter; they disturb her less and she is able to get some sleep.

†

Mary is staying with me again. Around four o'clock in the morning I awoke to hear her voice in combat and realized they were trying to get to me too. I had a headache and pressure along my body, like something large pressing against me. Remaining in bed I began praying, and knowing demons and Satan do not have access to our thoughts, audibly I told them I resisted them, and they must leave. Suddenly I recalled seeing a Joyce Meyer television show, where she had guests who worked through painful moments by singing praise to the Lord. Meyer said the Holy Spirit once directed her to sing at a particular time, and she sang a few words of *In the Garden*. So in my off-key voice, barely audible as I didn't want Mary to know I too was being harassed, I began singing one of the few songs for which I know the words, "Mine eyes have seen the glory of the coming of the Lord, He is trampling out the vintage where the grapes of wrath are stored ... " and following *The Battle Hymn of the Republic*, the *Doxology*, which goes like this:

> Praise God,
> From Whom all Blessings flow;
> Praise Him, all creatures here below;
> Praise Him above, ye heavenly host;
> Praise Father, Son, and Holy Ghost.

Deciding there was nothing more I could do, I asked God to send warrior angels to fight for Mary and me, and turned the whole thing over to Him. Then I went back to sleep.

When Mary came downstairs to breakfast the following morning, she said they had kept her awake.

"They said a lot of wicked things about me. They said I couldn't go to a restaurant because there was no chair, and he said 'we told them you're a 'puttana' and they won't give you a chair.'"

One of the evil three, Porgi, speaks Italian to Mary. Puttana is an Italian word for whore. She told me Porgi had got into her dream of being in a restaurant with a friend. They wanted her to remain awake.

May 11

I turned on the television, and Joyce Meyer was speaking on worship and spiritual warfare. She said Paul taught the Corinthians that complaining can open the door to the enemy. We need to say the right thing, and not complain, while we trust in the Lord, because the way we handle our battles shows our character and level of maturity.

Meyer said, "We think we're waiting on God, but the truth is He's waiting on us. Prophesy victory while approaching the battle."

She cited David's approach to Goliath in 1 Samuel 17:45-47 (NIV).

45 David said to the Philistine, "You come against me
with sword and spear and javelin, but I come against
you in the name of the LORD Almighty, the God of
the armies of Israel, whom you have defied. 46 This day
the LORD will deliver you into my hands, and I'll strike
you down and cut off your head. This very day I will
give the carcasses of the Philistine army to the birds
and the wild animals, and the whole world will know
that there is a God in Israel. 47 All those gathered here
will know that it is not by sword or spear that the
LORD saves; for the battle is the LORD's, and he will
give all of you into our hands."

Don't you love that! "Prophesy victory while approaching the battle!" We
all know the outcome. David ran toward Goliath, slung a stone at him
with his slingshot, and hit him square in the middle of his forehead. He
fell onto his face on the ground, and David ran up, stepped on him, drew
Goliath's own sword from its sheath, and cut off his head with it.

Meyer teaches us to approach our battles with praise for past victories,
and that worship wins the war. Our weapons are not carnal, but spiritual.
Something happens in the spiritual realm. Singing songs of worship is
warfare. Meyer told her audience to trade worry for worship, and to focus
on the answer rather than the problem. We can praise God, and we can
thank Him for what He is doing.

June 11

Connie is certified by the International Center for Biblical Counseling, and we believe she can help us. I initiated a conference call between
the three of us. She recommended three books and told us she would
bring a questionnaire to Mary to gain insight into her life history. Mary
and I already are reading through the second recommended book.

Mary continues to fight harassment and torment by demons both day
and night. I pray with her, for her, and help her find Scripture suitable for
rejecting the enemy. Connie gives us hope and encouragement, and with
her we increase our understanding regarding how and why these things
may happen. It is so good to talk with someone who understands Mary's
suffering.

Mary told Connie, "When they're with you twenty-four hours a day for one and a half years, you get to know them. I don't look forward to going to bed at night. They do things to me I don't like."

Connie reminded us that Jesus has discernment to know what Satan says is a misapplication of the Bible, and Jesus can get us back on track. She will bring a tract guiding Mary in giving herself to Jesus, and for Him to be in control of her life. She'll also bring a video and worksheets to use when we meet at Mary's place next week. Mary will fix lunch, and I'll bring dessert.

"Do you see them?" Connie asked Mary.

"No, but they put pictures of themselves up on my TV, blocking the program I'm trying to watch. They say they're not spirits, but men .... "

Connie recently moved to a new home and said,

"I've been under a lot of attack since I've been in this house, and my son too. Demons are legalists; they have doors open, they have grounds, they have rights."

Connie suggested I also complete the questionnaire, as I had shared with her some of my background. We told her about suicides on Mary's side of the family. Unconfessed sin can open doors, and we want to find every door that could be open to the enemy. When we walk in righteousness with God, we live under his protection. When we sin, we step away from God and his protection and become vulnerable to the enemy.

June 16

I drove to Walnut Creek to meet Connie at Mary's house. I brought one of Mary's favorite desserts, a pineapple upside-down cake. Connie and I had talked several times on the phone, and I felt a connection with her through Christ. Trained in spiritual warfare by several authors we have read, she has successfully helped others regain the freedom Jesus Christ wants us to have in Him.

Demons claim to have grounds, or rights, to enter into Mary's mind. This questionnaire will help Connie ascertain what those grounds are. Anderson's *The Bondage Breaker* includes a similar questionnaire, written to draw out experiences one may have forgotten or not considered relevant. The carefully designed questions evoke deep memories. Examples include involvement in occult practices, in cults, or in false religions. God loves us, and he knows how dangerous these activities can be.

Connie drove almost an hour and a half to get to Walnut Creek. As I opened the door at Mary's house, I was amazed. She stood there, gorgeous, glamorous, and blonde, professionally dressed in a mid-calf length navy knit dress and jacket. She had a pretty smile, and the color on her fingernails matched the color on her toenails. "Wow," I thought, "she's nice ... and pretty too!"

As it was almost noon, we ate lunch, got to know each other a little, and then got down to work. Connie wants to discover Mary's past activities and the values and actions of those who influenced her in her childhood and youth.

After lunch we watched the video Connie brought with her. Mary and I saw a kind, sensitive, and most remarkable man, John Regier. He was a pastor for twenty-four years before founding Caring for the Heart Ministries. Regier has extensive experience in counseling, and has recorded a series of sessions where counselees expose the roots of various relational problems. In a sensitive, discerning, and insightful manner, he speaks of generational sin being inherited as a weakness, as a stronghold (being bound by Satan), and as blind spots. He has helped many people find the root cause of the problem they experience. It interested me when he said eighty percent of people who go to doctors have spiritual problems, that when resolved, will fix their physical problem.

†

The following week Connie, Mary, and I met again in Walnut Creek, watched another Regier tape, and began discussing Mary's demonic problem.

"He calls me a prostitute," Mary said, referring to the demon who calls himself Walter. "He has a machine that can bring me to a climax. I cannot live with this. I lose sleep, and I have to get rid of them. They tell me they came here because they saw me masturbating ... but I had those desires, and that's what I would do occasionally. I prayed to God that he would take away those urges. I just have to get rid of this ... my nerves are shot. Well, I could go on, but *they* are listening to everything I say."

"They want to keep everything in the dark," Connie confirmed.

"They don't want me to talk about it," Mary said. "And then when I do talk about it, Walter punishes me."

Mary continued. "This is the way they punish me ... they do things like ... well ... I have to get out of bed. I cannot sit down. If I sit down, I feel them working on me. There's not a single spot in my house where they can't reach me. I get angry, and that's not good for me."

"Well, you can get angry with Satan and his wicked spirits; that's okay," Connie told her.

Mary continued, "Now this machinery they use ... it's degrading, it's awful, and I cannot get away from this. In the past couple days I have been very stressed, and I talked to God."

"I'm sure the Lord will make them go," Connie assured her. "We have to look at the people who have hurt you in the past."

"Well, maybe my step-mother," Mary disclosed, "but I have already forgiven her. It was like she was a stranger. She tolerated us. I don't remember her doing very much for us. I remember turning eight years old, and I was the one who fixed breakfast. Just coffee and bread. But she would have lunch for us. We moved when I was ten. I chopped the wood; we cooked with a wood stove. She couldn't read or write; she was ignorant. She made us feel worthless. I forgave her a long time ago. Later, when she was old, she said I was the only one who came to see her. She had a son. And her granddaughter was the apple of her eye. She showed favoritism. When she had oranges, Evelyn got the juice, and we got the part that was left over. One good thing about her; she was always home. I ran away from home when I was sixteen ... but after a week I came back.

"I met Lexie's father when I was seventeen and a half. We got married the day before my nineteenth birthday. To get out of the house, my sister had married the wrong man, and then when she couldn't stand the marriage, she attempted suicide. So, no, it was not a happy childhood. Luckily I had my sister."

Connie said, "I had a sister fourteen months younger also. Any other people who have hurt you? I know your first husband, Lee ... "

Mary replied, "I can't say he hurt me very bad."

Connie continued, "Well, you said he neglected you. He put hunting and fishing before you."

Mary said, "He was not a good provider; we didn't have much money. I fell in love with someone else. Had I read the Bible, I wouldn't have done it because Lee and I had a lot of good moments together too. But he made me feel financially insecure."

Connie added, "The enemy takes advantage of your hurt."

Mary spoke again of her step mom.

"She called me dirty names, like 'tramp.' I went to tell her we were married, and she told Lee I had been used. But he knew better. Can you imagine that? Because I had a lot of boyfriends and I'd been kissing. She thought if I did a lot of kissing, I was doing everything."

"How did that make you feel?"

"It made me feel terrible!"

Mary reminisced about the period after her mother died, and before her father remarried.

"Old Lady Julia moved in and slept in the kitchen. She told us scary stories at night. They were spooky, but we kept asking for them. Kind of ghost stories. Maybe that's what she heard in Italy. I don't know how long we had her before my father got married."

"Did you have bad dreams?" Connie asked.

"I don't remember, but my sister said she saw our mother as a ghost. I slept next to the wall to be farther away than my sister from any ghosts."

"Did you ever wonder why God let your mother die?"

"No. I accepted it. But I was afraid of it. They made us look at her body. My father made us go. I really didn't want to. I think my sister kissed her; I didn't kiss her."

"How did you feel about your father?"

"Oh, we loved our father."

June 23, 2006

If we want to believe in miracles, we must believe Jesus continues to perform them on earth today. Webster defines a miracle as, "an extraordinary event manifesting divine intervention in human affairs."

I left Mary's place, and was driving toward the freeway to go home. I was thinking about the events of the day and listening on CD to Randy Travis sing songs of worship. As I approached a red light, the Lord spoke to me. I heard the words clearly. He sounded like He was right behind me, over my left shoulder, in the back seat. This was an audible voice, not an impression in my mind. We are told to test the spirits [1John 4:1]. But we are also told " ... the sheep hear his voice, and he calls his own sheep by name ... " [John 10:3].

I was astounded by the words I heard: "You are released from the strangleholds of your asthma."

As I pondered that phrase, He said, "Rejoice and be glad in it."

Dumbfounded, while driving I reached for a notepad to write those wonderful words that I did not want to forget. But I was also thinking, "Can this be true? Is this really the Lord speaking to me?" We are in a battle, and the evil one can shoot thoughts into our minds. That very day we had intensely battled the forces of evil in an effort to free Mary. We had watched spiritual warfare recordings, and we had prayed a powerful prayer. Unconfessed sin can be like an open door for Satan to enter. I questioned whether these miraculous words were more deception or whether they truly were the voice of Jesus. In my heart it seemed unquestionable; it was the Lord. Thoughts flooded my mind, including thoughts about asthma drugs.

The Lord spoke to me again, "It's just that quick, Lexie."

"Wow," I thought, "he called me by name!" I have no idea why that surprised me.

In the early days before my dad left, both he and my mom smoked cigarettes. There was a lot of second-hand smoke in the house. Doctors diagnosed me with asthma at about five years old and I have been taking prescription drugs for the disease ever since. I didn't learn to play sports in grammar school because if I wheezed or choked the teachers made me go back inside and sit down. When playing with my friends outside of school, I noticed it too. I could do some things; I could ride my bike and roller skate, but if I ran down the street, I didn't get very far before asthma constricted my breathing.

Epinephrine was the drug I remember being available in the 1940s. I poured it from a tiny bottle into a glass tube with a rubber bulb on the end. I squeezed the bulb while holding the glass tube to my mouth and inhaled. Thankfully, drugs for asthma have proliferated and improved. Over the next mile I thought about the drugs I take, and I heard His voice again, "You've had enough for the rest of your life." He was speaking about my drugs!

I arrived home, awestruck. I believed what He said, but I wondered what "released from the stronghold" meant? Does being released from it mean I'm healed? I have been hospitalized with asthma, and I have spent too many nights sitting up in bed, struggling for breath. I prayed the Lord would cast out my feelings of doubt and forgive me for having them. He had given me a great gift. I couldn't think of anything better.

Usually asthma was worse for me at night, and it was time for bed. I inhaled. The air went in. I exhaled. The air came out. I knelt down and prayed, as is my habit, then got into bed. The inhaler was on the night-stand. I left it there, untouched. When I awoke at daylight, I looked at the clock—6:30 a.m.—and I recounted the events of the past day and night. I realized I was breathing comfortably. "Wow," I thought again. "This is powerful."

Today I have the day off, and I decided I'd like to go for a walk. I didn't think about running, this was all too new, and I worried this new free-dom could be taken from me. I didn't use the preventive inhaler which I take when I arise in the morning. It takes two hours to take effect, keeping me from getting out early to exercise. I went downstairs, half-filled a large mug with milk, heated it in the microwave, then dripped boiling water through a filter containing a heaping measure of coffee.

Asthma drugs were the insurance I carried with me whether I walked, hiked, or ran. I always had an inhaler in my pocket. Should I leave it home today as an act of faith? My natural common sense took over, and I put it into my pocket, even though in my heart I knew I would not need the drug.

God did not give us a spirit of fear or a spirit of doubt. When we feel those things, we can audibly say to Satan, "I resist you Satan and your spirit of doubt, in the name of Jesus Christ. Flee from me." I probably said something like that.

On Saturday I walked two miles, and the next day I walked to church and back, about four miles. I hadn't used asthma drugs since Friday morn-ing, before the Lord spoke to me, and I had no trouble. I was fine. Air went in and air came out. On Monday morning I did my first run without drugs.

I longed to get back to running. I ran regularly—with drugs—until I made a career change to sell residential real estate. Learning something new took most of my time, and I neglected training. I chose a three mile out-and-back Monday, with the out segment slightly downhill with a couple of minor inclines.

I stepped outside, locked the door behind me, walked down the walkway to the driveway, and began to run. Well, you must understand. When I use the word run, I mean jog; I'm not fast. I ran out of the court, down the street, through the intersection, past the horse ranch, and all the way to the turnaround point. I hadn't run this distance in a long time without walking at least a few steps. My muscles lacked strength, but the Lord was with me, and I just kept running. It felt great!

I value my running and walking time, because I can talk to the Lord. I can pour out my heart, my concerns, and my prayers for others. Getting tired, and as the trek home was mostly uphill, I ran part of it and walked part of it. The miraculous part was that I did it without drugs! Hallelujah! I thank you, and I praise you, Lord!

To me, this was absolutely a miracle from God. But why did he grant me this freedom now? Over the years I had asked in prayer for healing from asthma, and over the years I had thanked him for the newer drugs that allowed me to breathe normally. Was there something in my past that had opened a door and allowed Satan to hinder me with this affliction? We prayed powerful prayers that Friday at Mary's house, and after watching a couple of Regier's recordings that afternoon, we renounced all possible connections with dreadful stuff.

Connie gave us each a copy of the Prayer of Release for Freemasons and Their Descendants, from the book *Unmasking Freemasonry*. Mary's second husband, Russell, had been a Mason and his sister an Eastern Star. Dolores lived with us when Mary and Russell first married, and later she and I shared an apartment. As a young teen, before Mary met and married Russell, I had been invited to join Job's Daughters. All three organizations are Masonic. All three require one to take vows. I believe Russell and Dolores thought these were simply social organizations; that's what Mary and I thought when she encouraged me to join Job's Daughters. But I recall, after Mary and Russell married, whenever I asked him about his meetings or about being a Mason, he would tell me nothing. He said it was secret. Mary and I did not understand how dark and how deep and how dangerous these groups are. As Satan mimics God, these groups purport to be Christian organizations. They are not.

Mary and I each read silently the prayer Connie gave us, to become aware of its content. It reveals Masonic vows, and what I read shocked me. Once we completed reading this prayer of renunciation, we openly, honestly, and sincerely prayed it aloud. We each read aloud and asked the Lord to accept our prayer and to redeem us.

It was on the way home after praying this prayer that the Lord spoke to me.

CHAPTER 8
HOUSE CLEANING

But those who wait on the Lord will find new strength.
They will fly high on wings like eagles. They will run and
not grow weary. They will walk and not faint.
Isaiah 41:31

ONE AFTERNOON CONNIE, Mary, and I were watching a Regier video about moral failure. Suddenly Mary jumped up from the sofa, grabbed a three by five card with Scripture on it, and rebuked the evil ones. After she had read the Scripture aloud and sat down again, she told us they had said to her, "We will not release you; we will continue to use you; it's too much fun."

Connie brought our attention back to the video and said Mary needed to ask the Lord to break all soul ties created from past relationships. She said Mary needs to bring everything that might be immoral to our attention. Not only objects, but even relationships can carry demonic power.

July 9

I initiated a conference call with Connie and Mary.

Connie said to Mary, "Do you rebuke them?"

Mary said, "Oh, all the time. One of them is stuck on me; he says I'm his wife. The others want to leave, but he doesn't want to leave me. There is no privacy. What can you do? You can't 'shut the door.' I don't know how God allows spirits like these to wander around! Sometimes I think they are people."

Connie sighed, "Oh, no ... " Then said, "I feel the Steps to Freedom are good, and just about everyone will be helped, but Mary, yours is really extreme! When we get together this week, we'll watch a couple more videos, and then next week we'll go through the Steps. We'll pray through all the lists you're making, and the Lord will probably bring a few more things to your mind that we need to pray about. This will be a long day—so we can't plan anything for the evening.

"We must get things out of the house—the statue, the apron .... Pray to see if anything comes to mind, otherwise they'll be right back. It's important to cleanse the home."

Asian, African, American Indian, South American artifacts, and things like masks, can have demonic attachments. And especially so if people have bowed down to them or worshiped them as idols or gods. Together we prayed for a hedge of protection around Mary while she sleeps. When we finished, Mary said, "I'll have a better night tonight. They were saying to each other to 'leave her alone,' but I can't always count on that."

I reminded Mary she should believe *nothing* they say, that the devil may tell an occasional truth in his effort to get us to believe his lies.

July 13

Connie said, "That's talk. Jesus is the One. But I am concerned about *that* thing." She gestured toward the tall white porcelain statue of the woman known as quan yin, a part of Mary's home decor. Mary admires oriental art. Connie came to Walnut Creek with the intent to watch videos, but as she brought a different video than she planned for us to watch, we began Anderson's *The Steps to Freedom in Christ.*

"*They* say you won't do me any good," Mary said to Connie, speaking of the demons.

Connie continued, "Satan will use it all, and he will gain rights; he's a legalist. Is there is a Ouija board in the house? Even if it hasn't been used for thirty years, Satan will use it, and demons will reside there. They have rights and can attach themselves. They can come in and go out. Jim Logan learned this by working with missionaries. Yoga means 'yoked together with 300,000 demons.'"

It is important to get things out of the house that might have demonic connections. I hunted through Grandpa's handsome old chest of drawers located in Mary's entry way and used for linen storage. In the bottom drawer I found a large, square clasp envelope. I knew what it was and handed it to Mary. Inside was Russell's Masonic apron. Neither Connie nor I wanted to even look at it, but I saw some cords from the open flap. Immediately Mary took the envelope out to the dumpster area. It's best to burn these things, but as there is no safe place to do so, she tossed it into the trash [Acts 19:18-19]. Connie told us even books can bring evil power, and different medical practices also can bring evil power.

Back at my place, Mary had already gone to bed, so I said my prayers and climbed into bed. I wasn't quite asleep, when in my mind's eye I saw an image of a steep staircase with two closed doors at the top. I had not seen those doors in many years, but I recognized the place immediately. It was Irving Street, an Asian area in San Francisco. In an effort to eliminate asthma, I had taken a Qi Gong class there with a Chinese friend from work. The Holy Spirit brought that memory to my consciousness in answer to an earlier prayer. We asked Him to bring to our minds past actions we needed to confess and renounce to be clean in His sight. He also brought to mind my experience with acupuncture, which I had tried for the same reason—and all without hoped-for results. Occult practices are displeasing to Him. He knows how dangerous they can be to us, and He wants us to depend upon Him alone.

Mary checked all the non-Christian spiritual things she remembered participating in that were on Anderson's occult list. She spoke of her deceased sister-in-law, a tea drinker, who for fun attempted to read tea leaves remaining in the cup. She admitted her habit of reading horoscopes in the newspaper and told us she cut out and mailed these clippings to loved ones on their birthdays. As she hadn't read the Bible prior to the start of this trial, she didn't know this is an outrage to the Lord.

Mary told us her step mother had been superstitious, to which Connie said,

"'Luck' is of the enemy. When people put faith in 'a lucky rabbit's foot,' or 'a four-leaf clover,' we can open doors to the enemy."

Connie said organizations using New Age techniques of power and control—which is witchcraft—is abhorred by God [1 Samuel 15:23]. Instead we might say, "I yield to you Holy Spirit, Lord Jesus, and my Heavenly Father Jehovah." She said singing the Lord's Word is a great weapon against demons, and added, "*A Mighty Fortress is Our God* is a mighty song!"

"They sing when they talk to you," Mary said about the demons who have harassed her for so long. "When they're mad at me, when they want to punish me, I think my house will come apart—such terrible sounds! And then they've got that hissing. In fact, it's on now. It's all over. Sometimes I leave my bed and go to another room to get away. They throw darts at me, at my private parts. They made up a dummy of me and of Lexie. They'll punish me for talking about it."

I have been teaching Mary for months that demons are liars. She must not believe the things they say to her. She understands they are lying, but is still quite uncomfortable, especially at night, as she doesn't know if they'll carry out their threats or not.

Mary continued, "There have been terrible moments for me. They shoot these darts at me in effigy, and I tell you if they connect with me, I get a sensation. I fight it. It feels like ... "

Connie cut in, "Any wicked spirit ... our body is a machine; it will respond."

We progressed through the *Steps* and Mary confessed ways the world has deceived her, and she has deceived herself. The *Steps* help us understand and give up the sin of pride, replacing it with the humility appropriate for us before a Holy God. The Bible has dozens of references to pride.

We met at 10:30 in the morning, and although we took a break to fry burgers for lunch, it was now dusk, and we wanted something more to eat. We ordered pizza and continued to learn to recognize various sin categories. With insight from the Holy Spirit, Mary dredged up old sins from her memory, confessed them, and asked the Lord for forgiveness. Only by confessing and turning away from sin, which is repentance, can we be free. We either choose freedom or we choose bondage to sin. I believe we made great progress and closed a lot of doors tonight.

July 14

Back home, I tossed out the little metal Catholic saint an extended family member had given to me when I was ill with cancer. It had been hanging on the wall in my office for years. (We are not to pray to anyone other than God. Not even when a denomination canonizes a person considered " holy" while on earth and declares that person to be a saint. We are to pray directly to the Father, praying in the name of His beloved Son,

Jesus Christ [Matthew 6:6].) I resolve to go through my home and toss out any questionable items that accumulated over the years. I already discarded books given to me or that I had purchased in ignorance. We can ask the Lord for discernment.

Mary is a remarkable woman at ninety-three, both physically and mentally, even without adequate sleep for the past year and a half. But she has trouble understanding that demons can attach themselves to *things*. She remains hesitant to discard her white porcelain statue of quan yin. Our friend, a Buddhist from Vietnam, told her it is "a kind of Buddha," and therefore a false god. We removed several items from Mary's home yesterday. The quan yin and the fu dogs were placed outside her home on the front porch. She wasn't ready to destroy them, but we left them outside when we drove back to Milpitas.

Connie called to ask Mary if she was still having trouble. When Mary recounted the action endured during the night, Connie said, "Let's ask the Lord if at least Lexie and I should fast, and ask Him about Mary's statues."

Regarding the ceramic pieces, the spirits told Mary they had nothing to do with them, but they could be lying.

Connie continued, "I feel there's still something in Mary's house ... maybe books? Your mom has a strong resistance. People get attached to their art objects. They have a hard time letting go."

Mary joined the conversation. "I'm still in a quandary about God and my kwan yin. We left them out all night, so who knows, maybe someone will take them away. In Old Testament times, God didn't like those things. But people prayed to them; I'm not praying to them.

"These demons tell me they will go, but they'll be back, but I won't hear them or feel them, but they'll always be around."

Connie said, "You'll be free. They're even admitting they must go. When you read the last page in that booklet he mentions they came back to some lady and they said, 'we're back,' but she said, 'No! You are not coming back to me.' Keep saying 'No.' I think that's good that they say they can't touch you."

Mary said, "I still hear them, but they tell me I'll be able to go to bed."

Connie agreed, "I'm sure we got back a lot of ground and closed a lot of doors. Lexie and I may do a fast to see what God feels about your ceramic decorations. They're created by people who are not Christians.

Asian Christians know they need to get anything created for the Buddhist religion out of their home. If not, they'll never be free to understand the Bible the way God wants them to, because Satan will blind them. It will be better for you to leave them outside, because if the demons have a right to be in your home, and if you're starting to hear them again … "

Mary said, "They tell me those objects have nothing to do with them."

Connie responded, "That's a lie. So don't listen to those guys."

We told Connie we would call her back in the evening.

Then Mary said to me, "I need the truth on this."

A while later I was upstairs in my office, when Mary came in.

"I just had a thought come to me," she said. "There were four more men in my life."

Whoa! I thought to myself. This explains it! This is why Connie and I feel not all ground has been taken back, and not all doors have been closed; it's because there is more unconfessed sin. This may explain why the spirits can still talk to her mind.

"I can't remember all their names," Mary continued. "One I will call Bolestero. Three of them were malfunctioning, but I enjoyed one. Two were sailors. One was a second Paul. He said he was a doctor, a good-looking guy. He shouldn't even have attempted it. But according to God, that would be having sex."

I told Mary the Lord had brought a sailor to my mind, in a mental picture of the duplex where Mary and I lived. I was about ten years old. I got up one morning, went into the living room, and saw a man sleeping on the couch. When I asked my mom about the man, she told me he had stayed too late and missed the last bus and could not go home. I distinctly remember his white sailor cap, common at that time. The Lord told me she should remember this man especially, but when I told her this, she still didn't remember him.

Mary said, "There were two sailors; I forget their names. Oh, one was Frank. It was fleeting, not a complete sexual act. The other was a one-night stand. I remember him being short and stocky. I met him at the Ali Baba dance."

Regier teaches that the process of sexually arousing another person is defrauding that person.

†

Dinner was over, the dishes were washed, and Mary and I were working on Step 7, Ancestral Sins, in Anderson's *Steps to Freedom*. Mary told me her step mother, Maria, had insinuated that Mary's biological mother, Giulia, may have had an affair. She called out another man's name on her deathbed.

"He was married," Mary explained to me, "but his wife was in Italy. He was my father's friend and a close friend of the family. His name was Pete. Later, after my mother died, my father told me, 'I could tell you things about your mother.'"

Mary and I prayed together, and she confessed the sexual sins the Holy Spirit had brought to her mind, and the possibility her mother may have sinned. She asked the Lord to break any unhealthy soul ties, or bonding, that may have occurred.

CHAPTER 9
SORCERY AND INAPPROPRIATE PRACTICES

And the rest ... repented not of the works of their hands,
that they should not worship devils, and idols of gold,
and silver, and brass, and stone, and of wood; which
neither can see, nor hear, nor walk. Revelation 9:20 KJV

M OSAIC LAW PROHIBITED magical arts under penalty of
death. All the occult, including sorcery, witchcraft, divination
etc., is inappropriate for followers of the Lord [Acts 19]. Connie and I
talked about these practices. We discussed breaking any curse of words
that may have come from Mary's step-mom and asked Jesus to heal the
abusive pain of words. I told Connie Mary did not want to give up her
quan yin statue, or her fu dogs.

"We're up against some strong blinding from the enemy," Connie said.
"We need to fast before we get together and ask the Lord to take the scales
off Mary's eyes. Don't argue with her; you're arguing with the enemy. This
is beyond your mom. Tell her to ask the Lord to show us the truth.

"It becomes generational sin. In fact, there're more areas the Lord
brought to me, two areas where the enemy still has ground. A twenty-
four-hour fast seems to be very effective in seeing people get free. I know
it's a big weapon against the enemy, from Isaiah 58. We'll watch another
video, pray, and hope the Holy Spirit will bring the truth."

I conferenced Mary into our call.

"Most of them have left, but one still wants to "f" me," she said.

Mary began abbreviating the "f" word after hearing the demons use
the full word. Before this trial she neither used the word nor any abbrevi-
ation of it. Foul language has never been part of her vocabulary.

"I don't know if they're lying or not," she continued.

Connie and I rushed to tell her it was a lie.

"Yes," Connie said, "They always lie! They have a stronghold in someone's life, but the Lord is stronger. If Mary comes under attack, play songs about the blood of Jesus."

"I think some are gone, but I have a stubborn one," Mary added.

"You will be free," Connie assured her.

"Go! Just go!" Mary said aside, rather loudly.

"We want to see you get complete freedom," Connie said. "But it's better now, right?"

Mary said, "Well, I'm sleeping better, yes."

Connie said, "When we pray together, ask Jesus. The Holy Spirit can go into the past; he will bring it to you, and then we'll renounce it and get back the ground. I have an idea." And she explained to Mary that she and I would fast before getting together for battle.

July 17

In Milpitas, Mary and I sat down to breakfast, and I said it was her turn to say grace. She thanked the Lord for the food, and also for a good night's sleep.

"So you had a good night's sleep?" I asked.

"Yes," she said, "but they woke me up at 4 o'clock. All that talking ... and they blew smoke in my eyes. I know it's fake smoke, but it still smells. It's like cigarette smoke."

"That's funny!" I said.

"Yes, but not funny to me," she replied. "They can be funny," she added, "I have gotten some good laughs, but I've gotten angry too. They have a one-track mind."

"And what's that," I asked, although I knew the answer.

"Sex, constantly. They're incapable, but they've got it on their mind all the time. They say they've had a whole group of people have sex with me. They seem to gloat over tormenting me, either verbally, or mentally, and I resent them touching my body. They say they're touching me all they want when I'm drugged. All lies. Immature. I want them out of my life! They keep saying they'll never be out of my life. I don't want to hear them;

I'm tired of their kind of truth. It's funny how they talk differently in the daytime than they do at night. I get laughs in the day; at night I get anger. They're like Dr. Jekyll and Mr. Hyde.

"You need to get those trees pruned one of these days," Mary said, changing the subject as she looked out the window at the backyard landscape. "Get someone that will chop it up and then put it around and use it for mulch. Yes, I notice that tree is too thick and too tall."

†

It came to Connie's and to my attention that I have not yet been through the *Steps to Freedom* and still have unconfessed sin. Connie told me her prayer partners usually go through the Steps. Is it possible I am a hindrance to Mary's freedom in some way? As we go through Mary's issues, I have been confessing my past sins as the Holy Spirit brings them to my attention. I want to do the exercise myself. From leading Mary through the process, I have learned we don't realize that things we do—or people near us do—are sin, displeasing to God. We must acknowledge sin and ask for forgiveness. To get clean we need to be washed in the blood of the Lamb, Jesus [1 Peter 1:19].

July 18

The phone rang midmorning. Mary said, "I'm going to do some washing today, then maybe go to the gym, and then I want to go find a street. I was told she's in a wooded area. I'm kind of curious, and I've never driven around that neighborhood."

Mary was invited to a jewelry show by a woman she met some months back, when she began going to Bible study. Since going through the *Steps to Freedom in Christ*, she has been getting more sleep, because of less interference from the demons. Not all issues are resolved, and the demons have not left her, but her progress is notable. "Wow!" I thought. "Good progress. Praise the Lord!" Mary's innate, God given joy of life was coming back!

"This is where you're going Thursday?" I asked.

"Yes, and I want to know where to park."

July 19

Connie and I remain concerned about Mary's figurines. "Walk through the house and ask the Lord what needs to go," she suggested.

"Let me conference Mary into the call," I said.

Connie commented, "It would be good to ask Jesus if there are other things in the home that need to be out of the home. There's a lot of stuff that can come into your home. Even Feng Shui."

We discussed how Feng Shui has become of interest to Realtors. Real estate boards offer classes to discuss how the arrangement of furniture and accessories is used "to maximize the energy flow of the room."

"It needs to be renounced," Connie said. "There are so many ways the occult comes into our houses."

Shortly after our conversation ended, Mary called me back.

"*They* say it's not the figurines, it's something else, but they won't say what it is. And they don't want me to talk to Connie."

The demons have told Mary innumerable times they don't want her talking with me either. "I tell Lexie everything," she tells them. She's not supposed to talk to them, but respond with Scripture, and tell them she "resists them in the name of our Lord, Jesus Christ." (This works only for believers in Christ [Acts 19:13-15].)

Usually our weather is perfect, but this week we are having a hot spell. So when my neighbor Donna and I went for a morning walk, we left early and walked on the shady side of the street. Donna and I share our faith in Jesus and attend the same church. She knows Mary is going through a trial. On our walk we talked about giving up objects or idols in our homes that may displease God, and which could have an evil spiritual attachment.

I told Donna I'm considering getting rid of three ceramic pieces, purchased years ago at Macy's. I bought them because I liked the color, a pale green celadon. One piece is a vase, one is a ginger jar with a lid, and one is a wee small dragon. I told Donna I looked closely at the five inch long dragon and realized the base of the figure looks like waves of an ocean. The dragon has a pointed tail. I took it outside, along with my hammer, and gave it a whack. Then I picked up the pieces and tossed them into the garbage sack that was already at the curb, awaiting pickup.

After our walk, Donna came into the house to see the remaining ginger jar and vase, and to give me her opinion. When I brought the vase to her, she said, "Oh yes, this looks bad. Look at the expression on its face! It's got a human head, and animal legs."

The ginger jar also was decorated with a dragon-like creature. We put all three objects, including the cover for the jar, into a plastic bag, tied the top, and brought them outside to the curb, near the garbage bag. After praying together that Jesus would bind any spirits that may have attached themselves to these objects and not allow them to bother anyone, we asked that any power they had would be destroyed. Then I smashed each one with the hammer and put the bagful of broken pieces into the garbage. When Paul was teaching at Ephesus, many of the new believers in Jesus brought their occult items to be destroyed by fire [Acts 19:18-20].

Earlier I had searched the internet to learn about quan yin, the lovely white porcelain statue Mary is so reluctant to give up. During the two years she lived with me, it was placed on Mary's organ. The statue is about twenty inches tall. When she bought it, one hand of the woman was removable, but Mary had it glued in place so it wouldn't get lost. If she was told the statue's significance, it has long since evaded her memory.

I found a long list of quan yin items on eBay. Following is part of one seller's description. His item is a smaller, soapstone statue, not nearly as beautiful as the one Mary purchased years ago to be part of her living room decor. Frankly, these ads shocked me. By reading the Bible I learned how God feels about false gods. But it hadn't occurred to me that even today people worship items made of metals or stone or wood that can't see, hear, or walk.

"THIS IS A POWERFUL COMPASSIONATE LIGHT WORKER SPIRIT KWAN YIN ALL SOAPSTONE CARVING Mr. [name removed for his privacy] had on a special altar which was surrounded by the most amazing ritual tools that are all up for auction all week long. This goddess love and blessings for you may help with your prayers and wishes for yourself and others.

"SHE IS POURING HER HEART OUT with love for you and part of that is the fact she is pouring her elixir of long life so that the good energies surround you and where she is placed at all times.

"This goddess is a representation of the LOVE and COMPASSION and CREATION forces of the divine she. Created by early man with symbolic meaning to many great mother figures in all religions and transformed into many images she is the LIGHT that pierced the VOID LIGHT goddess of all creation, you came through her portal. Thus the mere fact of worshiping her and honoring her powers to give life and support to you is of the greatest thanks and faith of all and in that moment of sharing and thanking you are connected to the trinity which you are apart of always. This goddess will get you there, she will make you think, she will expand your wishes and worship and mind and her presence is so powerful to have around you. Psychic intuition will be enhanced by your sharing with her in your sacred space. Mr. [name] worshiped her and you will feel his love and compassion and the moment she enters your divine space you will be one with some amazing powers.

"ENDLESS LOVE and LIGHT ~ [another name] empowered it with the most powerful vibration in the universe the OM as you see she is WHITE the COLOR OF PURE DIVINE LIGHT, she is the compassion and vibration of the OM and if you chant her mantra or [OM xxx xxxxx xxx] you will feel an every present in any room this sacred one resides in that is so wonderful and warm and as your spiritual wealth energy grows so to will the blocks stopping your from all wealth you seek begin to open again for you to receive everything you need and want. Its simple and this statue will help you to focus your attention to what is really important right now.

"SIZE OF THIS BEAU TIFUL AND RARE SACRED STONE FEMALE DEITY OF DEVOTION is 5 ¾ inches TALL by 1 1/2 inch WIDE and by 2 + inch LONG. A sacred power tool to work with in your healing and spiritual practices that you may take and cherish with you where ever you go."

Talk about the devil's lies! The Word of the Lord states clearly, "You shall have no other gods before me." [Exodus 20:3]

I called Mary and told her my internet search confirmed to me that the quan yin was something to which demons could attach themselves. I read to her the description of a quan yin item currently for sale.

"Well, that certainly is something ... " she hesitated. "Well," Mary said, "check out the fu dogs. They're so pretty; I love their color." Another pause.

"Well, for that matter I like quan yin too; she's a beautiful woman," Mary said.

"Yes, Mom," I said, "it's a beautiful statue, but it's an item of worship for people who are worshipping a false god, and the one true God hates that."

Mary said, "That makes me wonder ... there're a lot of people who have these items in their homes. Why aren't they suffering?"

"Well," I responded, "possibly they are suffering, or perhaps they are not followers of Jesus. Maybe the devil doesn't always torment people who are already his."

Mary knows that only people born again who are alive spiritually in Christ are saved and will go to heaven to live forever with the Lord. The rest of mankind will be cast out from God's presence to reside in darkness until the second death, the great white throne judgment, and the lake of fire [Revelation 20:11-15].

Mary sighed and said, "When I get the report on the fu dogs, I'll do it all at once. You need someone to lean on, and who else but God? Well, I'll let you go."

I feel better. At last Mary understands quan yin should not be in the home of a Christ follower. I hung up the phone and searched the internet for the fu dogs to see what I might learn about them. Mary said they were guard dogs. "But what are they guarding?" I wondered.

My search didn't turn up much. There were a lot of Fu Manchu items for sale, but I didn't find ceramic fu dogs. The results I did see were heinous. Descriptive words I found included: insidious; hallucinating; brides of Fu Manchu; vengeance of; blood of; daughter of the dragon; fiendish. Certainly none of these descriptors were fruits of the Spirit, (love, joy, peace, patience, kindness, goodness, etc. [Galatians 5:22]).

†

The telephone rang, and I heard Mary's voice. "You know, I can't even play the organ in my house! They say it's keeping them awake," she said, referring to the demons.

"Play your organ anyway," I replied.

She hesitated, "They know they can't touch me."

We have seen improvement since taking Mary through the *Steps*. The demons admitted they are no longer allowed to touch her. But they still talk to her.

"Gee, I make so many mistakes," she said regarding playing the organ. "I need practice. You know, in a couple months it will be two years since I've been here.

"I think I'll go down to the gym," she continued. "I was in my office and outside the window in that ivy on the slope was a big buck, a two-pointer," she informed me.

It isn't unusual to sight deer, although I see mostly does and their off-spring, few bucks.

"He was out in the heat," Mary added. "I hope the lions are sleeping."

I told her what I had found on the internet regarding the fu dogs.

"Oh dear," she said, "I'll have to chop 'em up."

"Just use a hammer," I said.

"I'll have to put them in a plastic bag, break them, and put them in the dumpster," she said. "I'll do it now, get rid of it, and then go to the gym."

We prayed together. Mary confessed to God in Jesus' name. Although she had been unaware these items were objectionable to Him, now that she knew differently, she wanted them out of her home. She wanted nothing in her home that would displease Him. In going through the *Steps to Freedom*, she had dedicated herself to Jesus. We asked Him to break any attachment those items may have to evil spirits.

I'm interested to see Mary's results after destroying the abominable objects. We try to pray effectively, but I'm still learning and recall we didn't use the word "renounce." However, God knows our heart.

Mary called in the evening. "I performed that duty. I put them in a double plastic bag and went to the garbage, and banged, banged away. And they're gone.

"I felt relieved," she added.

"They said I wrecked their code, so now they can't do something to me, and they say they can only keep me awake until midnight. I don't rely on it, but that's it. That's what the demons said.

"Then I went to the gym. I discovered all three of the 'one-steppers' were in use. You sit on it, and your arms and legs go back and forth. So I went over to the treadmill, and my poor heart wouldn't take it; it was too much for me. I did about ten minutes on the treadmill before I did twelve minutes on the other machine, which became available."

CHAPTER 10
RESOLVING TEMPORAL VALUES AND REBELLION

Know that the LORD is God. It is he who made us, and we are his; we are his people, the sheep of his pasture. Psalm 100:3

AFTER TALKING WITH Mary, I typed an email to Connie, telling her our progress in removing and destroying objects from our homes that could be considered idols or false gods.

Mary had let me know the demons don't want her to go to see Connie. Wanda [another demon] told Mary she would "die on the road" if she went there. More lies. Mary laughs at them sometimes. They tell her she is driving too fast; they say she scares them. She thinks it's funny. I told her she does drive too fast. When she laughs at them, she told me, one of them says he likes her laugh, and he "wants to 'f' her."

"I'm very sick of it," Mary said, "and I think Connie may be able to do something."

All Connie or I can do now is try to help her bring up past sin and pray with her about it. We have found so many pieces of this puzzle.

Mary said, "Walter got alarmed that he'll lose me. He said he can't reach me up there at Connie's. He said I would never see him again. It's so silly; sometimes it makes me laugh, but it annoys me. That business when I go to bed at night. That armor I use to protect myself."

Mary began talking about her early memories.

"I remember we had a two burner gas hotplate. Our stove was a wood stove."

She recalled memories of her biological mother, including the time a large wooden garage door had fallen on her.

"She was holding me on the back porch and washing the blood off of me. I knew I was in my mother's arms. I remember this touring car took us to the hospital. We didn't have a car; we took the streetcar. My mother never came to visit me in the county hospital. It was 1918; she was pregnant before she got sick."

Her mother's pregnancy ended when their baby brother was still born the day before she died in the flu pandemic.

"I could have been four, when they had a party. I remember it being at the beach, a dreary day. They had cooked up stuff like a torta made of rice—we had that a lot—and chicken, a lot of food. People went into the water. I got kind of sick, but on the way home, on the street car, Sally and I ran up and down on the Potrero line. We lived on Utah Street, the end of the line. They were having quite a conversation, my mother and father. I have limited memories that stand out.

"The only feeling I got about my mother is that she let me do whatever I wanted to do. She trusted me. They just let us grow."

July 22

It's over one hundred degrees here in Milpitas and also in Walnut Creek today. I called Mary.

"It's too doggone hot to go out," she said. "Monday I have plans with Elizabeth to go to a strengthening class. The time is good; I need to get stronger if I want to hit some golf balls. I'm deteriorating little by little. If this ordeal goes on, your mother is on her way out."

I knew Annie would be melting in Mill Valley, where they too expected a high today of one hundred degrees. My step-mom, Ann, lived much of her life in San Francisco and likes the fog that cools the air there. Ann's home in Mill Valley is a little flat-roofed cottage. It's adorable, but has no air conditioning. When I called she told me she took a shower in cool water, but can't stay dry.

Ann also was born in 1912, two months before Mary. She's been a good friend to me since we met, after my mother and father divorced. Ann worked in the same building in San Francisco as my dad. She worked on street level in the delicatessen, and Dad worked upstairs in the fur department. He was a furrier, a trade he learned from his father, a Danish emigrant.

I talk with Ann almost daily. Today I called to see how she was doing in this heat, and after she asked about Mary, she too began reminiscing. She led me back to World War II. She began talking about how my mom, along with my dad's niece, used to go to Pittsburg [California] to a prisoner of war camp where the U.S.A. interned Italian military personnel during World War II. Mary speaks Italian and she and Jean danced with the Italian prisoners. That's one of my early memories too. I remember a large hall with tables and benches along the sides. A red Coca-Cola machine was at one end. I had never had a Coke before. One man put a coin in and out came a pale green bottle of Coca-Cola. Using the bottle opener built into the machine, he opened the bottle and handed it to me. It burned my nose; it made me burp, but I liked it. I felt so grown up. His name was Franzini.

"Ann!" I exclaimed. "That could be it!" In a flash all the pages we had gathered on Mary's history, while going through the *Steps to Freedom in Christ*, came rushing to my mind. I didn't recall seeing the name Franzini anywhere! Jesus said, "When you lust after a woman [or man], you commit adultery in your heart [Matthew 5:28]." Mary was married, but felt neglected by my father, and although the friendship was innocent, this Italian attracted her. Lustful thoughts about this man may be a sin she has not yet confessed.

After talking with Ann, I called Mary.

I said, "Mom! I think we have the key!"

Mary said, "Oh golly, do I ever hope so. Well, tell me later; they hear everything!"

"Okay, Mom," I said. "Be happy! I think we've got it!"

Mary called around 9:00 a.m. the next morning.

"Everything's okay. I had a fairly good night's sleep. Now they say they're all homo- and bisexual, and one is a pain in my butt and we constantly battle. They say they want to hold me another day because they want to conquer me."

After reminding Mary about Franzini, she agreed to talk to the Lord about him.

July 25

I was sitting at my computer yesterday typing, and I had just begun the sentence, "Yes, the devil is real, and we need to understand his role. It doesn't matter if you believe that or not ... " when instantly my keyboard and mouse froze, and I could not record the rest of my thought.

After turning the computer off and on again a few times, after plugging in another mouse and rebooting, I called Dell support.

A nice man in India kept me on the phone for an hour and twenty minutes. He determined the problem wasn't the mouse, but the operating system. He told me to back up my data, and said he would call me in three days, as he had the next two days off. As it was ninety-five degrees in my office, I decided to back up my data in the morning.

The next day I turned my desktop computer on in safe mode, as instructed, and copied a large folder containing photographs onto an external drive. Next I wanted to copy this book so I wouldn't worry about losing work I had done. Still in safe mode I moved my mouse over to that folder ... and instantly the computer froze.

Do you see any coincidence in that? The enemy does not want this story told. My computer has stopped twice. Since becoming a follower of Jesus Christ, I attribute much less to coincidence. I believe Satan attempted to thwart my plan. But he will not! 1 John 4:4 teaches us that "the Spirit who lives in you is greater than the spirit who lives in this world."

That evening on the telephone Connie prayed with me about the computer; she asked the Lord to fix my computer for me. The following morning I turned it on again before calling tech support, and it worked just fine. Thank you, Lord. You continue to amaze me. You make each day a joy!

July 27

Mary called and gave me elaborate descriptions of what they said and did to her.

"You should see what I do," she exclaimed, "I even have a big box on top of the bed for when they shoot those things at me. And I have a stack of pads for protection. They hurt my behind! They started in early, while I was watching the television. I don't like people touching my body!

"I went to the gym. I did the treadmill twenty minutes and the new stepper fifteen minutes. You haven't been to the gym here have you?" she asked me.

"No," I told her, "Not yet."

"You can come as my guest," she invited.

I asked her to tell Connie the same story she told me, and she said she would.

Demons continue to harass Mary and intrude in her life, both day and night. They torment her in every way they can, and Connie said we should sit down and watch the videos we missed earlier.

†

We put popcorn into a bowl, and sat down to watch the Regier tape, *Resolving Temporal Values*. When the video finished, the three of us talked about what we learned. Connie reminded us that demons have rights, that God hates divorce, and that Satan attacks marriages.

Of her childhood Mary said, "We lived in a shack. I can remember the salamis my father would buy in North Beach hanging in one corner of the room. San Francisco didn't get too hot so we could do that."

Connie said, "You need to see that to God marriage is a sacred union. Be like Jesus; give up your rights. Most people would counsel people to just leave, but the Bible and Jesus talk about how we are to live as Christians [1 Peter 2:1-3; 1 Peter Chapter 3; Romans 16]. Don't let your mind be forced into the mind of the world. The spiritual gift exhorting would be counseling. In the book of Romans it is written, 'Be not overcome with evil, but overcome evil with love [Romans 12:21].' Pray, 'Lord, take the scales off; let them be born again.' Where the sin came in was in letting the marriage go—marriage is sacred to the Lord."

Mary reminisced, "He liked the way I kept house, and he liked the way I cooked. He told me, 'It was so nice to come home to you.'"

Connie explained, "What I want you to see and repent of was filing for divorce. You wanted money and security."

Using a Temporal Value sheet as a guide, Mary prayed. Then she continued talking about Lee, my dad and her first husband.

"I could have had him back, but Ann gave him a car. He needed a woman; I knew that. With Ann there was no problem with money for his hobbies, but he always asked her first if he could go away for the weekend or if she had plans."

We began to watch a second video, *Resolving Rebellion*. We learned that God designed each of us to respond in submission to others. It could be our parents when we're children, our employers, our spouse, our spiritual leaders, even our government. It does no good to change someone on the outside; the heart has to change first. Jesus leads gently as a shepherd. He doesn't force change as that can lock one up spiritually.

Connie said, "Rebellion usually comes from being hurt."

Mary shared another childhood memory. "We were at a boarding house after our mother died. My father only came for us on Sundays."

They left the boarding house when another family friend, a woman named Julia, came to live with Antonio and the girls in order to care for Mary and her sister Sally.

Mary continued, "Julia slept in the kitchen on a couch. She lived there with us until my father got married. At least we had food. He got married because his paesani [friends, countrymen] told him about a widow who would take care of the kids."

I cut in, "But she didn't take very good care of them."

Connie said, "Let's ask Jesus to heal the pain that came when your mom died, because you were suddenly orphaned."

Mary told us about Maria, the widow who became her step-mother. "She married my father when I was seven. Evelyn, Maria's grandchild, was born when I was eight. I already fixed the coffee for my sister and myself for breakfast. I grocery shopped for my stepmother at seven. My hair was pulled back, and I wore overalls. 'Is that a boy or a girl?' I heard people say. I was too young to fix my hair. Don't you think my stepmother would do something for us? She didn't do much."

Connie spoke up. "Let's pray through that and forgive your stepmother."

I added, "Maybe that's why Grandpa drank, because he married her, and he may have regretted it."

Mary continued, "She never bought us a raincoat. We walked two miles to school; we got wet. Evelyn's mom bought us a raincoat."

We went back to the video and learned that God has established all authority for our good. Submission brings a clear conscience and peace. Rebellion may be acceptable in our culture, but the Bible says rebellion is as the sin of witchcraft [1 Samuel 15:23]. It takes us away from God's protection and allows the enemy to influence areas in our life. A case study in the video showed us that breaking a stronghold of rebellion also breaks the desire for temporal things.

July 31

Mary called Monday, and it thrilled me to hear her say she had a good night.

"Best sleep I've ever had!" she said. "I had myself well-armed and protected, so I decided I would close my eyes. I was so tired. They couldn't reach me, but they're still with me."

I pray for Mary every night before I go to bed, and I ask the Lord to have mercy on her. Was her good night a respite, as He has graciously allowed her periodically during this trial? Or was it an indicator we're coming to the end of this trial?

"They don't want to go," Mary said. "They want to remain in my family. They say they like my family. I used to say I loved them, but now I say I hate them. 'You are all part of the devil, and I cannot love the devil.' I hate them," she repeated.

She learned from the Bible we are to love our enemies. I told her I think the Lord means love other people, not demons. She understands it now. I reminded her she shouldn't talk to them.

"I have little slips of paper taped up to remind me not to talk to them," she added.

Mary used to say, "Lexie, if you had someone with you, talking to you twenty-four hours a day, you couldn't help but talk to them." I have told her to respond with Scripture, using the sword of the Spirit [Ephesians 6:17]. She had responded that she didn't know enough Scripture to use it appropriately. I've since typed various scriptural verses she can read and use against the demons. They tell her they don't like hearing it. She also tells me they know Scripture. They quote it to her.

"But they twist the truth!" I cried out.

CHAPTER 11
I WILL *NOT* HAVE SEX WITH THE DEVIL!

Go away, all you who do evil, for the Lord has heard my crying.

The Lord has heard my plea; the Lord will answer my prayer.

May all my enemies be disgraced and terrified.

Psalm 6:8-10 NLT

I DIDN'T HEAR from Mary until after 5:00 p.m. when she returned from having her hair done. "I had a bad night!" she said. "What did they do last night?" I asked.

"It's always a battle to rape me, and it's sickening. He says I owe him. He's got to make me." Mary sighs.

"All this trouble. I have to protect myself. This woman demon even tells him, 'She doesn't like you.' She knows I can't stand him. He's a little fart. He's the one who gives me all these bad nights. It's a battle *every* night. They blabber on and on. I'm a wreck. Something's got to be done. I don't know what, but I *will* resist him; I will *not* have sex with the devil! I'm down to 84 pounds. I look disgusting when I'm naked. I know I need to eat."

I mentioned the time I was sick for three years, when I lost so much weight. Hopefully, I encouraged her by reminding her I was brought through that trial, and she would be brought through this one too.

The next morning Mary called and said, "I made it through the night. I slept on the couch all night, but they couldn't reach me so I did pretty good. But they awakened me with a lot of noise, and I'm exhausted. I'm not dressed yet, and the coffee tastes bad to me. I don't get enough proper rest; I'm disturbed too much.

"Here I am quietly sitting here, and someone has his hands on my private parts. And then I have the other one. She's milking me. I feel a little wet, and I know he's down there. It depresses me so much. I get so desperate in my thinking; I just want to cuss them out."

After a momentary pause, Mary continued, "With so much of this, my thinking isn't good. They're wrecking me. I get so sick of it I don't want to eat. But I can eat fruit. I thought about taking a nap, but I can't do that because there's always one or the other fooling around with my private parts.

"I can't escape it. If I go out, they get me in the car. They say how bad I am, they say I'm their toy, and they can do it because God hasn't released me yet. I told them my Savior will protect me. I told them Jesus is watching you. You are just building up more and more sin against yourselves. And sometimes when I talk about Jesus a lot he doesn't want to do things, but next time it's the same. They are the lowest kind of scum to pick on an old lady like me. They say I owe them. I don't owe them nothing!

"There is one guy, and well, this is boring stuff to listen to."

She stopped speaking, but then continued, describing how she must protect herself.

"I don't know how my nerves stand it. They're frayed. I jump at the least little thing now. I'm living on nerves in the night. I am battling."

"Maybe they're stepping up activities because they know it's ending," I offered.

"Yes," she replied, "I have thoughts about this too."

Mary said, "I already told God I'm not eloquent with words, but I mean what I say. I think I have accomplished something in my prayers. The Bible opens your eyes to a lot of things you're not aware of."

We ended our conversation with her telling me she had tomato soup, a spoonful of cottage cheese, and a plum for lunch—but had skipped breakfast.

†

Connie called today, and I conferenced Mary into the call. We haven't talked with her for over a week.

I said, "We've got three more sets of issues. Maybe we'll meet one more time. We need to go over the sins of temporal values and rebellion."

Mary added, "And pride."

Connie said, "We really want to see you get free, Mary. Rebellion and unforgiving are big openings for Satan to come in with sexual spirits. It starts with hurt feelings, then goes to bitterness, then rebellion, then sexual spirits."

We all prayed for true repentance, and to see our sin from the Lord's point of view. For it is written in Scripture, " ... every man did what was right in his own eyes [Judges 21:25]." Connie asked Mary to ask the Lord if there was a time she felt hurt. A time when those who were supposed to take care of her didn't and did she decide to take care of herself?

Instead of praying, Mary answered Connie and said, "Yes, I was around fifteen. I took off for about a week, but I went home. But I didn't stay home for long, I went to a home for young women in Oakland, the Blue Triangle Club. And I did have sex before marriage; I was eighteen. We had gone together for over a year, and we knew we were going to get married."

Connie asked, "Do you remember what happened with your step-mother that day?"

Mary recalled, "Well, she had never hit me before, but she hit me, and I kind of struck back. We were both serious. But we were good friends afterwards. I'm not the kind to hold grudges."

Connie said, "A child should not strike an older person; they should show respect to authority, so that gave Satan some ground."

Mary added, "She used to accuse me of having sex all the time, and it wasn't true. She told my husband I had fooled around. He knew better. She always accused me."

Connie said, "That's another thing. I don't know if we did other boyfriends with you."

Mary responded quickly, "No, no, I did nothing. We just kissed. I forget what she accused me of, but I didn't do it."

Connie said, "You should forgive your step-mother again. So she hit you that day. That's physical abuse."

Mary added, "And I took up smoking."

Connie said, "That's a badge of rebellion. Making your own decisions."

Mary confirmed, "My father didn't like it."

Connie said, "Disobeying your dad is another seed for the devil to come in. I want you to renounce that rebellion to your dad. Can you tell the Lord, 'I'm willing to forgive my father, and step-mother for hitting me, and for this rage?' Ask Jesus, 'Can you show me where you were when I was not getting the love I needed?' Let's ask Jesus to heal the hurt inside you when you were a little girl."

Mary prayed, "We were not happy little girls [referring to her sister and herself], but if I'm in any way hurting unconsciously, please heal me. Thank you, Lord Jesus."

Connie said, "You can confess it again, and ask for the gift of repentance. It broke God's heart, and it broke God's commandment. It hurt other people. Psalm 51:10 says, 'Create in me a clean heart, O God, and renew a right spirit within me.' And verse 17 says, 'The sacrifices of God are a broken spirit: a broken and a contrite heart, O God, thou wilt not despise [KJV].'

Connie encouraged her, "Don't ever give in."

Mary quickly responded, "Oh no! I tell them I'll die first!

†

Mary is staying with me in Milpitas, and this morning she has a dental appointment. When she got up, she told me she had a bad night; she had gone downstairs to get away from the demons.

Mary said, "Boy, are they mad! They're furious! They tell me they can kill me off. Now they say they're going to give it to me worse than ... " She shakes her head, "I've had it! He *will* pull the plug and free me."

I commented, "They're mad because they're losing you."

Mary said, "They don't want me to tell anybody about their tricks. But of course what I'm hearing could be lies. Sometimes when they're very bad in the daytime I don't get the bad treatment in the night, and sometimes when they're not so bad, they really give it to me."

They said something to Mary about, "giving it to her when she's under anesthesia," and it brought tears to her eyes.

I spoke, "It's good news that this activity is so ... "

Mary interrupted, "He just said he's not going to see me anymore, but he'll keep torturing me until I die, even though I won't feel it. And they said earlier they'd be incinerated, but not right now. I thought that was kind of funny."

After we returned from the dentist, Connie called and said, "I'm sorry you had to move downstairs last night."

"Yes, I did. They can't reach me there with those little darts they shoot at me."

"Are you playing praise music? Keep it on, even at night. I know that when I've been able to do that it helps, because I am awakened at night too. I think I'm targeted too."

I added, "Yes, and I am too."

Mary said, "They're telling me today that I will not have any sleep at night and they'll punish me until I die. Oh, they're saying they're going to punish me."

Connie said, "On the internet, find the New Creation Singers. They have a CD *Sweeter than Honey*. It's all Scripture, put to music. It's singing the Psalms."

Could the root cause be Satan influencing Maria, the step-mother, to say mean things to and about Mary? Maria sinned by lying and hurting Mary. Mary sinned by lashing out at Maria, and in rebellion moved out, to "take care of herself."

As God wants us to depend fully upon Him, He appoints authority over us (government, church leaders, employers, parents, etc.). As Mary rebelled against the authority God gave to her parents, she sinned against God. We move away from Him when we sin, and by moving away from God we provide openings to evil.

August 19

Brushing my teeth this morning, a thought came to mind; could there be another area of rebellion? During my childhood, I heard many times over how Mary had "given up the church." She wouldn't step foot inside a church door. Her step mother had, out of obligation Mary said, taken her through the process leading to her First Communion in the Catholic church. But afterward, Mary gave it all up. And it wasn't just apathy; Mary was adamant.

I asked God to bind the evil one and to open Mary's eyes, ears, and heart to the truth. I asked that she would reflect on her early years, and with her new knowledge in Christ, understand what led to this stronghold. Downstairs, and as we sat together at the breakfast table with our bibles, I explained this to her.

We talked about the trinity again, a difficult concept for many of us. I reminded her that before she came to know Jesus, she had always said, "My God knows me and understands how I am." She learned from the book, *The Purpose Driven Life*, that we can't have God "our way," but we must conform ourselves to His way. He is the sovereign being. He created us. As Isaiah said, "We are the clay, you are the potter" [Isaiah 64:8]. With her newfound knowledge of Christ, and now being in Christ, she agreed. I told her we would pray about it when I returned from a conference today, and I hoped this would be the key to her freedom from the tormenters.

August 21

"They haven't been keeping me awake too long," Mary said. "From midnight on I get about six hours. I woke up at 5:00. I consider that a pretty good night. And I get sleep during the day. They keep talking about leaving, but they're such liars."

Connie called, and I put the telephone on speaker. "Well, thank God they're saying they're leaving."

Connie explained that our sin nature causes us to make wrong decisions.

"It's a huge area," she said, "because all the sins in our life come down to whether we are the boss or God is the boss. We take our own lives into our hands and not let God make our decisions for us. We think it's us, but it's really Satan."

Mary admitted, "I haven't called on God to make my decisions."

†

At the breakfast table again with Mary, she began telling me what the demons had been saying. She said she knows it's not true, but this is the kind of thing they say to her.

"They tell me I don't know how to pray. They said they wrecked my house. They said my bank account has been cleared out. They said we don't like you, but we love you. They said now that Jesus Christ is not helping you, we're going to keep tormenting you.

"I say to God, 'Lord Jesus, see what they're doing now.' Of course he sees it; he can see it all. I can't understand this spirit stuff. I keep thinking 'can they be real?' In one breath they tell me they're spirits and in the next breath they tell me they're business men ... gambling and prostitution. They want me to be a madam, not a prostitute. They say I'm not a good 'f-er.' What gets me is they keep me awake with that lousy music. They tell me it's canned music; they say they put it on because they know I don't like it. And they have a thing they do ... just as I go to sleep they jolt me awake. They don't like me telling you things. I tell them I tell you everything, and there's nothing he can do to hide.

"They have a hisser and an electric jolter. When I'm jolted, I jump. They can't actually touch me, but it feels like they touch me. I'm in my house, but they say they're in their studio. They can make noises that shakes the house like a thunderstorm. They say I'm the only one who hears it. But I'm getting smart; I can kind of block them on some things.

"That hisser is in my car, and everywhere! They follow me! They heard us talking, and they said there are a lot of them going around."

I said, "I bet that part is true."

Mary said, "They don't like what I'm saying, and they say they'll punish me. And they do punish me in their way. And because I block myself—this is kind of funny—because there's a woman there, they say she's a lesbian, and she says she wants to free me."

I cut in. "That's a lie. They're playing you!"

Mary continued talking about the personalities of the demons.

"This old buck thinks he's married to me. He says he's 97 years old. And he goes after all the chicks. He's short, but he's popular because he's got a big one. Then the woman demon says, 'He's up to something.' He can do all kinds of things to irritate me, like make me itch and scratch. But she says because I'm blocking them, they can't get near me. She says he's coming with a big long thing to shove at me. They do things to keep me awake, and they say they have a big bunch of people lining up to "f" me. They say they'll charge them and make money off me. Some things are really funny.

Mary added, "I guess I'll get punished tonight for telling you these things, but I'm firm in my stance."

I commented. "It's just all lies, all torment."

Mary said, "Yes, I'm getting nothing but a bunch of lies. But that old guy doesn't love me; he wants to conquer me. This is the kind of crap I listen to that's keeping me awake. It's awful. They're using me."

August 26

Mary continues to suffer the same torments.

"I had a hectic night," she said when I called, "but I survived. Things are not good at all. I can't talk now; I have to go get my car."

We ended our conversation so she could pick up her car, which she had serviced. When she called back, she asked me about tampons, which she has never used.

Mary said, "I need to block them from getting to me. I'm having too much trouble. They are persistent, and I thought it might be worth my money to take a chance and try tampons.

"Well, I've done my praying and reading my Bible. I'm waiting for the insurance guy, and after he leaves, I will take a nap while *they* are sleeping."

†

Connie said the Lord brought to her mind that we should walk through the house as there may still be things in Mary's home.

"What type of church does Mary go to?" she asked.

"Methodist," I told her. "It meets on campus, so it's easy for her to get there."

"Repentance is essential," she continued. "Some churches are loving and don't tell people anything they do wrong. They allow people to open more doors to the enemy. It's more than an intellectual belief in Jesus. It's wanting to obey Him and feeling bad about the previous stuff you've done in your life. A repentant heart is the key to being and staying free."

She said she has been doing a lot of prayer. She said, "Let's you and I do a fast before we get together and walk through the house."

The next day I called Mary and asked if she had anything to tell me.

"No. I had an uneventful night. But they told me I'm incompetent, and maybe they shouldn't leave.

"I put stuff around me at night to block my private parts. I have cardboard and pillows. I must fool these spirits somehow. I can't even go out to my front porch; they reach me there. They reach me if I go out to the car. I have to find a spot where this hisser can't reach me.

"I don't mean to burden you. I'm just trying to figure out what else I can use as protection. I have some ideas, but they're so horrible."

I said, "Mom, if you want to come down here, I'll come get you."

Mary said, "I'm in a fit. I waste days because I'm kept awake all night. They say they program the hisser to follow me—and it does follow me. The sun porch here is out, but I've got another idea. He's listening to me; I don't want him to know .... My nights are turning into days. I didn't get up until 10:00 and I haven't had breakfast yet. And I'm concerned about this birthday thing. What can I get for Jack?"

I replied, "Homemade cookies? Or how about a golf hat with the community logo?"

CHAPTER 12
THE ENEMY SHOWS HIS HAND TODAY

If you continue in my word, you are truly my disciples, and you shall know the truth, and the truth shall make you free. John 8:31-32 KJV

MARY WAS ALREADY up when I gave her the 7:30 a.m. wake-up call she asked for last evening. Today is the first day of her fall Bible study, and she's looking forward to seeing the women she met last Spring. She had hoped to reread Nehemiah before the class, but hadn't yet accomplished it.

While talking with Connie last night, the demons disconnected her phone several times during the conversation, requiring her to redial Connie's number. They disconnected the phone during our conversation as well. While waiting for Mary to redial my number, I prayed the Lord would smash their hands so they would not again disconnect Mary's phone. It's new for me to be so harsh, but I'm learning from David's psalms [3:7] that we must be effective warriors. Mary has told me repeatedly the demons hate her to tell others what they do to her, and one result of not complying with their wishes has often been disconnected telephone conversations. This has continued for over a year. I used to blame the phone lines in her old building, but no one else in Mary's building has had the problem. And each occurrence is too selective to draw that conclusion.

I also talked with Connie yesterday. She explained that to her it felt like Mary doesn't have a repentant heart. She felt resistance. I love Connie. She is so kind to us, and she knows so much about spiritual matters. She has driven over eighty miles quite a few times to come to Mary's house.

"I've spent a lot of time at Mary's," Connie told me. "Most people get free."

We talked about Mary's frustrations. Yes, Mary absolutely wants this to end. She's been fighting this battle for close to two years, and it has taken a toll on her body, her mind, and her spirit. I told Connie that Mary weighs only eighty-four pounds now, whereas she used to be quite shapely. I told her how much Mary has grown spiritually. Although she believed in God, she made Him someone who fit her own wants, needs, and desires. And now she has become someone with a real understanding of our true Sovereign Lord. She has learned who Jesus is, and what he has done for us.

"She loves the Word and reads it daily," I said. "She started with Genesis, and already she's up to Isaiah."

I told her about the previous evening, when Mary took Sally, Jack, and I out to dinner for our birthdays. For years Mary has enjoyed taking family members to lunch or dinner to celebrate. It's a treat for us; it's so fun to get together. We selected a place boasting Northern Italian cuisine. Jack drove down from his home in Quincy to join us, and on his birthday, September fifth, we walked through the door of Massimo's.

Jack prefers not to pray with Mary and me. Until one has an experience with demons, I guess it's difficult to believe. Or scary. Back at Mary's place after the birthday dinner, I put my arms around my mom and prayed. As I related this to Connie, she quoted, "Two in agreement make 10,000 flee."

Prior to the birthday dinner I prayed to God, in the name of Jesus, that Mary have several good nights to get caught up on her sleep. When I picked her up I asked, and she confided to me she didn't get to sleep until 5:00 a.m. Those creeps [demons] are totally wretched, totally malevolent, totally evil! However, on Wednesday, the morning following our birthday dinner, her tone was upbeat. "I did pretty well last night," she told me.

I ask Mary to call me before going to bed, so I can pray with her, but she doesn't always call at bedtime, and I hesitate to call her because she may have already gone to bed, or I may interrupt her prayer time.

One night recently I called Mary around 11:00 p.m., but she did not answer the phone. Worries pop into my mind when this happens. But I shoved them out of the way, left a simple upbeat message, and asked her to call me in the morning. "Where could she be?" I wondered, as I put down the phone. "In the bathroom, not hearing the phone, or has something happened to her? Hopefully she's asleep," I tell myself. But she is ninety-three years old. The truth of God's Word overrides my fears and fills me with hope. The words of a familiar song (from Philippians) include, "He who began a good work in you, will be faithful to complete it. He'll be faithful to complete it in you." And Paul wrote, in his letter to the Romans,

> And we know that God causes everything to work together for the good of those who love God and are called according to his purpose for them.
> Romans 8:28 NLT.

Connie and I continued to brainstorm, to find the elusive door that remains open giving the demons their right to continue to harass and torment Mary. I told Connie about the night I called Mary late in the evening. Mary explained to me later she was just too tired to answer the phone. She explained that once she was in bed, it was hard to move because of all the paraphernalia she uses to keep the demons from touching her body. "You don't know what this is like, Lexie!" she repeated to me. She finds it imperative to "protect her private parts." She sleeps using thick padding and a large metal cooking spoon to block the demons, and she places a large cardboard box over herself, on top of the covers. I saw the carton one day. She had cut an arch in it on both ends, so it fits over her body.

Connie and I both know spirits are not hindered by physical resistance, but I didn't question Mary about the box. "Whatever works," I thought.

"Maybe it's her faith, not the objects, that keeps them away," Connie said.

Connie has successfully counseled a woman who also had sexual spirits, and she has talked about Mary with another counselor. In a conference call with Connie and Mary, Connie said we can ask the Lord to reveal Mary's blind spots, generational sins and strongholds. We can ask Him to reveal sins of our ancestors.

Connie and Mary prayed on the telephone. Mary got through generational sin issues okay, but when Connie led her to ask the Holy Spirit to show her things in her house that were not pleasing to the Lord, Mary stammered and could only get a word or two out at a time.

Connie said, "There was a long pause between each couple of words ... it sounded like they got her in a grip. The enemy showed his hand today. That is the stronghold; he has a lot of control over her."

Connie suggested I go to Mary's home and walk through the house and pray. She reminded me to bind the enemy first and pray over Mary and her household. (Matthew 18:18 teaches that whatever we bind on earth, using the power of Jesus' name, is bound in heaven, and likewise whatever we loose on earth, is loosed in heaven. When confronting the enemy we must first put on the full armor of God as described in Ephesians 6.)

Later that evening, when I spoke with Ann and told her what Connie had said, Ann said,

"Maybe it's jewelry."

I thought that was rather insightful. Mary had a pair of gold and jade earrings given to her long ago. The jade was carved figures of Buddha. I convinced Mary to destroy them a few months ago, but perhaps there is something more. We must look in every drawer and closet.

†

Mary called. "I had one of my bad nights with only a few hours sleep. I'm used to it, but I didn't like it. I lose a day, and I lose a meal because I don't have any appetite.

"One of them is trying to pass for someone I went to school with. He has named people in my school. Real people! Their names!"

I told Mary that although we can't see them, they can see us, and they do have powers. I told her they "walk up and down on the earth [1 Peter 5:8]." I said they could read her name plate outside her door.

Mary said, "I know they can do that. I know they have powers. They make my private parts all warmed up so I want sex."

I said, "They are sexual spirits."

Mary said, "They've got stories. They say I will be released from them. I tell them they stole me. They moved in and took away my privacy. They say they will eventually seduce me. They say they'll do it when I'm asleep."

I said, "They won't Mom."

Mary said, "I tell them I'll die first! They are making me so miserable.

They don't want you to know all the things they do. I tell them I tell my daughter everything. You'd be surprised if you knew *all* the things .... "

We again discussed there might still be things in her house Satan may use to establish his right to be there. I mentioned the books about healing and herbal medicine that Connie pointed out when she was there. When Mary said, "I don't see how that could be it," I explained how the devil can blind her to the fact that there might be importance to certain objects. She understood—praise the Lord!—and took the books out of the house to the laundry area for others to take if they wanted them. I would have preferred for her to toss them into the dumpster, as she has no way to burn these items, but just getting them out of her house is good.

I agreed to come to Walnut Creek on Friday, to pray through the house, including closets, and again ask the Holy Spirit to show us anything that should not be in the home of a follower of Jesus. When we have done that, I will bring her home with me for a few days.

As we proceed through this trial I learn more about spiritual warfare and deliverance ministry, and I observe more people in need of help. It seems to me quite a few people suffer in their bodies from demonic influence. Those demons may not speak as Mary's unwelcome spirits speak to her, but many people who shouldn't be ill, are ill, some even becoming mentally and or physically disabled. Doctors aren't able to help; most haven't gone beyond prescribing drugs to suppress symptoms. Apparently this has been going on for a long time:

> [35]Jesus went through all the towns and villages, teaching in their synagogues, preaching the good news of the kingdom and healing every disease and sickness. [36]When he saw the crowds, he had compassion on them, because they were harassed and helpless, like sheep without a shepherd. [37]Then he said to his disciples, "The harvest is plentiful but the workers are few. [38]Ask the Lord of the harvest, therefore, to send out workers into his harvest field." He called his twelve disciples to him and gave them authority to drive out evil spirits and to heal every disease and sickness. Matthew 9:35-10:1 NIV

Mary and I have asked the Holy Spirit to tell us what still is not right in Mary's life, as she cannot rid herself of these unwanted visitors. The word "tithing" came to me. I shared this concept with Mary and looked up relevant verses in Scripture [Malachi 3:10-11]. I asked about her income. When I calculated the figures for her, she was amazed. Ten percent seemed like so much; I could sense a strong block. She remained hesitant about giving a tithe, or ten percent of her monthly income. She said her adversaries told her not to do it.

†

Connie told us about a woman who suffered seventeen years before she got free. Mary compared her own story with that woman's story.

"It started with music; that was in November," Mary said. "And then different noises, like a loud hiss, like a snake, or a steam engine. I told Lexie it sounded like an animal [perhaps a mouse] was running around my kitchen. The music always started at night. By January they spoke to me. When they talked, it startled me."

Connie asked, "Did you ever see anyone or a shadowy figure?"

Mary replied, "No, the only things I've seen were pictures of them in the glass door of my microwave. They talk and they say they'll never be seen."

September 16

"How was last night, Mom? Did you sleep? I asked."

"I had a little action, but they let up last night. The hisser came in; it's still here in the house. It followed me when I went to bed on the sun porch. It starts by coming in and hissing a lot—like a steam engine—and it's so loud! It's a power thing, and they can lower it, but he doesn't. His cohort, Porgi, doesn't like it, so sometimes he turns it down.

"Once I got to sleep, I slept good. I kind of woke up by myself this morning, but it was late, already daylight. Usually they wake me up while it's still dark and I lose all that sleep I need. I feel good today."

Again I suggested that when they talk to her, she should block them out and not listen by singing a praise song to the Lord.

Mary replied, "No matter what I say or do, they're right here. I might as well listen."

"Didn't you tell me they said, 'Their contract was up?'"

"Oh yeah, they said their contract is up, yet they laughed. I can't help but laugh too; you'd be surprised how funny they are when they talk among themselves. Their reactions. You can't imagine. But they're always on to that horny sex. But they talk about other things too, and when I'm cooking they say, 'Oh, we do it like this.' Porgi says it reminds him of home. He says he's a Genovese [native of Genoa]. I can tell; he speaks it. And I have Jewish people and a black man. They invite me to come over there. In the daytime they're nice, but at night they torment me. They say they make their living with porn. In some ways I can't help but laugh; it's very funny, but they can be so cruel."

†

Last night was Mary's third consecutive good night. "I slept very well until this morning. Then he touched me and woke me up. But it was only one touch, and I think he's getting the hint. He wants to show his authority over me. He told me I will not be going to my Bible class next Thursday, but he's wrong. He's wicked. But I'd say there has been improvement."

I emailed Connie. We're still looking for clues to get Mary free, and I told her it seemed to be a "heads up" when she said, "you might as well listen." It's not good for me to hear her say they tell her to "come over there" with them. I told her we discussed the tithing issue, and I wonder if that could be another stronghold. Mary agreed to increase her giving, but still thinks ten percent is too much. After six nights together, I took Mary home to Walnut Creek.

September 22, 2006

Around 11:00 a.m. Mary said, "I slept good. I had a good night's sleep, but they're still here. I believe we're past the peak and are on the way downhill now. I got those pants I ordered from Land's End."

"Good! I hope you like them."

"It was not a good night from 3:00 a.m. on. I had a lot of action, which wrecks my day. I pray to God, 'Can't you punish them? Listen to how they talk.'

"I read this morning in Luke [8:26-33] where the demons in the man from the Gadarenes, near Galilee, recognized Jesus. They begged him not to send them to the bottomless pit. These demons are going to get it. And they don't like it."

†

Connie called and said she talked with Jim Logan, who said, "Pride is a root behind every sin. Pride doesn't go away with just one prayer ... there will be a natural tendency to operate that way, although you'll be able to notice it more."

Connie repeated that pride can be overt or hidden. She suggested that before the three of us meet, I ask the Lord to bind the enemy and open Mary's eyes to understand the video and be able to apply it to herself. Connie said we have four weapons: (1) The name of Jesus; (2) The blood of Jesus; (3) The finished work of the cross; and (4) Our position in Him.

> Greater is He who is in me than he who is in the world [1 John 4:4].

Giulia and Antonio, Mary's mom and dad, holding Mary (left) and Aunt Sally (right). Their parents emigrated from Italy, but met each other in San Francisco.

Mary, a young woman, and still a teen.

Mary, Grandpa (Antonio), and Aunt Sally. They lived in San Francisco where Grandpa made his own wine.

Mary and Lee (Lexie's dad) at the ranch in Sonoma County.

Aunt Sally with Cousin Sally on the left; Mary and Lexie on the right.

Russell and Mary.

Mary preparing a holiday dinner.

Mary and her cat, at Christmas.

Mary being recognized for volunteer work after retiring from the telephone company.

Mary with her golf buddies.

Lexie with Mary at her 90th birthday party.

Mary and Lexie at Massimo's.

Mary blowing out the candle on her sundae at her 95th birthday party.

Mary and Ann saying goodbye after Christmas dinner 2009.

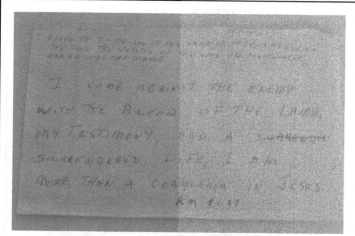

One of Mary's handwritten notes used in battle.

CHAPTER 13
OUR WORDS HAVE POWER

Resist him, firm in your faith, knowing that the same experience of suffering is required of your brotherhood throughout the world. 1 Peter 5:9

ONNIE CALLED SUNDAY to see how Mary was doing and to pass along some instructions for her. "Don't talk to them," Connie said, "Read Psalms 145 and 73, and read the end of Revelation, about the lake of fire. Read Psalms 91, 18, 27, and 32, about our position in Christ. Read the Bible and play Christian music. Praise God, and also praise him in song, even the doxology."

Mary and I have tried to sing the doxology together; she doesn't know the words yet, and I get off tune.

"And especially sing songs about the blood of Jesus; singing is a weapon the enemy can't stand. Before being cast out of heaven, Satan was in charge of the music. David used music to make demons leave Saul," Connie said.

The following day Connie called again with suggestions for Mary.

"Music is a big weapon, and singing God's word defeats the enemy. Praise is a weapon. It's important to use the Word of God when speaking. We should put on the Armor of God daily and also pray for those in authority. Ask for a hedge of protection about you. Ask for the mind of Christ. Ask to be filled with the Holy Spirit. Put off the old man and put on the new man [Ephesians 1:3-12 and Ephesians 4]. Ask the Lord to reveal generational sin, and pray to the Lord before bringing antiques into your home, because demons can attach to them. Demons are afraid of prayer. Mary, pray out loud and especially speak the Word out loud."

†

Mary came to Milpitas on Saturday. I read to her the gospel story about the unjust judge who finally gave justice to the widow, lest she weary him with her repeated requests [Luke 18:2-8]. We read Scriptures encouraging us to continue to ask God, and that our requests will be given to us. Jesus said to pray always, and not to give up [Luke 18:1].

Mary said to me, "Even when I pray, I'll be saying 'God, please send them away,' and the demons will say, 'Please God, let us keep Mary, we want to keep her, we want her to stay with us. We want to torment her for the rest of her life.' They keep mimicking me, but I know God knows better.

"When I'm praying to God and he [the demon] is praying too, to keep me, he says he knocks out my prayers. He says I owe him. I can't believe this is happening to me. I just can't believe it."

After a pause—because what can I say after that—I asked, "So how did you sleep last night?"

Mary said, "Well, they started in, but I was so fortified they got tired of me and they gave up. And they didn't wake me up at 3:00 o'clock, like they said they would."

I said, "Good!"

Mary said, "They say they will go. They're talking all the time. Then they tell me it's all lies they're telling me about leaving, and they'll be with me forever. They say I won't feel or hear anything, but they'll be tormenting me."

I took Mary back to Walnut Creek on Wednesday.

†

Connie will mail me a copy of the tape about pride. She suggested we pray together by phone before watching it. We must ask the Lord to bind the enemy so Mary can hear the Lord and the Holy Spirit. Connie thinks that is a blind spot, and she may be right. Mary has told me more than once she doesn't hear the Holy Spirit.

Connie said, "Pray that the Holy Spirit will bring whatever is relevant to Mary's attention, and that the mouths of all the demons will be shut. Satan keeps us blind to our own pride. That was his sin. I just want Mary to know she's not the only one that has pride. Satan's kingdom is built around that—the entire world system.

"They can do things to the phone lines. These guys that teach warfare, they backup systems, everything goes wrong. I do believe the enemy has power to mess around with our inventions, like television, DVDs, computers, phones, and all that stuff."

Connie will do no counseling from Thanksgiving through the rest of the year, except maybe by phone. I told her Mary had prayed to die if this doesn't stop.

†

When I talked with Mary this evening, she told me she had no sleep last night, for the third consecutive difficult night.

"This is wrecking my nervous system. If there isn't a sound, then I feel something crawling on my body. I know they're doing it; they told me they were. And then they fool around with my genitals! I can't stand that! In the morning hours when I should be asleep, they come on talking. But today it was a lot of their lousy music, and their hisser was hissing around my head. I'm getting so I can kind of take it because I've heard it so much. Sometimes I can sleep with it because it's the same tempo.

"Like I told the Lord, if only I can go to bed with no hindrances on me; if only I can go to bed and put my legs where I want. The Lord knows what's going on. There must be a reason. I don't know why I'm going through something like this. There's no privacy! I can't even think without them responding to my thoughts. It's a helpless feeling. I'm one against four. But I feel much braver tonight; I'm in a fighting mood. I can't run and hide."

†

By telephone I learned Mary finally slept better last night. "I slept on the couch," she told me.

This morning she read from the book of Revelation. "And *they* didn't like it," she said. "They say it disturbs them."

She's looking forward to her Bible class tomorrow. She said, "I put my place in order in case anyone should come by afterward. It takes time. I

129

read my prayers, and then I read my Bible. I tell the Lord in the daytime it's good to be alive. In the night I wish I was dead."

†

On Thursday, October 12TH, Annie became 94 years old. In the morning I picked up Mary in Walnut Creek, and we drove to Mill Valley. We picked up Ann and one of her neighbors and went to lunch. After our visit I brought Mary home with me.

Sometime after 3:00 a.m. I heard the crinkling sound of sheets of plastic. Now awake, I got up to use the restroom, and saw Mary walking down the stairs—in the dark—carrying things. Having trouble in her room, she was on her way to the den.

We have been talking about generational sin. As the demons listen to our conversations, they know we wonder if their "right" to be tormenting Mary might have come from some sin of her ancestors. She began telling me some lies the demons had been saying.

Mary reported, "They said my mother was cute, good looking. She had a lot of men before she married my father. They said she was like her mother, that her mother had lots of children, but they weren't all from the same father. You and I were talking about generational stuff, so those liars brought all this up. And they brought my father up. 'He was good looking, but he wasn't very sexy,' they said. I don't think he was ever a rounder, which was like a promiscuous guy. I don't think my father was that way.

"And then they added, they're not through with me. You know? They're not through with me until I give in! They say they're in the prostitution business. They say they can screw me through my fluids. Then Porgi [a demon] comes out and says, 'Don't believe that.' They are *not* very funny. Anyhow, that's the kind of stuff I have to listen to. They're not going to let me off easy, they're going to my house to 'fix it,' and when I get there .... Well, that's what I got this morning. Just evil!

"And this is what gets me. Because I don't want this disturbance to go on, I have to battle and pile stuff up around me so they don't get to my genitals. They make me itch and they give me a pain here and there. It's peculiar how they have power. And they keep telling me they can really hurt me. How did I ever get *into* this mess? How did I ever get into this *mess?*"

She shook her head.

"And when I recite Scripture to them, they repeat it to me and say, 'That isn't the one you should use to say something to us.' The woman demon says she wants me to be free. They're kind of funny sometimes, but it's not too funny when I want to sleep and they say, 'If we can't sleep, you can't sleep.' They say they work at night and don't like it when I tell you things. They say it hurts their business."

†

Mary came into the kitchen after saying her morning prayers and told me they woke her at 5:00 a.m. talking among themselves. But she said she slept well. We spoke with Connie who told Mary about Lucia (not her real name), a woman who had similar sexual spirits for about three years, but who has come to freedom. Connie told us she has known Lucia, who is now 86, for about eight years. Lucia said the worst thing is that the demons want to engage you in conversation. When they talk, Mary should either sing or quote Scripture.

"They're out to kill you; don't talk to them!" Lucia had said.

When Mary and I talked later on, I recounted this conversation and told her again, "they want to kill you." She said she knows that. Lucia had memorized a lot of Scriptures over the three-year period in which she combated demons, including Psalm 18, and she sang whenever the demons attempted to talk to her. Possibly because she is older, Mary hasn't memorized many Scriptures.

Connie said Lucia told her, "Mary needs to be in the New Testament, especially reading the gospels. She should read something from the gospel daily so Jesus can talk to her. Praying confession of generational sin can break underworld evil connections and the transference that can occur during sexual relationships and even through friendships."

November 4

Mary and I didn't get to bed in Milpitas until after 11:00 p.m., after praying various written prayers. She reads them to God; some are from Anderson's twelve steps booklet. She said they express her own thoughts.

Just as I drifted off to sleep, the loud sound of Mary's voice—almost yelling at the demons—jolted me back to consciousness. She had the light on and was reading Scripture to them. The battle raged for a couple of hours.

Last night after dinner Mary and I discussed the fact that we haven't yet prayed through the pride area, confessing sin, including ancestral sin. Twice we watched the video Connie sent on pride, as the evil one kept putting Mary to sleep the first time.

On a sheet of paper near the bottom of the page I drew a circle and stick picture of Mary with her smiling face. Above her I drew two circles to represent her mother and father, Giulia and Antonio. I drew an arrow from each of them, pointing toward Mary. Above her parents, I drew circles for each of Giulia's and Antonio's parents. We filled in only the name of Giulia's mother, Maria, which Mary learned from her cousin Teresa. Mary didn't know her father's parents' names. I added eight more circle faces, without names, above those four on the sheet of paper, until we had four generations, a total of fourteen ancestors. The Lord tells us in the Bible that he will punish the children for the sins of the parents to the third and fourth generations [Exodus 20:5].

Mary had shared with me earlier that her step mom, also named Maria, had made innuendos about Giulia having been unfaithful to Antonio. Mary confided that after her mother had died, a friend of the family also had said something like this to her. What could we do?

With my Bible open, I prayed with Mary regarding those passages. We told the Lord we have no knowledge of behaviors of Mary's ancestors, but "the buck stops here." We are both readers of His word, and we are learning his rules for our behavior. And because we love Him, we would "sin no more," as far as that was possible for us.

Earlier in the evening, Mary told me how much she longed for a peaceful night. She wanted to go to bed and lie down in peace, like she used to. She dreads going to bed. It's always worse for her at night. They torment her and steal her needed sleep.

Being tired last night, I fell asleep right away. In the morning I realized I had heard nothing from Mary's room during the night. She was still in bed sleeping when I got up. I feel hopeful.

Friday, November 10

Mary now fully understands she has strength and authority over evil in Christ, but these demons have not obeyed her orders for them to leave. Nor have they obeyed anyone else's orders to leave Mary.

The disciples came to Jesus and exclaimed, "Lord, even the demons obey us when we use your name!" Jesus told them, "Rejoice not that the demons are subject to you, but rather rejoice that your names are written in heaven" [Luke 10:20]. When the disciples asked why they could not get an evil spirit to leave a young boy, Jesus replied, "This kind can be cast out only by prayer" [Mark 9:29].

I have told Mary to depend on the strength of our Lord, but she says the demons are relentless, and she must cover herself with all those implements or they attempt to rape her. And having sex with the devil is a horribly disgusting thought. I'm grateful she gets some relief, and hopeful the Lord will shoo the evil ones away so she can sleep a few hours before they return to awaken her with loud noises, usually around 5:00 a.m.

"It's a difficult battle—more than you know," Mary said. "There are too many personalities to put up with. And those evil things touch me! I can't stand it! After the workout they gave me I slept fine, until they awakened me while it was still dark."

I believe when this is over we will laugh about it. When the Lord's purpose is served, when she is released from this suffering, we will look back and remember how she looked when she lifted up her nightgown to reveal the big red Macy's star on the plastic bag she cut into the shape of underpants, to wear to bed over two pair of her own underwear. At least I sure hope we can laugh about it.

December 1, 2006

Mary has been watching Andrew Wommack on television. After his show today, she phoned me.

"I was exhausted last night. I threw up my dinner—and all I had to eat was soup and cornbread and cottage cheese and pears. I don't understand why I threw up. Was it the Roquefort cheese with a little muffa [mold] on it?

"I slept well, although I slept on the couch as a precaution because they can't reach me as easily there. And of course there's always activity going on that I do my best to block out—noises and music I don't like."

We believe that Mary has finally learned what she needed to learn, confessed what she needed to confess, that God has changed her heart, and that this trial must soon end. However, several times during the past two years we thought freedom for Mary was just around the corner. And then the Lord showed us something more.

Now we are learning the power of the words that come out of our mouth. Both Joyce Meyer and Andrew Wommack have been talking about this. James, in his letter, teaches us about the power of the words we say:

> So the tongue is a little member and boasts of great things. How great a forest is set ablaze by a small fire! And the tongue is a fire. The tongue is an unrighteous world among our members, staining the whole body, setting on fire the cycle of nature, and set on fire by hell [James 3:5-6].

The Scriptures talk about the power of our words [Proverbs 18:20,21, et al.]. In the beginning God created the heaven and the earth by speaking things into being [Genesis 1:3, 1:6, 1:9, 1:11, 1:14, 1:20, 1:24, 1:26]. And in Romans 4:17 Paul writes that if we call that which hasn't happened yet, as if it has happened, we can bring into existence what didn't exist before. The King James version says "God ... calleth those things which be not as though they were."

Meyer, in her book *Me and My Big Mouth*, includes a summary of Scriptures on the mouth. She recommends we have "a list of confessions—backed up by the Word of God—which we speak out loud over our life, family, and future." (She also warns, "This practice can work against us if we are calling for things that are not God's will but the enemy's.")

The point is, we can steer and change our lives by the words we speak. If we make up a Scripture-based confession list, and say it out loud every day, or more often, we can become what we say we are. Conversely, people with negative attitudes about their lives, who go around speaking negatively, may bring about the very things they fear may happen. That is prophesying against oneself. An example of unwise words would be to repeat something like, "Oh, I'll always be too fat." Yes, you probably will. You just prophesied defeat over yourself. However, it is beneficial to speak positive phrases over oneself, especially phrases found in the Scriptures that conform with God's will for our lives.

For some time I have been bringing particular Scriptures to Mary's attention that I felt would be helpful in her struggle. I typed a confession list of warfare Scriptures for her which we both read aloud. We can personalize the word of God. We can change the word "you" to read "I," and say it aloud in a personal way. Following are some verses on Mary's list:

> I don't give the devil a foothold in my life. I humble myself before God. I resist the devil, and he flees from me. Ephesians 4:27; James 4:7.

> I bow down before the Lord and admit my dependence on him. James 4:10.

> I am strong with God's word living in my heart, and I have won my battle with Satan. 1 John 2:14c.

> I am a believer—not a doubter. Mark 5:36 KJV.

> I take every thought captive unto the obedience of Jesus Christ, casting down every imagination, and every high and lofty thing that exalts itself against the knowledge of God. 2 Corinthians 10:5.

> I catch the devil in all of his deceitful lies. I cast them down and choose rather to believe the Word of God. John 8:44; 2 Corinthians 2:11.

> I cast out devils and demons; nothing deadly can hurt me. Mark 16:17,18 KJV.

Last night a couple from Jakarta visited the small group I host at my home. The young woman told us she battled with the devil and had experienced a period in her life hearing voices. She said she was a new Christian and thinks she may have been victimized by Satan because she once practiced Buddhism. The Lord rescued another attendee from a similar circumstance.

†

On my walk today I talked to the Lord about Mary, and it seemed like he told me she had nothing to do but trust Him, cast her worries on Him, and wait. I recalled that Abraham waited a very long time before he and Sarah had the child God promised them [Genesis 21:2]. Mary amazes me; she can function with little sleep and with little food. It seems God has his hand on her situation; it seems supernatural to me.

Tuesday

Mary called. "I had a really good night; I slept in my own bed! It wasn't bugged! I slept well, and I thanked the good Lord."

"That's great, Mom! I'm happy about that. Why can't you sleep in your own bed every night?"

"Well, they bug 'em [her bed and her guest beds]. I get into one and then they screw 'em up. They can reach me better with their little hisser around."

"But last night wasn't like that?"

"I'm going into my own bed again tonight. The time has come to revolt. Can I call you back when I get these in the oven?"

(She was baking pumpkin muffins.)

I replied, "Okay. I may bake something too."

When Mary called back she said, "I see pictures of demons reflected on my windows. I saw their eyelashes move. I stared one down once."

"No, Mom, don't do that. Don't look at them. Thumbtack a sheet over the window."

December 11, 2006

Mary called and said, "I'm not so great, but I'm still alive. I'm going to read Scriptures to them. That takes a long time."

She called again in the evening and said, "I get so sick of hearing them with their rotten, nasty talk. Sometimes I sit in my car when I come home before going into my own house."

Mary talked about balancing her checkbook and writing checks for charities. Then, complaining about the demons, she said,

"They watch everything. They watch me balance my checkbook. They're always wrong. Today my nerves are very shattered, so I yield; I told them to shut up and get out. It's like having someone in the house you can't stand. They are leeches, and you can't get rid of them, and they do terrible things. And they keep me from sleeping when I'm piled up with so much stuff. Oh well.

"I was telling the Lord I'm losing days when they keep me from sleeping, but then I trust in the Lord ... that's all I can do. And they tell me I'm incompetent. Oh Lexie, you have no idea."

December 18

Today is Mary's 94TH birthday. She was pleased to receive a phone call from Enzo, our Italian cousin who lives in England. She told me that despite a bad night, she got up early and listened to Wommack, teaching on television. I talked with her again in the evening, and she told me what the demons are doing.

"They put pictures of faces up in all my windows, and in the dark I even see them on the ceilings. When night time comes, they get terrible."

I said, "I don't get it. I don't get why the Lord allows this to go on. What's the purpose?"

Mary said, "That's what I wonder too. What have I done to deserve this? I know I'm not an angel, but sometimes I don't quite get it. And especially this sort of thing. I said to Him this is offensive to You and to me too. I'm not this type. I found a prayer in my spiritual warfare folder. It has a couple of prayers they don't like."

I replied, "Good! Read it aloud morning, noon, and night!"

Mary continued, "Well, maybe I'll fix a potato to go with that corned beef. Well, Honey, see you in a couple days, God willing."

December 29

It's been several weeks since Mary started reciting her confession list out loud. I have amended it for her periodically, as I read the Word and come across a Scripture that I believe applies to her in this trial. It seems like when she recites these Scriptures throughout the day, she sleeps better with less interruption, harassment, and torment.

Wommack has been talking about his book, *You've Already Got It*, and as some of his teaching seemed particularly relevant to Mary's case, I ordered it for her.

I've been busy with the things life calls us to do, besides earning our living, while Mary has been under siege for the past two years. With Christmas coming, the thought of decorating the house—usually a joy—seems like too much to do right now. Both Mary and I need a break. We decided to escape the commercialism of Christmas by flying away to a warm place where we could worship our Lord quietly and celebrate the anniversary of his birth.

Neither of us have had a vacation in a while, so I made reservations and we flew to Scottsdale, Arizona. We shared a room, and I wondered how much sleep either of us would get. I wondered if Mary would be jumping out of bed, rebuking devils. We tried to keep positive thoughts, we each read our confessions lists, and I am happy to say Mary did very well. She had hoped to leave the demons at the airport in San Jose, but somehow, they followed her. She doesn't always tell me when they speak to her. She is learning to ignore their chatter, and she is getting better at reaching for Scripture to stop them.

We allowed ourselves five nights, but looking back, we should have taken a full week. Mary had a lot of catching up on rest to do, and some days we didn't get our breakfast much before noon. We did some sightseeing, but not as much as we would have liked. The time flew. We visited a wonderful church on Christmas Eve, a Sunday this year. Their parking lot was landscaped with many of Arizona's state tree, the Palo Verde. We learned that Palo Verde means "green stick" in Spanish. It's a gorgeous tree, with a beautiful green trunk, green branches, and small leaves, common in an arid climate.

We visited Frank Lloyd Wright's western home, Taliesin West. We planned to visit the Desert Botanical Garden, as both of us are interested in plants and the desert has a special beauty, but it was closed on Christmas Day. "No problem," I said to Mary. "We'll get up early and visit the Garden before we go to the airport tomorrow."

About 5:00 a.m. I realized Mary was awake. She spoke to me.

"I haven't been asleep yet," she said. "They're giving me a really hard time."

"Oh, Mom!" I exclaimed.

She had not had a bad night since we arrived in Scottsdale. Although she could hear them talking in the background, and although they did sometimes speak directly to her, she had been sleeping rather well. I was so pleased. Wasn't this the purpose of our trip? But last night they ganged up on her.

"Okay," I said, "try to sleep, and we'll skip the Botanical Garden."

CHAPTER 14
DEMONS BRING IMAGES

But those who wait on the Lord will find new strength.
They will fly high on wings like eagles. They will run and
not grow weary. They will walk and not faint.
Isaiah 41:31

MARY HAS BEEN making calls from a list she was given of people who drive seniors around when they no longer drive themselves. While she still drives, she prefers not to go onto freeways, and she has been longing to get to a particular butcher shop in San Leandro. She claims their meat is the best, and she wants the best for the cousins who will visit this month. Tony and Enzo arrive in a week, and we both look forward to seeing them.

Mary has had better control of her situation even though demons harass her day and night. Recently, with help from the Holy Spirit, she has been speaking the Word out loud (which demons cannot stand against), and life has seemed a little closer to normal. So we were both surprised when the phone disconnected immediately, as I mentioned to her we should get together and pray through sins of pride. However, she heard what I said, and she knew *they* were continuing their evil tricks. She dialed me back, and we finished our conversation.

We want to continue with Anderson's twelve steps to freedom. We will ask the Lord to reclaim ground that inadvertently may have been surrendered to the realm of darkness.

It didn't seem relevant to mention earlier, but I am having trouble with my hands. Some time back, maybe six months ago, I noticed that using my left thumb for my cell phone was becoming difficult. Picking up a plate from the kitchen cupboard with my left hand was painful. The condition worsened, and I visited the doctor.

"It's tendonitis," he said. "Take over-the-counter anti-inflammatory drugs."

I dutifully took ibuprofen twice a day for a couple of months, but saw no improvement, so I stopped taking them. Other than using my cell phone, I couldn't see how this condition might have developed. Around November my right thumb began to suffer the same painful inflammation. The condition made the Thanksgiving meal more difficult to prepare.

I wondered why. Well, yes, I probably was overusing my right hand since my left thumb had been affected. Had I strained it opening jars? No, I couldn't believe both of my thumbs were impaired by opening jars.

Over the course of Mary's trial, she has mentioned that the evil ones told her they will go after me. She would hate that, and I'm sure they delighted in her horror of the idea. But I must consider this possibility. When we worked with Connie, she was constantly on the alert and prayed for protection against being targeted by the enemy. Doesn't it make sense that demons might attack those whom they perceive to be attacking them by rescuing those whom they are tormenting?

Mary and I have been using the Word of the Lord against them. Paul, in his letter to the Ephesians, tells us to:

> Put on the full armor of God ... and take the helmet of salvation, and the sword of the Spirit, which is the word of God [Ephesians 6:11,17].

If I use the sword of the Spirit against them, they may fight back by disabling my use of the sword. In the Old Testament, when a king was defeated, the victors cut off his thumbs so he could no longer hold a sword. They also cut off his big toes so he could not chase after them.

> But Adonibezek fled; and they pursued after him, and caught him, and cut off his thumbs and his great toes. Judges 1:6 KJV

And Wommack, in his book *You've Already Got It!*, tells us,

> "God's Word is spiritual. The Bible tells us what's truly going on in the spirit realm ... God's Word is a spiritual mirror."

"You'll never move into the supernatural things of God while being dominated by the natural realm—what you can see, taste, hear, smell, and feel. If you can't believe anything beyond what your five senses can tell you or confirm, then you are carnally minded. If something must be proven in a test tube, scientifically, before you'll believe it exists, then you're trapped in the natural realm. 'God is a Spirit, and He moves in the spirit realm. (John 4:24.)'"

Once I realized the demons had targeted me, I found and spoke appropriate Scripture verses, and healing took place.

January 11

I called Mary as she was preparing her lunch. She had not slept as much as she would have liked—and she has minimized her standards for sleep—but she got up early to go to Bible study, the first meeting following the holidays. She had no breakfast. How can one exist without sleep and without food? She had coffee, which these days is heated milk with two large spoonsful of instant coffee in it, so she got a little protein and calcium. She told me they served the group a fruit cup, which she enjoyed very much.

I read a few passages of Wommack's book to her. I believe he is on track, and my plan is to explain his ideas to Mary. We may change our thinking as he's coming from a position of victory in Christ, and all of us born again in Christ have that ability. Either not trying or unbelief keeps us from accomplishment. The instructions we need for success in life are in the Word of God. We benefit by reading it, and subsequent readings provide greater understanding.

> Verily, Verily, I say unto you, He that believeth on me, the works that I do shall he do also; and greater works than these shall he do; because I go unto my Father. John 14:12 KJV

Wommack writes, "As I have drawn on the joy that God has already placed within my born-again spirit, I've lived a consistently victorious life .... "

I recalled the joy I felt when Mary told me she was a "born-again Christian." I felt so good! She truly understood! I remembered the time the Holy Spirit told me I had been born again. Hallelujah!

January 28

Mary slept well on the porch. She has been sleeping with her robe, raincoat, and comforter on top of her for protection.

"Some things are different now. They said they're going to leave me with music."

Mary tells me they talk of leaving, but they haven't left. Her comment left me hopeful.

She continued. "They watch me all the time. That lesbian demon is fooling with me all the time—it's terrible! I'm sick of them! All they talk about is f-ing me." But she added hopefully, "I feel the Lord is with me; he will make it go away. They have kind of decreased it, except that female. Oooh ... ugh!"

January 29

"Not a good night at all. I'm a rag today," Mary said.

She explained how the past few nights have been difficult for her.

"You're sleeping and it's like they shoot something at you—it's just like a needle. They torment me! They can be ruthless."

It's late morning, and over the phone I hear a clinking sound.

"Are you drinking alcohol?" I asked, thinking about the sound ice cubes make, clinking in a glass.

"That's my coffee," she said.

She was stirring it. She has been having brandy over ice before dinner each evening for the past few months.

"I drink one drink in the evening. It increases my appetite. I think I eat more," she explained. "I watch the gardening show from 6:00 to 7:00, and then I eat. But I didn't even eat my tapioca last night; I was so tired."

February 1

While talking with Ann last evening, I told her Mary has had several tough nights.

"Why doesn't she go to a psychiatrist?" Ann asked again.

Many people ask that question. Mary fully understands her situation and knows the Lord is in control of it. She also knows an unbelieving psychiatrist will know only to prescribe drugs for her. She doesn't want to suppress the problem with drugs, if that were possible. She wants the demons to leave her. Rather than treat the symptom, she wants to be cured, to be healed. And the cure is to cast them out, just as Jesus cast out demons years ago.

Mary took the drug prescribed by her primary care physician to help her sleep. At his direction she even doubled it for a while, but after sleeping a few hours, she would awaken to hear the tormenting noises of the demons. So she gave up the medication.

February 13

Mary stayed with me for more than a week. I wanted her to read Wommack's book and understand that God's Word is spiritual. Just as we have physical laws on earth, like gravity, there are spiritual laws, which differ from ours. He talks about faith and unbelief. He draws an analogy about a horse (faith) trying to pull a cart in one direction, while another horse (unbelief) attempts to pull the same cart in the opposite direction. When this occurs, nothing happens. The cart doesn't move. We must pray for the Lord to take away unbelief. (The New Testament has multiple references to unbelief.) Wommack helps us see the Scriptures perhaps differently than we have before. I felt blessed by his writing, and I knew Mary would as well. God is faithful. He will bring her through this. Neither of us doubt that.

After studying Wommack's concepts, I tried to cast out those ugly demons. But even as a born-again believer with authority over them in Christ, they did not obey. If I can gather several believers together, and if we pray for Mary together, then in Jesus' mighty name we command them to leave, they must leave. The difficult part is finding believers who have faith, without unbelief, who are willing to have a go at demons. Many Christians are unwilling even to speak of demons.

Days go by quickly. There's shopping, meal preparation, and laundry to do. There's business and Bible study. I spend hours daily reading the Bible and Christian authors.

Former Oakland Raiders player, Napoleon Kaufman, pastors a church near us. I have watched his teachings on television. One evening he introduced a woman who talked about deliverance ministry. I called them. Their program was four weeks—the first three weeks of this and that, and then prayer the fourth week. Mary has done that.

Wommack doesn't think it's necessary to go through a person's life history before commanding demons to leave. But others are doing this. We spent a lot of time going over Mary's past, her relationships, her entire life. She listed every sin she remembers committing. She confessed them all and asked the Lord for forgiveness. But she still has demons tormenting her, keeping her from sleep, shocking her awake, and putting their pictures on her microwave's window and her glass sliding doors.

When I told her about Kaufmann's church, she asked me how they get demons out. She's tired of endless questions, even from loving people, who could not help her. I'm at the point where I believe if we can just get some strong believers, who don't doubt, we can cast them out.

February 28

As I hadn't heard from Mary, I called her. She had a terrible night and began telling me about it. After listening for some time, I grabbed my note book.

Mary said, "I need a prayer for demons; my prayers just don't work. I have my spiritual warfare prayer, which they don't like, but it doesn't seem to be working. If they don't get out of here, they'll wreck another Spring."

(I could hear her tearing up, almost crying a little.)

"It's demoralizing," she continued. "You don't want to think about it, but you can't help it ... they torment you horribly. They torment, abuse, and molest you. And they have stuff working on you. I put a scarf on my head for protection. They use feathers or something on my eyes. It's awful. And they fire something into my vagina. And I'm battling that. I know there's nothing there, but I feel it. So I fight it. And then they say, 'She has broken the string.' And they say all these guys want to 'f' me. I know they're capable of these things because they've hurt me. But I don't like these surprises. It's gruesome. And that horrible music is going on. You can't sleep!"

Before dialing her number I put a piece of French toast into a frying pan, on low heat. But as I listened to Mary's story I forgot about it. I could now smell burning and turned some attention to it. As she continued her story, unaware of my late breakfast, I grabbed the handle of the fry pan and flipped the bread over. I turned the heat lower, then decided to turn it off.

Mary was saying, "It's bad on my nervous system. I haven't been up very long. At 4:00 o'clock they told me, why don't you go into your own bed? I haven't cracked up yet, but my nervous system is shot. At the least little thing I jerk and I get jolted. I say, 'Dear Lord, forgive me for sinning, I hate them.'"

I interrupted, telling her to stop blaming herself, that it's okay to hate the devil. I assured her their doom is predicted and sure—that God has prepared the lake of fire for them.

Again I asked her not to focus so much on the demons, but to focus on God, and to ask Him to fill her with His Holy Spirit. Although in my heart I know that's easier to say than to do, especially when one is constantly under attack. Mary continued her story.

"I'm trying to sleep. You always hear it. You never know what to expect because sometimes they do to me what they say they'll do. I'm surrounded with enemies, and I'm battling. They're usually in a good mood in the daytime, but at night time they're awful. I want to kill them.

"I know they're not real," Mary repeated regarding the images they post on her sliding glass doors, the microwave, the television screen, and even on the curtains. "But they look ugly! When I first saw one that wanted to come in, I swung at him with my big spoon. Well, then they retreat backwards and they fade away. You could write a book. They're the scum of the earth.

"Oh, one evil one is also fooling with my behind. They say they want to 'defrock' me and make me a little boy and do me in my butt. They think because God is doing nothing they're okay, but I have not lost my faith yet. I'll endure. I don't know how long I can go without sleep though; it's not good for my heart."

"People are praying for you." I said.

March 5

It's almost 5:00 p.m. and I'm tired. I jogged a couple of miles earlier today, but the fatigue is from insufficient sleep last night. My heart goes out to Mary. We said prayers and went to bed around 11:00 p.m. I had just fallen asleep when I heard Mary reading aloud and I saw light coming from her room. She was sitting up in bed, with a scarf on her head, reading Bubeck's prayer against demonic oppression. We prayed together and asked the Lord for His power to cast them out. Then I summoned my courage and my voice and told them that by the power and authority of the Lord Jesus Christ they *had* to go. Mary was quiet, listening to their sounds and speech.

"He's getting all emotional," she said. "He doesn't want to go; he said, 'Jesus will send him to Hell.'"

After several brief speeches, we both went back to bed. An hour later Mary was reading aloud again, light flooding down the hall into my room. Once again I got up, put on my robe, and marched into her room to command the demons to leave. When it seemed quiet, I got back into bed. Not long afterward, however, I heard Mary descend the stairs to sleep in the den.

†

As I came downstairs this morning, the doors to the den were closed and I let her sleep. I heard a sound a little after 10:00 a.m., and I walked into the den bringing Mary's coffee. She spent the latter part of the night on the unopened sofa bed covered with her robe. When I came in she sat up and pulled out that large metal cooking spoon.

"Wait," she said to me, "I have another one." She stood up and looked about saying, "It must have fallen between the cushions."

She opened her robe, reached up under the hem of her nightgown, and the first thing she took off was a pair of Depends.

Mary said, "This is what they use for incontinent people; see how thick they are? But see how loose? The demons can't go through terry cloth. I wear my own underpants. The Depends goes on next, and then another pair of my underpants—to keep it all snug. It's an awful big nuisance, I'll tell you that! Next I adjust a towel so it comes up over my behind and the excess covers the front.

"Those demons can get into the darnedest spots. As they get in, I can move that spoon. I need to block the entrance to my vagina. If they're getting close with their arrows or darts, I use the spoon—I move it around—but it sure hurts my hands to move it."

Mary's hands have become arthritic, and sometimes some fingers on her right hand become numb.

I said, "You wear a scarf on your head at night too. Why is that?"

"Well, that's because if I'm making it tough on them to get to me, then they want to mess with my eyes. You know how you feel something on your face? The scarf works pretty good in keeping that away. Remember, they don't want me to sleep; that's a punishment for me."

She added, with resignation in her voice, "I've been hearing the same stuff for two years, and I know they must be ugly. I hear so much stuff … yeah."

"What's that?" I asked, pointing to a canvas tote bag with handles.

"They can't get through canvas very good. That's my supplies. I load up with everything I can so they can't reach me. They say they can't get through the robe, but I don't know. I get those darts, so I pile up another blanket on top of me and a pillow on top of that. Well, they couldn't reach me last night, but they kept trying.

"Oh, they're so clever. They say they can have me killed … they say they will rape me … and then they say they've made up a dummy. When they work on the dummy, I feel it. But if I protect myself, I don't feel it. There're all kinds of crap, Lexie, you wouldn't believe it. I get such stories. They tell me I'm an old, used-up prostitute, and they'll dump me like a has-been. They say they 'want to throw me out because they know they can,' and it goes on and on."

Later March 5

Mary was inattentive to our dinner conversation. She seemed to focus on the conversation between the demons she heard going on in her mind. When I asked her what was going on, she said, "They're listening to everything we say; can you tell me later?"

Well, that got my dander up! Immediately I began reading aloud from the "Defeat of Evil" list of Scriptures I had compiled and typed for myself and for Mary. As Mary repeated some of his mocking to me, I told him he must go where Jesus sends him. I cast him out by the name and authority of the Lord Jesus Christ of Nazareth. When I said that, he said to Mary, who repeated to me, "he could hurt me." So I continued with Scripture, reading aloud Luke 10:19 and Mark 16:16,17. At that point I remembered I was to bind them first; so I said, "I bind you in the name and power of Jesus Christ and whatever I bind on earth is bound in heaven." [Matthew 18:18] Then I shot up a nonverbal arrow prayer to the Lord, saying the power was His and asked Him to make them leave Mary forever.

A little later while we were still at the table Mary leaned over and whispered to me, they said they "would not keep Mary awake past 2:00 a.m. tonight."

"But," she continued, "You can't count on them." And then added, "One is a real devil, but the others are wimps. They told the leader they should leave, but then this is probably all a part of their act and lies."

March 12

I enjoy learning from Christian television networks. "Nada es Imposible para Dios" followed a program I watched. I know a few words of Spanish, and I spent a little time watching the program. I learned they are a Christ following ministry, located less than an hour's drive from my home. Their ministries include praise and healing services.

Recently I received an email response to my request for help for Mary sent to another ministry. The respondent, from their Encouragement Department, took time to write many pages to me, which I passed along to Mary, but the first line really said it all. "For the most part, in the Bible, demons were cast out by a person who is directly there dealing with the person in the midst of the situation." Well, I tried that, and I'll continue to do so until they have left, but meanwhile I'll look under more stones. I called the number on the screen for Nada es Imposible para Dios.

Spanish words tumbled out of my handset, much too fast for me to respond to, so I stammered a bit, then asked the female voice if she spoke English. "Yes," she said, and asked how she could help me. As briefly as possible, I explained Mary's situation.

"My mom, who's ninety-four, is oppressed by demons; can you help her?"

"We have a pastor who can help you," she said. "She has written two books. She speaks English and she preaches deliverance and interceding one Friday a month. She has a heart to help people, and her next time to preach is March 9TH."

I was speaking with a woman about demons! "They don't want to leave; they claim a body for their home. They think they have legal rights to stay there, but they don't. They have to leave. They don't want to listen to you. They will put up a fight. They don't want to obey right away, but you have to stand on your belief."

"Hallelujah! Praise the Lord!" I said silently in my mind. "At last, someone who understands, who speaks this spiritual warfare language!" She gave me a few Scriptures, and continued, "At the end, when you insist, he won't even want to come around you."

Yes! The best news I received in two years! I believed this already, but it helped so very much to hear it from another person. She gave me the pastor's name and phone number. "Joyce Martinez teaches spiritual warfare and prayer and healing," she said.

After taking a minute to let the conversation sink in, I picked up the telephone and called Reverend Martinez.

"I do have the gift of spiritual warfare, and that's to bind up and loose the spiritual forces of evil," she said. "I am anointed since 1991. Do you know Morris Cerullo?" she asked.

I did not.

She was on his team; he was a prophet. She has been under his teaching since 1991, and she confirmed she would preach March 9th.

"Come to our church that night. You will see, the gates of hell will tremble. I KNOW she will be delivered. It's a spirit of harassment. She WILL get delivered and set free," she said to me in a strong voice indeed.

She said to come to the front row and sit with her.

"I have blonde hair and blue eyes," she added.

"I do too," I said.

March 9, typed April 3

We wanted to be on time, find Joyce, introduce ourselves, and sit with her in front, as she had suggested. It was already dark. Fortunately, we found a parking space a few doors down from the church. Walking toward the entry, we passed double glass doors with closed curtains inside. Through a separation between drapery panels I could see a large room with neat rows of stackable upholstered chairs.

"This must be the place," I said to Mary. "There are lots of chairs inside."

We continued to a second set of doors and entered. We found ourselves in the back of the room. To our right was a counter with several young men standing by, speaking Spanish.

"Oh yes," one of them said to me in English, "Joyce Martinez will be here. The service starts at 7:30. Have a seat."

In the front of the hall a raised stage held musical instruments, a podium, and a container of lovely cymbidium orchids. Mary and I walked toward the front and took seats on the left aisle about seven or eight rows back.

People drifted in. One young man, on his knees, faced the back of his chair. Across the room another young man was kneeling, facing the wall. As I looked around, I noticed several people praying alone. Others were chatting. Occasionally women came and welcomed us.

I felt a commanding presence and looked up; I knew this was Joyce. She was a large woman, compared to Mary and me, whose frames are small. She was nicely dressed in a black dress with beading on the bodice and a short white jacket. Her fluffy hair had been bleached blonde, and she wore dark red lipstick. Her dark eyes peered at me through blue contact lenses, giving me a bit of an eerie feeling, quite frankly.

We stood out as much as she did, I'm sure, as everyone else present had brown to black hair. I introduced myself and Mary to her, and she invited us to sit with her in the front row.

The music began. I had been told this service lasted from 7:30 until

10:00 p.m. I hoped Mary could handle the length of time and the loud music, as she has often mentioned when music is too loud for her. Five women and a man were on stage singing praise songs to the Lord. The keyboard guy, the drummer, and other musicians were giving it their all. The music was great! I knew a couple of the songs, as we sing them (in English) at my church. I glanced to my left to see Mary joyfully swaying to the music, smiling, hands raised in praise.

When the music stopped, Joyce took the stage and was introduced. She gave a powerful sermon on spiritual warfare, pausing between sentences, waiting for an interpreter to translate her English words into Spanish. That gave us time to grasp and understand each thing she said. I heard, "Amen" a lot from the congregation, indicating to me they understood, believed, and agreed with what she was teaching us about the powers of darkness in the spiritual realm.

"We are all in this battle, and if you don't fight, you lose," she said.

Following the sermon, people who needed help or deliverance came to the front where others prayed for their healing. They called Mary forward. She stood before several men who prayed that the power of the Lord fall upon her and release her from the clutches of the devil. Like others that evening, she too fell backward, being caught by a man standing behind her for that purpose, and helped to lie on a mat on the floor, where she rested for a few minutes. Based upon my understanding, these wonderful people did everything biblically. Unfortunately, the demons went home with Mary.

March 17

I was sitting at my computer when Mary called. She sounded down, and said she didn't get much sleep.

"There was a lot of noise, the loudest hissing I've ever heard. It sounded like a circus going on. But I know it's something he puts on. It sounds like it's outside."

Walter continues to tell Mary she is married to him. When she told me that, I told her to respond by saying "It is written, I belong to God, I have been bought with a price."

She responded saying, "Yes, that's good, but you're thinking more clearly than I am. I'm without rest. I get all kinds of noises and then I get these faces ... and if I close my eyes, I can still see those ugly faces. The one with the big nose is supposed to be him," she said, referring to Walter, the leader and the worst one. "I endure because I can't fight. I just wonder what kind of spirits I've got. They keep telling me I'm not praying right. It's such a stronghold. I feel a little dejected because I feel that my springtime is being wasted."

March 20

Mary said, "I'm reading Wommack's book. He's great, and I'm learning. I slept, but not as good as I would like, but I got enough sleep to sustain me. I don't feel so dragged out. I was very glad to get up and hear Wommack on television. He even impressed the evil ones. I didn't say a word. They are so foul. But wouldn't it be good to get some evil ones to repent?"

I told her to say Ephesians 4:29 out loud when they use foul language.

"Let me write it down," she said. "Let me put this phone down while I get my little pad."

March 21

I had just turned on the computer when Mary called. I put the phone on speaker and began typing.

Mary said, "Nothing is changed around here. I'm still working hard on it, and I'm still bouncing around from one place to the other in the wee hours in the morning. I'm being aggravated beyond measures. Their little faces and bodies; they're looking in the windows. So I got a spray gun and they took off. I slept with the light on; they don't like light."

"What do you mean, a spray gun?"

"A spray bottle with water in it. They're life size. Even if it's just an image, they look so alive. And they blink."

"They blink their eyes?" I asked.

"Yes, they do. Out of the corner of my eye I'll see a dark shadow, and I ignore it, but it's so annoying. And then I see something like a big black fly. And they say, 'that's one of our restructured spirits.' I say, 'I'll smash it to bits!' And then it leaves."

I reminded her of a particular prayer, addressing restructured spirits.

"They don't like that prayer; that gets to them. It says here, 'I also bind all replacer spirits. I forbid any dividing, restructuring, or multiplying of wicked spirits.' They say they reproduce themselves. The funny thing is, they have a regular man-sized head on my porch. Nobody sees this but me. It's like a head and an egg below it that's all dark. What they're trying to do is scare me. And you know my skylights? They look down on me from there, like putting a big man's head on the skylight ... you know, when evening comes, when it gets dark. Oh Lexie, if you only knew what they do to me. It's disgusting. They change, and none of them are nice faces. And they get up against my window."

I said, "Are they on the outside?"

"Yes, they float around. It's dark, but you know, one morning when I was sleeping in my own bed, I looked out from my bedroom window. It's like there's a platform with something on it, and they float off of the platform. It's goofy. I'm seeing things they're doing only for my benefit."

"Not for your benefit, Mom, for your destruction."

"They want to scare me, but they're not scaring me. You know, when I'm at your house, I see them too. When we're watching television, like when we were watching Charles Stanley, they were out there looking at me. But not as many as I get here."

"Were they outside here too?"

"Yes, they're always outside, but one night they were in my bedroom. I have a lot of light that comes in, enough to see them. And when I swat at one of them, it backs away. You'd be surprised. This is really crap, but it does something to you. It's like you've lost control in your own house. I want to regain control. I'll get it back. I had to get out of that bed last night; I had too much action. I got disgusted, so I take up all my stuff and move to the next bed. And when I see those little spooky things I turn on the light. They blink at me. And I told you one night they came into the house on stilts. One would seem to be coming from the window to the porch, and then they'd come out dancing. They'd come toward me, but never touch me.

"They've started a new torment; they give me 'the heats.' When I'm prepared for battle, I have a lot of stuff on me. So they use the hisser to turn up the heat, so I'll get hot and take away my armor, so they can get at me at that spot. So I decided if they come in again, I'll put the bathroom light on; they don't like that. I put the light on last night when I moved out onto the porch.

"Today I told him don't talk to me because it's always lies, lies, lies. I said anything you've got to say, you swear by Jesus Christ that it's the truth, so don't talk to me. I thought, 'Oh boy, this is it, I won't have to listen to them.' But they go on and on, whether or not I want to listen. But it is quieter this morning.

"I didn't get to sleep until after 3:00. Instead of going to my bed, I read my prayer in the dining room, and when I went to bed, they didn't bother me. When I woke up this morning, it was still dark. I looked around from the bed on the porch, and these four voices were saying they were going to kidnap me and use me for sexual purposes and for wickedness. And I will be under the leader's control, like a puppet. Oh gawd, you ought to hear it. Later, when I woke up again, there was no talking; I woke up to silence. But the light was on, and I wondered where I was, and then I realized I was on the porch."

I said, "No Mom, they can't do that; they can't kidnap you."

"I know that, but I hear it all the time. And they don't want me near you because you influence me. It's so much. It's an ugly atmosphere I'm under. This is their time to sleep, but they're listening to every word."

I offered, "I don't think spirits need to sleep. That's probably a lie too."

Mary continued. "It's so demoralizing to listen to them. And if I'm in the house, I just get it. Whether or not you want to listen to it, you get it. And now they say they like Wommack. I hope he has an influence on them. There's a bunch of them—blabbing all the time. And that female, she's pretty sharp.

"Well anyhow, I've said my prayers to the Lord, and I tell him I know there're other people with worse problems and I know he'll free me when he's ready. I praise him, and I don't bring my problem up very much."

I said, "Yeah, that's good. Because he already knows about your problem, and remember Joyce Meyer said "praise and be raised, complain and remain."

Mary said, "Walter said, 'I guess you won't get rid of me unless you give in.'"

I said, "That's a lie. Say to them, 'I belong to God, I've been bought with a price.' Say, 'I cast down imaginations.'"

"They wait for my prayers. And then they dispute them. And they wait for me to read *Our Daily Bread* so they can dispute that too. I don't have much time. I don't think I gave the Bible an hour yesterday."

"That should be your focus now."

"And I have my Bible class to do. That's the Bible. I don't have time for the study questions, but they want you to come whether or not you do the lesson. Well, look at the time. I've got to take a bath and get dressed."

"Tell me how much sleep you got last night."

"Probably four hours. Let's see, I don't know for sure because it was after 3:00 ... well anyhow, I've lived on four hours of sleep for some time."

"Find that Scripture, 'I take every thought captive unto the obedience of Jesus Christ, and I cast down imaginations ... ' [2 Corinthians 5:10] You *will* drive them out!"

"Yes, I've got to do it. I'll talk to you later. Bye."

"Bye Mom."

March 27 At Milpitas

After finishing our lunch of leftover pasta (always delicious!) and some celery sticks, I asked Mary how she slept. Before going to bed, we had sat at the table and prayed. We praised the Lord, and we thanked him for many of our blessings. We read one of David's Psalms and asked for angelic help in the battle Mary is forced to wage with the spirits from this present darkness. Then I told the spirits they were bound, and commanded them to leave, by the power and the authority of Jesus Christ.

Mary said, "They awakened me at 2:00 a.m., and they really gave it to me. They told me how stupid I was and that I can't get them out, only you can get them out. They think I'm too passive, that I don't holler and scream at them, and they will be with me forever because I'm too dumb to get them out."

"Oh, Mom. We know that's not true. You can't believe their lies. When you believe them, they win. To quote Wommack, the battle is 'between your ears.'"

As frequently as I advise Mary not to believe their lies, she reminds me she's simply reporting what they say to her.

Mary said, "You did a good job on them. They say when they get me at home they'll give it to me. Last night you know what they did? They had you on the wall. They send all those spooky things. Gee, I thought, it looks like Lexie, but that's not the way Lexie looks. And they said that's the way she'll look when she gets older.

"And you know what's at my house now? I'll be busy and something goes by me, and I look, and nothing's there. They are little (she waved her hand, showing about two feet tall). I never saw one so small, but when I go to bed, they bring up one with a human-sized face, up by my window. And they change. And they're ugly. They've never had a good-looking one! He makes them, so he says. He's the one who drew you. So that's what I'm hearing."

I told Mary about our friend Olivia seeing a demon in the baby's room, crouched down, hiding. Olivia said it was small.

Mary said, "Yes! They're small. The head is like an actual person, but it's dark and difficult to see. I don't have my glasses on and it comes toward me and if I swat at it, it evaporates and disappears. It looks at you and it's a real face. And Walter says, 'That one wants to 'f' you, so you better look out for him.'"

We laughed.

"In the daylight, Lexie, it's funny, but at night it's spooky. I get so sick of that kind of talk. 'We don't like you, but we all want to 'f' you.' He is so obsessed with me. I said 'nobody will get to my body; I'm dedicated to the Lord ... and furthermore you all will go limp,' and then they all went limp! And then he said, 'Let's get out of here, she's a witch!' But they don't go. They acted like they were afraid of me, but they didn't go. They shoot their arrows at me and I wave my spoon at them and tell them, 'those arrows will go back to you,' and you know, they go back!"

CHAPTER 15
DEMONS LOOM AT MARY

The Lord is my light and my salvation; whom shall I fear? The Lord is the strength of my life; of whom shall I be afraid? Psalm 27:1

WHILE MARY STAYED with me in Milpitas this week, we focused on "calling into being those things which are not" [Romans 4:17] and talked about the power of our words. The Gospel of John—the good news—begins, "In the beginning was the Word, and the Word was with God, and the Word was God" [John 1:1]. John, a disciple who spent time with Jesus during His ministry on earth, tells us Jesus is "the Word" and that Jesus is God. In the first chapter of Genesis we note that "God *said*," and called things into being. God also said in Genesis 1:26-27 "Let us make man in our image, according to our likeness ... in the image of God he created him; male and female he created them."

In his book, *A Better Way to Pray*, Wommack suggests, "Don't speak to God about the problem, but speak to the problem about God." Isn't that what Jesus taught in Matthew 17:20 and also in Matthew 21:21? Wommack teaches us to speak death to cancer, while we speak life to our bodies. He references the fig tree Jesus cursed as an example of the power of our words [Matthew 21:19]. And he teaches that prayer is a process, that things go on behind the scenes in the heavenly realm when we pray.

†

While sitting at the breakfast table I observed, "You don't look joyful."

Mary said, "Well, I would like to be, but I'm not. I feel like nothing is changing. And I think Jesus, Jesus, Jesus. The background sounds I hear in my mind are still rotten. I said to the Lord today, 'I am free, thanks to the Lord.'"

Mary was "calling what is not yet, into being."

I said, "Repentance means changing. It takes time. You've been one way for ninety years. You're intelligent and you're learning."

Over the past few days we prayed and took charge of the situation. We used our words and the authority we have in Christ to cast out the evil ones, and now Mary is waiting for her freedom to manifest. The demons have quieted down, but she still has awareness of their presence. Just as it took a day for the fig tree to wilt after Jesus cursed it, I told her it may take time for the evil ones to leave.

Roses were on the table that Mary had cut from the rosebush in the backyard.

I said, "You cut these roses from their life source, the rosebush, and even though these blooms are beautiful, they're dead now. It'll take some days for all the life to drain out of them, and during that time we'll enjoy their beauty and their fragrance. But those cut roses won't grow again or produce more roses."

April 30

Back in Walnut Creek, Mary sounded fine, said she slept pretty well, but was awakened too early. She talked about her orchids, saying she wanted to buy fertilizer. Although she hasn't talked much about the problem, this morning she said, "I want my freedom and I want my privacy."

She has learned from Wommack that when we pray within God's will, we are to believe we have what we ask for, although we may not see the results until later. He says a process occurs as the answer to the prayer manifests from the spiritual realm into the natural or physical realm. We are to believe, have faith, and know that once we pray, God answers immediately. But with things going on in the spiritual realm, sometimes there is a delay before we receive God's answer to our prayer. He illustrates from the book of 2 Kings, Chapter 6:8-17.

> When the king of Aram was at war with Israel, he would confer with his officers and say, "We will mobilize our forces at such and such a place." But immediately Elisha, the man of God, would warn the king of Israel, "Do not go near that place, for the Arameans are planning to mobilize their troops there." So the king of

Israel would send word to the place indicated by the man of God, warning the people there to be on their guard. This happened several times. The king of Aram became very upset over this. He called in his officers and demanded, "Which of you is the traitor? Who has been informing the king of Israel of my plans?" "It's not us, my lord," one of the officers replied. "Elisha, the prophet in Israel, tells the king of Israel even the words you speak in the privacy of your bedroom!" The king commanded, "Go and find out where Elisha is, and we will send troops to seize him." And the report came back: "Elisha is at Dothan." So one night the king of Aram sent a great army with many chariots and horses to surround the city. When the servant of the man of God got up early the next morning, and went outside, there were troops, horses, and chariots everywhere. "Ah, my lord, what will we do now?" he cried out to Elisha. "Don't be afraid!" Elisha told him, for there are more on our side than on theirs!" Then Elisha prayed, "O Lord, open his eyes and let him see!" The Lord opened his servant's eyes, and when he looked up, he saw that the hillside around Elisha was filled with horses and chariots of fire.

God opened the servant's *spiritual* eyes. Faith bridges the spiritual world to the physical world. We find another instance of delay in receiving an answer to prayer in Daniel 10:12-13.

Mary is intently believing her prayers for release have been answered, and she is waiting for the manifestation—the moment when she will no longer hear the demons or see their "imaginations." She told the demons she is free.

Today she shared recent experiences.

"Last night I slept on the couch, and they made these big heads. They mock everything, even when I pray. And this thing was leaning over me— it was on stilts—and as I reached out toward it with my spoon, he evaporated. I turned on the light."

"Why did you turn on the light?"

"They evaporate quicker. It annoys me immensely! I finally tell myself to talk to the Lord and I tell Him. And then I shut my eyes, and that's it. They are the most evil! They are on the subject of sex and that drives me bats! I've been so un-private for so long."

May 3

Mary called today after noon. "I'm so sick of this thing! They put their ugly faces up on stilts, and they covered my slider! He produces restructured stuff, and they float around. They're supposed to be paper, but I know they're really nothing; they're unreal. He puts them on stilts so they look like they have legs, but they have no arms. When I'm in bed, if I happen to open my eyes, there they are! They come looming toward me, and even though you know it's not real, it comes toward me, and I say, 'I'm going to crack that head,' and it vanishes. Last night they were coming toward me. I know they can't touch me, but seeing those grotesque things, larger than human size ... "

I said, "Say to them, 'I catch the devil in all his deceitful lies, I cast down imaginations, and I choose rather to believe the Word of God.'"

Mary said, "I've told them. They get tired of hearing it. So I just keep my eyes closed, but they still have their racket going on. If I can get to sleep, they give me a jolt, and I'm startled awake. I can't make much noise because of my neighbors, and they take advantage of the fact that I can't scream at them. I read to them from *The Blood of Jesus*, and that gets to them for a while, but he's becoming hateful."

"He's always been hateful ... "

"Yes, but now they're worse. But the day will come. It's coming.

She continued, "They had them come over and walk up to me. I was so mad! I thought, if I could just grab that head! But I can't. They kept me awake all night. I ended up on the chair, and then I got a couple hours sleep. But it's an ugly situation. There's got to be an answer to it, so I'm going to call up that television station that sends those materials to me. They say call for prayers. I get so furious because I can't retaliate the way I want to. So I'm getting a beating all the time, and I hate listening to their vulgar mouths; they want to 'f' me until I die. Oh Lexie, I hear so much trash. Thank God I'm not weak because it's demoralizing. Anyhow, I went to my Bible class, which I enjoy very much. I like those ladies."

"That's wonderful!"

"I do, I like them very much. One of them knows what I'm going through. It's an interesting group, but I've got to get a hearing aid. But here I am, without sleep again, and in no mood to go out shopping."

We ended the conversation when I told Mary I would ask Sally if she would take her to buy handles for the cabinets she's having made. She wants counter space on the sun porch for her potted orchids.

May 5

The phone rang before 9:00 o'clock, earlier than usual. Mary hadn't slept. The past couple nights weren't bad for her. I always think this trial is about over when she has a good night. But this morning she described the previous night to me.

Mary said, "He [Walter] says they're not leaving until he gets what he wants, and that is so ridiculous to me. Of course I will not consent, so he decides he's going to scare me with these big things on stilts that go around staring at me. 'They will not touch me,' I tell myself; 'I will go to sleep.' And when I wondered what time it was, I opened my eyes, and you know what's staring at me? A horse! It was 2:00 o'clock."

I responded, "A horse?"

"Yes, well, a head of a horse. It looked like he would walk through the glass door. It shocked me, because when I opened my eyes I saw a big thing to represent you, and on the porch one that looked like a horse. They had lights in his mouth and I could see his teeth. Lights were flashing. Earlier in the evening I had faces around and I took a flashlight and flashed it in their eyes. That makes them mad. Nonetheless, it isn't an inducement to sleep. So I put up with that. But I flail a cane at them. If I get up they evaporate, but it seems so real. Their faces are realistic, and they're so ugly. So that's the kind of night I've had. It's unnerving."

"How many faces were there?"

"Oh ... I'm trying to think of all the faces ... well, I'd say six. And there's one who's really ugly. And he's got them blown up; one is as tall as that door. I'm in my sound mind, but this is something I see, and I know it's not real, but it *is* real. They just do it to scare me, and they don't like the lights on. I know he's got stilts on them, and I know it sounds foolish, but he was about to lean over me. As soon as they get close, I strike out at one of them, but I can't connect. He moved away. It's not that I've got so much fear, but I'm uncomfortable. Do you know what I mean? They have those gruesome faces."

"Yes, I know what you mean."

"They don't want me to sleep, so I'll be weak, and then they'll rape me."

"Tell them ... Jesus ... " [I don't always have time to type my response, as I'm busy typing her responses.]

"I tell them; they know. I've been holding up to them. Well, I've got to die first."

"Don't say that! Don't say you'll die first!"

Mary has said this before. She tells the demons she will die before she allows them to rape her. As our words have so much power, I have admonished her several times not to say things like that. We both believe with all our heart the Lord will release her from this trial. I have known of several people who went through an experience of demonic oppression, including myself, and everyone has come through it okay. Well, everyone except our dear cousin Matteo, who committed suicide. We doubt his problem was recognized as demonic, and he didn't get the help he needed.

I asked Mary if she wanted to stay with me a while.

Mary said, "No, I've got to fight them. I want to go to my church tomorrow because we have a new minister. I keep reading to the demons from the Bible that they're defeated. He's been defeated at the cross. I haven't eaten anything today; I should eat a piece of toast. I don't know what Sally has planned, but I'm dressed. I got up at 7:00. I want to be ready when Sally gets here. It's getting so I don't know what to tell the good Lord anymore. But he knows. Just praise Him."

I said, "Yes, praise Him. Someday we'll understand, and someday you'll be sitting alongside Jesus, feeling His love, and those demons will be in the lake of fire, in torment forever. God is faithful."

We ended our conversation discussing breakfast. She doesn't feel like eating, and yet she must. I told her when I was young, and had stayed out late and didn't get much sleep, I always ate more. I suggested she have an egg.

"You need the protein; eat a muffin with it, and a piece of citrus."

"Yeah, I have fruit," she said.

I have prayed more during this trial than any time in my life. We are taught to pray as a first response, not a last resort. That's good advice. After this morning's conversation, I went into my room to pray—to talk to the Lord about Mary's trial. And I asked the Lord if he had anything to say to me, and I knelt there quietly for a few minutes.

As I read what I had written while on the phone with Mary, I noticed she said, "I've got to fight them." I decided to remind her once again—I've mentioned this a lot—to focus on Jesus and not on the demons. The battle is the Lord's [1 Samuel 17:47].

May 7

Mary let me know she didn't get much sleep because she can't yell at the demons at night.

I said, "You don't have to yell at them, just *saying* the Word is effective. It's not more effective when it's said in anger; it just has to be verbal. I'm praying now to oppose demonic suppression of God's answers to your prayers."

Mary said, "I'm at a loss. I'm waiting, but I'm getting a little on the desperate side. The things they say; the things they do. I had to go to another bed, and finally to the porch, where they had enormous things—as big as the porch—all lined up. Of course I shut my eyes, I don't keep them open, but I'm hearing all of their crap. This does not induce sleep. And they give me that electrical jolt. As soon as I'm going into sleep, I'm jolted."

I said, "I'll pray about that jolting specifically."

Mary said, "I pray with my God-given power. I'm not very good at it, but I'm getting better. But, this thing is not getting better.

May 8

On his television program Wommack explained that Old Testament saints, i.e. believers, had no authority over Satan. But by Jesus's work on the cross we now have authority over Satan. However, demonic influence can hinder or delay an answer to prayer. Whether we are aware of demonic influence or not, as believers, we are in a spiritual battle. Ray Pritchard, author of *Stealth Attack* said, "It's like having a bull's eye target on our backs." Satan uses discouragement, fear, criticism, resentment, and so forth.

Pritchard, a former pastor, believes, "We need to *read* the Word, *know* the Word, and *memorize* the Word" to be safe. He said an attack shouldn't surprise or frighten us, and we should not fight alone. He talked about the effectiveness of God's music as a weapon. Sing along with it, he urged, and as Connie also told us, keep Christian praise music playing day and night. And remember, we are on the victory side.

†

Mary sounded pretty good when she called. We talked about Sally's birthday lunch, scheduled for the 26TH, and about the anticipated construction work on her porch. Then she updated me on the problem.

"I'm very much annoyed with these devils in my life. I was listening to Wommack, and the demon distorted the picture; he put a wig or something hanging down over Andrew's face. After a moment, I realized *he* did it. 'It's startling,' I said to myself. 'What am I looking at?' and then I realized what he had done.

"They listened to Wommack too and told me they're not hindering my prayers."

I said, "They're liars."

"Yes, I know they are. I read off Joyce's book and told them they were finished. I have their number. They are such evil …. It leaves me kind of speechless, this evilness. I don't know what to say.

May 11

Mary had her hair done Thursday instead of Friday because the cabinet maker was coming Friday to install the cabinets he had made. I told her I would come up in the afternoon, giving them the time they needed. Mary has an appointment at Gateway City Church in south San Jose on Saturday at 9:00 a.m., so she will stay with me tonight. I left Milpitas at 4:30 p.m. to drive to Walnut Creek. Highway 680 is backed up with traffic on Friday afternoons, with many people heading north. I didn't mind the stop-and-go today, because I received a CD set in the mail, which I listened to on the way to Mary's house.

The CD ran a little over an hour, and after pulling into the guest parking at Mary's place, I sat in the car to listen to the last few words. Getting out of the car I noticed a chill in the air. I walked to Mary's building and up the nine low rise stairs to find water on the porch. Anticipating being away a few days, she had watered her potted plants. I knocked on the door and tried the door handle, which surprised me, as it opened. Clearly, I was expected.

I caught a glimpse of the recent construction from the dining area. I followed Mary through the living room, through the sliding doors, and onto the porch. It looked good; a massive improvement over the ugly cabinet in place when she moved in. Now she has cabinets above and below, and a waterproof wood-tone countertop upon which she had already arranged a few potted plants. The new coleus is beautiful—such colorful leaves.

She filled a shopping bag with artichokes, left over polenta, some uncooked chicken, and a small watermelon. I was getting hungry and was looking forward to implementing Mary's suggestion that we eat before we get on the road back to Milpitas. She suggested Chinese at the restaurant we had recently discovered and enjoyed. Having left my light jacket in the car, with guest parking about a dozen car lengths away, I decided that together we could make it in one trip.

Snapping my fanny pack around my waist, I wheeled her suitcase out the door, lifted it down the nine low rise steps, and set it down. I brought out her canvas bag containing her Bible and reading materials, and the watermelon, in a plastic bag with handles. Pulling up the handle on the suitcase I hung the two bags over it. Mary picked up her purse and the bag with her vitamins and drugs in it. I gathered the other food bag and her CD player in my left hand, leaving my right hand to control the wheeled suitcase that was now also a cart. She locked the door, and we walked to the car.

Even though it was dinner hour—on a Friday—we were quickly seated at a corner window table. Mary looked out onto landscaping and fountains, while I had a wonderful natural view of 50 foot trees, creeping ground covers, and a creek running through. Mary always wants pork fried rice—I think it has something to do with her generation—and she also loves bean sprouts. This place actually lists bean sprouts on their menu, and they are delightful. I can taste vinegar, soy sauce, and sesame oil; the sprouts are sautéed quickly, with green onions cut on the diagonal into two-inch lengths. We began our meal with barbecued spare ribs, and added a beef dish with asparagus and black bean sauce, one of my favorites.

Before taking her last bite, Mary began asking me about the fortune cookie.

"Yes, he'll bring them," I assured her.

We both got fabulous fortunes that night, but I don't remember either one.

Typed Tuesday, May 15

Mary and I were greatly anticipating our meeting on the 12TH at Gateway City Church. They have a vibrant deliverance ministry, operated through the Cleansing Streams program. I enjoyed speaking with a woman who understood the problem. I inferred from her speech she had experiential learning. She asked questions, and I supplied answers, pertinent and specific to Mary's case. I told her where Mary lived, when she moved there, and when she first heard the music that sounded to her like music from the 1930s. I told her how demonic activity had escalated, how Mary believed some of their lies, and what we did when I recognized Mary's problem as demonic. I recounted the journey the Lord has taken us through, mentioning teachings we studied after Mary accepted Jesus as her Savior. Authors we read were named, and I told her how Mary studiously recalled her lifetime, listing sins and sin areas, and confessed them to the Lord, asking His forgiveness.

Upon arrival at the church Saturday morning, we were met by a woman who placed us in a "soaking room," a large multipurpose room without windows. It contained a few tables, in no particular order, and a scattering of folding chairs. There were music keyboards on a couple of the tables and a small CD player on the floor, near an electrical outlet. Two other people were present, and a Christian music CD was playing. Lights were on, but soon a young man switched most of them off. We sat quietly in the darkened room. I prayed silently.

Soon the door opened, the lights went on, and first the man and then the woman present were escorted out of the room. Soon someone came for us. She introduced herself as Joy, and brought us to a smaller room with a sofa, several large comfy chairs, and a few folding chairs. People began filing in.

Once everyone was seated, we all introduced ourselves. Joy remained, and I got to meet Carina, with whom I spoke on Friday. Carina told us she had researched the land where Mary lives. She said the 1930's music makes sense, because in the 1930's an estate was constructed where show horses were raised. I told her Mary reported to me that an apparition she saw looked like a horse. Carina said, "It's the land—not the house."

She talked about freemasonry being a covenant with the land. I don't remember telling her about Russell's baby cup, or if it just came up that Saturday. But as Russell had been a Mason, she suggested the cup could be an open door to demons. This was welcome news to me! Last year we went through Mary's house, discarding items demons might attach to, but neither of us thought about Russell's personal possessions; we only thought about things related to Masonry. We prayed and renounced everything to do with that insidious group, which deceives men into believing they will have camaraderie with other good men; then sucks the life out of them through satanic ritual and curse. Why is this a secret organization? Why does one have to be a Christian to join? Because Satan hates Christians!

While talking about Russell's silver baby cup, the Holy Spirit brought to my mind a ceramic leopard that Russell owned prior to marrying Mary. It has now made its way into my home. I never liked it, really. This long black cat, reclining with its head up and alert, had gold circles all over its body. They looked like gold Cheerios. Mary brought it to my home when she moved in with me, and when she moved to Walnut Creek, it remained in my den. It's best to burn things that could have a demonic attachment, but how do you burn a ceramic cat? That evening I placed it in a bag, smashed it to pieces, then tossed the bag full of pieces into the garbage, destined for some landfill.

Mary spoke, bringing my attention back to the meeting.

She said, "The demons keep saying they want my house!"

"Yes," someone responded, "but your body is also your house."

As a group we prayed aloud, as the Holy Spirit directed us. Most people present shared specific Scriptures, including Luke 10:19-20 and 2 Corinthians 10:4-5. With my eyes closed, as I was praying earnestly, I heard a couple of women praying in tongues. All present prayed over Mary. One broke soul ties with Russell, and renounced and broke words and curses having to do with Freemasonry, now and in the past.

"The yoke has been broken off; you are a free woman," one man said.

And another man said, "We aren't going to cast anything out today ... " at which my heart sank. Jesus drove out demons. They don't leave by themselves.

They anointed us with oil and prayed for us both. I don't know how long we were there, but it was a good session. Kind people prayed wonderful prayers and gave us good suggestions that confirmed the prayer attitudes I have been teaching Mary to practice. As a born-again believer, Mary is renewing her mind and focusing on Christ. I believe this entire trial would be finished by now if Mary was a little younger. At ninety-four, learning new ways takes longer. It takes more repetition. She had her own way of thinking for ninety-two years; she has been reading the Word and renewing her mind for two-and-a-half years.

May 15

Mary was in the den sleeping when I came downstairs to make my coffee. I determined not to awaken her before ten, but she was up shortly after nine o'clock. I had already eaten my breakfast, and hers was prepared. Her coffee was ready to go, her cantaloupe was cut, trimmed, and on her plate. The English muffins she likes were in the toaster ready to be toasted, and water was hot on the stove, ready to soft-boil her egg.

"So how was your night?" I asked.

Mary said, "It wasn't the best. They tormented me. I don't know when I went to sleep. I didn't want to sleep late this morning; it wastes my day."

"How would you compare last night to previous nights since Saturday at Gateway?

"I forget ... "

I reminded her to hold on to the belief they could no longer torment her. If she would focus on Jesus whenever she heard something from one of them or saw an image they created for her to see, they would soon be gone. I acknowledged that if they spoke she would hear it, but she should turn her attention away from them, and onto the Lord. We talked about this last evening before bedtime too. Instead of listening to them, she could focus her mind on something Jesus said or did, something she has read in the gospels. I suggested she could focus on Jesus writing in the sand, or preaching from inside the boat, or any of the many mental pictures of Him we see in the Bible.

Mary said, "Well, as far as they're concerned, nothing is changed. I'm not supposed to pay attention, but that's what they say. I want them to go!"

"It's a discipline. That's your challenge, to believe they're gone, even though they may attempt to continue to harass you. You can't acknowledge they're doing that."

May 16

Mary said, "It's still around *all the time*; nothing has changed."

I reminded her we still need to destroy Russell's cup, which is in Walnut Creek.

"They want me awake," she said.

We sat down at the breakfast table and read our morning devotionals. As Mary was still hearing voices, I prayed for her.

Mary came into my office later and said, "I don't just go to bed and go to sleep. I get tormented before I fall asleep. So I took my putter to bed."

I asked, "Why take a putter to bed with you?" (I asked, even though I knew why.)

"To flail at their images when they get too close to me. They're intimidating. And it works. They back away."

"That's a problem. The Lord wants you to depend on Him. Not a putter."

"I do depend on Him. After I have battled a while, I go to sleep. Then when I've had about three hours sleep, they wake me up."

About 9:00 p.m. on Thursday, the 17TH, Carina from Gateway City Church called. She said she got notes from her team, and she'll forward them to me. "Her team took to us," she said, and about Mary she said, "She's pretty strong even though she's lost weight. She'll probably live a long time."

Carina said she was continuing to pray for Mary. When I told her Mary was going to bed with the putter, she said,

"Maybe go to bed with the Bible."

She talked about Mary possibly, "praying over olive oil when she buys it, and then she can anoint things with oil. Just pray over the oil."

She said, "God is not in it. It's representation, and it trains us to have faith."

Carina continued, "Definitely continue to pray for her. I will pray for her daily that God will strengthen her and grow her up. We know His voice, and a stranger we will not follow. It has to come into fruition."

She concluded with the reminder that patience is a fruit of the Spirit [Galatians 5:22-23].

May 18

When I talked with Mary, who was back at Walnut Creek, I told her Carina had called.

"Did you ask her if she ever got anyone out?" Mary asked.

Perhaps when Mary has learned what the Lord wants her to learn from this experience, he will deny the demons further access to her mind. We have found no one to cast out demons, and they haven't obeyed me when I commanded them to flee. Meanwhile, we rely on the Bible verse that tells us "some can be cast out only by prayer" [Mark 9:29].

May 21

It's already noon, and not hearing from Mary, I called her.

Mary said, "I had a terrible time last night, hopping back and forth between beds. I lose so much time this way, because I'm so tired the next day. I'm kind of cramped, and my back bothers me."

I asked, "You ended up where?"

"In the chair. My third stop was the chair. I've landed there before. They were very wicked last night. They seem to think they can get away with murder. I don't seem to be able to reach them. But today I'll read Scriptures to them if I have to."

I said, "Mom, I don't think you're getting it. Remember when Paul and Silas were in prison, and they were singing praises to the Lord, and the chains fell off of them, and the prison doors opened [Acts 16:25-26]? Well, the same thing happened for Peter [Acts 12:7] and to Brother Yun,

The Heavenly Man! Have you read his book yet? He too was in jail, and he too had a supernatural experience, and he walked out of the prison right past several guards, and the prison gate opened by itself. He walked right through. When we praise Him, God acts."

Mary said, "I told the Lord, I just don't know what to say to Him anymore."

I said, "I know it's difficult, but ignore them as best as you can, and focus on Jesus. The Lord lives in our praises. Your focus seems to be more on the demons than on God."

Mary said defensively, "You've never experienced in your entire life what the kingdom of darkness is, what an interference it is! I don't have very many quiet moments! They don't sleep much. They talk constantly. It's difficult. You have no privacy. None."

I ignored she had forgotten my experience with demons living in my mind, and I said, "Mom, write this down to remind yourself today. 'Praise God; ignore the demons.' I guarantee you if you do that today, you'll sleep well tonight."

Mary replied, "I expect to sleep well tonight."

I said, "When they talk to you, start praising Jesus. Talk over the demons. We have so much to praise the Lord for. Talk to Him about the blessings you enjoyed in your past. You'll think of lots of things. Weren't you happy when you learned you were pregnant? Praise Him for that."

This trial is a strain for me too. It's time consuming, and it hurts me so much to know how my mother is suffering. There is no escape for her; they torment her day and night. And the nights are always worse because they don't want her to sleep; they want to weaken her. The enemy comes only to steal, kill, and to destroy [John 10:10]. We have spent weeks and weeks, months and months, reading through and learning from God's Word and learning also from many books addressing spiritual warfare issues. Mary has been under siege two-and-a-half years.

Fortunately, Mary is a strong, optimistic person. She learned to be strong growing up in a household run by a stepmother who showed her no love. She and I both know God loves her, and he is renewing her mind as she reads his Word. He is teaching her to be more like his only Son, Jesus Christ. His love sustains her. We praise you, Lord!

CHAPTER 16
ARE CHRISTIANS AFRAID TO CAST OUT DEVILS?

God is our refuge and strength, a very present help in trouble. Psalm 46:1

ONE EVENING A woman hosting a writers' critique group brought me the book, *How to Try a Spirit* by Garrison. Glancing through the small book containing lots of scriptural references, I noticed the author identifies various evil spirits by name. The back cover indicates the book can aid in recognizing principal evil spirits. Garrison writes about bondage, fear, infirmity, jealousy, et al. and lists each spirit's manifestations. For example, the spirit of fear is possibly responsible for fright, torment, trembling, horror, dread, anxiety, worry, and others.

This made sense to me, and gave me hope. Many of us are in spiritual battle—not only those who hear voices. I called Mary to share my overview of this new treasure. We can demand the spirits to leave Mary, because we can call them by name. We can bind the spirits and loose Mary!

May 25

Mary called to say she slept okay, not great, but okay.

"Yes, I slept in my bed. I had the fan on top of the bed blowing all night, because they make me hot so I'll take my stuff off. It was a godsend when I thought of that fan."

I said, "Do you think the Holy Spirit suggested you get that fan?"

Mary said, "Well, I think it's Jesus. I credit Jesus with whatever I come up with. Well, I will get dressed and throw stuff into the wash before I leave for my hair appointment."

We also talked about Ann and her niece JoAnn, who flew to San Francisco from Butte to visit with Ann and go with her to a cousin's wedding.

Mary said, "It bothers me about Annie. She doesn't think right anymore, and she's still in control of her own affairs. She would be better off in a retirement home, especially since she took that fall. Yesterday JoAnn told me Ann had arisen during the night to go to the bathroom—after taking a laxative—and fell down in the bathroom.

"What can they do? If it's a rib that's broken, they do nothing. I wonder how she fell. Maybe she hit the tub."

I said, "Perhaps her leg collapsed."

Mary said, "She does say she gets kind of numb. That's not too good."

We focused again on Mary's problem, demons disturbing her sleep.

I said, "You have the power of Jesus running through you. You have been cleansed by the blood of Jesus, and they have been defeated by the blood of Jesus. You must take that authority. And you are. You slept in your own bed. That's good. Take your authority and tell them to leave with their dirty mouths."

She asked me about my plans for today, and I told her I planned to finish the Garrison book. Also, I would email Carina to ask if she would join us to get these spirits out. I specifically remember Michael saying when we met at Gateway, "We will not cast anything out today." I wonder if Carina would like to witness spirits leaving. I should call Connie back too. She wants to go over a prayer of revocation with me.

June 1

Mary's mother Giulia had a watch that disappeared after she died. Mary lamented its loss—it belonged to her birth mother—so much so that even I had been told about it. We have a photograph of Grandpa and Giulia on their wedding day, with Giulia wearing the watch. Round and decorated, with a locket, it has a chain that one can wear about the neck, and also pin to one's blouse. Mary believes it should have gone to her and her sister (now deceased), but there was no watch.

Mary has a niece called Evelyn who is eight years younger than Mary. Maria, Mary's step mother, was Evelyn's grandmother. Maria had a son from her first marriage named George; Evelyn was George's first daughter.

Evelyn called Mary recently and said George's second daughter gave some old pieces of jewelry to Evelyn's daughter. One item probably was Mary's mother's watch. On Tuesday Mary and I drove to San Mateo where we had lunch with Evelyn, and she passed the watch along to Mary.

I took Mary home yesterday, and today on the phone she said to me, "I was thinking about my mother's watch." She reminisced about dinners of polenta and castagne (cornmeal and chestnuts). Her family was poor.

Mary said, "The watch has some filigree design work, and the initials M.S. Whose initials are they?"

We don't know. She also told me her step mother's brother lost his leg in the mill and said they must have had wheat to grind into flour.

"He was an alcoholic," Mary said. "He's the one I caught having push-push down in the woods. The other guy, he drove Uncle Charlie out. He was kind of wimpy—lean, not confident. His wife was a skinny little thing. I don't know if he was out walking around or what, but here's Uncle Charlie on top of the other guy's wife. That shocked me. You know, even when you're a kid you know when something isn't right."

I hate it so much when Mary doesn't sleep. I praise and thank our Lord Jesus Christ for His care of her. He imbues her with supernatural strength through this trial. How could she survive this siege for two-and-a-half years otherwise? She agrees and said He keeps her going with His strength. She told me not to worry when she goes out today to the store and post office because the Lord gives her the strength she needs.

As I walked into church this past Sunday, I saw David. Having not seen him lately, we spoke briefly as the worship service was about to start; I said Mary continues to suffer from the torments of the demons. I told him about Garrison's book, and how she learned to deliver people inspired by the Holy Spirit. I asked if he would look over her book and then come to my house to help me, to agree with me, and to cast those devils out. He told me to send him an email about it.

I've been busy with real estate these past weeks. On Sunday I told David I would email to him, and it's already Tuesday. I will drop off the Garrison book for him.

July 10

At 6:15 in the evening Mary called and said, "They are so big! They're everywhere! This morning there were images under the blotter on my desk! Sometimes I wonder, 'Dear Lord, how can you let this go on?'"

Mary continued by telling me about her next-door neighbor, changing the subject to not think about the images.

Thursday, July 12

Mary was talkative this morning. She asked about my ESL class last night and talked about differences in the Chinese and English languages. She discussed getting estimates for remodeling her bathroom, and what her neighbors are remodeling. I asked how she slept, as we had prayed together before she went to bed.

Mary said, "Not too bad, not too much action before I got to sleep. But being awakened at 5:00 a.m. is not getting much sleep."

"Didn't you go back to sleep at 5:00 o'clock?"

"Not when they keep waking you up. And he blows in a stinky smelling stuff through that hisser, and I keep the fan on to blow it away. You don't know the treatments he gives me."

"Don't believe those lies he tells!" I commanded, raising my voice in emotional fury at that devil. "Tell him he's a liar and the father of lies and to get out!"

"He's sadistic; he gets a jolly out of tormenting me. Anyway, that's the way it seems to me. He's going to let me have it. He's going to punish me."

"Mom!" I implored her, "You've got to watch your mouth! There's power in your words! He is a defeated enemy! You know that! Yes, he has influence, but your words have more influence! God will enforce your words. Please watch what you speak."

July 28

I received a discouraging reply to my email to David. I haven't answered it yet; it's difficult. He wasn't sure about Mary Garrison and wanted me to go through proper church channels. I have asked several people. The hard part is that no one will join with me in prayer and in casting out those devils. I don't blame them, because even Mary Garrison says it's dangerous to do unless one is filled with the Holy Spirit. I am anxious for Mary to be free. She does seem better since the two of us have been binding, loosing, and casting out. They haven't left her, but a couple of nights ago she said she had the best night's sleep ever. Praise the Lord! I was so happy about that. The previous night was good too. I know we are almost there—almost total freedom. Through the power of Jesus Christ I have been loosing Mary too, from the grip of the enemy.

I thought Connie might pray with me over Mary, so the Lord could use us to cast out those demons for once and for all. So when she called last evening, I told her about the Garrison books. The disappointing part of our conversation was that she continues to assume Mary's problem is due to "something in her home," because the problem began after she moved there. She thinks there is still ground, and she may be right. She repeated that Mary needs to hear from the Lord where the ground is and then confess it and renounce it. I told her Mary has confessed and renounced everything that has come to her mind.

When I asked her specifically if she might pray with me for Mary, and cast the demons out, she refused.

"No," she said, "that's too dangerous. They can come back worse than before."

"That's if the person isn't filled with the Holy Spirit," I argued.

She said Mary must cast them out herself. I responded that I didn't recall anyone in the Bible with demons able to cast them out of themselves, and I reminded her of John 14:12.

July 30

Mary called, sounding out of breath. "I've been up a while. That rug in the sun porch was crooked, so I was out there, pulling at it to straighten it."

I asked my inevitable question, "How did you sleep last night?"

Mary replied, "Not as bad as the night before. At least I got some sleep, but I slept in the office. I had to get out of my bed; I couldn't take it. Finally I raised my voice, and they left me."

"See, doesn't that prove that if you resist the devil ... "

Mary interrupted, "Oh Lexie, I resist every night!"

Today the new pastor at Mary's church is coming to visit. Mary is hopeful because she read that the woman has some "spiritual experience," whatever that means.

August 2

Mary had a pleasant visit with her pastor, but not helpful regarding spiritual warfare. And last night was difficult for Mary, as the past three consecutive nights have been. My heart breaks when I hear her morning reports.

I'm swamped for time today and it's already 3:22 p.m. I haven't finished Garrison's teachings, and I meet prospective tenants this evening. I must pick up and deliver a prescription to Ann, who recently moved from Mill Valley into a retirement home closer to me.

August 11

I talked with Mary this morning about the Garrison book. She has a copy, but I don't think she's read it. The first time through is a little tough, but I'm going through it a second time and it's much more clear.

Mary mentioned that a couple days ago she "just had a thought pop into her mind," a recollection of an experience from her youth. "I was only eighteen," she said. She had a friend named Dorothy, whose husband (coincidentally) was named Walter. Mary was blessed with a lovely body, and men liked looking at her. I'm sure she enjoyed the attention. Walter said he was a photographer, and he wanted to photograph Mary in the nude. She did not agree to do that, but one day they were in Salinas, and Dorothy insisted she allow Walter to photograph her. Mary's picture was taken outdoors in a woodsy environment. She took off her clothing, but held a large handkerchief in front of her, covering critical parts. I saw the picture several times when I was a child. If she still has it, maybe she'll be willing to burn it. By today's standards, it's tame, but we're not living for the world; we're living for Jesus.

I told Mary I believed the Holy Spirit revealed that old memory to her. I told her I had prayed that if there was still some ground, he would reveal it to her. I asked how she would have felt at the time the picture was taken if she knew God was with her and watched what happened that day. She said she would have been embarrassed.

I suggested she confess that activity as sin and renounce it. She agreed, and we planned to get together on Sunday afternoon. After all, we want Mary to wear white robes washed in the blood of Jesus, not robes that still have spots on them.

While on the phone with her I perused *How to Try a Spirit*, and my attention went to the chapter "Spirit of Whoredoms." Mary recalled her day in the park posing nearly nude. Garrison lists manifestations which she defines as "consorting with the devil; unfaithful to Christ ... unchaste ... a backsliding Christian–Ezek. 16:15." Included are harlotry, love of the body, etc. Under love of the body, she writes, "fornication and adultery; sexual sin of every type; exhibition of the body of all types–exalting the body, such as lewd pictures of the body, nudity, pornography."

One can see, even from this brief glimpse of the work Garrison has done for us, that it takes time, thought, and Bible study to determine which spirits are the offenders. And can they be cast out if we don't know who they are? She writes that once a particular spirit accomplishes its purpose in a person's life, it brings in other spirits who then begin their evil work as well.

The more the human spirit is oppressed, the more difficult it becomes to cope with life. The manifestations, Garrison teaches, "are the goals that demon is striving to attain." She writes:

> "The amount of fruit he has been able to produce in a certain life depends upon the length of time he is permitted to work ... uninterrupted. He knows that he could easily be resisted, overcome, and thrown out, should a true believer command it."

August 16

Mary's night was particularly bad. They had exhausted her. She missed a meal, critical for her now. I got so angry with those devils when Mary told me she had no sleep, that when she and I prayed together, I really let them have it. I bound them; I loosed Mary's spirit; I cast them out in the name of Jesus Christ. I identified the strongman as the spirit of fear and used words from the Garrison book. Mary whispered to me over the phone; they were active and angry.

After hanging up the phone, I continued in prayer before getting into bed. As usual for me these days, I spoke a couple of Scriptures aloud before going to sleep. Was I dreaming? I awakened around 1:00 a.m. when I realized I was seeing disgusting images, and even in sleep I knew it was Satanic. When it happened a second time, even more blatantly wicked and repulsive than the first, I realized I was being targeted. I got up, used the restroom, prayed about the dream experience, and asked the Lord for protection through the night and for peaceful sleep. When I went back to sleep, I slept well until morning.

When I talked with Mary in the morning, she reported she too had a dreadful night. And then something wonderful happened. The following morning she called me and said they did not disturb her during the night, and she awoke all by herself. Hallelujah! Praise the Lord! At this writing, I believe she had several nights without being awakened before dawn; she was able to sleep until she awoke naturally, as God intends for all his children.

August 18

Last night I prayed with Mary, a personalized version of a prayer Garrison includes as a help to those who minister to persons under attack. I have prayed this prayer before with good results; this morning, however, she said they interrupted her sleep last night.

"During the wee hours," she reported, "and then again later in the morning they kept telling me what time it was. They wanted me awake! 'That's part of the punishment,' they said."

Mary told me they're now saying I have the power to get them out.

Well, I know they are liars, but this time they've got it right! The gates of hell shall not prevail against the church! [Matthew 16:18].

August 23

After Mary and I had made our coffee, I asked her to tell me about her night. She began her story.

"They say I won't remember all the pins they put in my head all night. I remember him saying I'll be in such a state I won't know where I'm at; I'll be a dummy. 'And no one can take the pins out,' he said. That's the kind of crap I hear."

I replied with my standard line, "How did you sleep?"

"I slept good, but intermittently, and that's when I hear those things. They want to awaken me every so often so I'll be real weak, and they can grab me. Lexie, I get this all the time. I hear it, but I dismiss most of it because it isn't worth hanging on to. I kind of want to be one step ahead of them though, because I have to deal with them."

I replied, "You're not to converse with them. Just say, "I bind you, spirit of fear, and I cast you out ... ""

"He listens to every word. Even last night he heard you say that one drink a night is okay, but to be careful. And he said, 'we can use that against her,' and the others said, 'No, she can have one.'"

August 31

Mary said she slept okay, but when she awoke about 7:00 a.m. they were chanting. She wanted more sleep.

"They tell me they won't leave me because there's no one to get them out. They put faces on my television screen. They have a face there with white teeth, and I'm telling you I just lose my patience. But the Lord knows. I talk to Him every day, and I tell Him."

I said, "You've given me an idea. It may be the house. We need to focus on the house and getting them out of there. It started two months after you moved in, right?"

"Exactly. Tomorrow is my 3RD anniversary here. I just wrote a check for my HOA fee."

We talked about the possibility of the demons being attached to the house, not Mary's body, but Unit 7. And isn't that what the people at Gateway Church had said?

Sunday, September 2

Mary has been beyond tired the past few days, as in 2004. After moving to Walnut Creek, she had internal bleeding and received a blood transfusion. She is anxious for the results of a recent blood test.

When I asked how her night was, she said, "Sometimes when they're going on, they give it to you so strong! I can see how people lose their minds with these tortures they go through. But I'm a strong s.b. too, and I'm fighting them differently. They're trying to back me down. They keep saying they're not giving up until they get what they want. They say they'll break me, and I say, 'Never!' And they say, 'one more night.' In the daytime they go on like they're sorry for me and they love me and they don't want to go elsewhere. They say I'm more interesting than the others are—and this goes in one ear and out the other."

Mary is making progress. Before this trouble began, like many, she made up her own god. Now she knows who God is, and from reading His Word is better able to discern truth from error. She no longer believes the lies of the devil.

Mary continued, "They're such actors. They have fooled me time and again, but when they give me that old spiel just before night time ... they are so evil. Sometimes they can be kind of funny, they have given me a laugh sometimes, especially the way one talks, but they wear me out. They go on and on and on. And sometimes it's exaggerated, which is worse. And sometimes, like he did this morning, he starts to saw—it sounds like he's sawing something—and that got me so mad because I needed to sleep. I got up and turned on Joyce Meyer's CD because they don't like her. The little one is so mean—he wants to kill me. He hates me because I won't give in. And he says to another demon, 'It's your fault, you've aggravated her,' and then they have a parade. They send those fabricated spirits marching through and they enlarge magically before you."

At this point, I asked her to hold her thoughts while I went upstairs to my computer, as I was taking this down in shorthand. When I sat down at my computer keyboard, Mary said, "They don't like me telling you anything. I said in the beginning you should know everything. They say to me, 'we can really harm you.' I know that; the books say that.

"In the morning hours, when they're supposed to allow me to sleep, they weren't letting me sleep, and I think they were tired too because they were babbling away. They berate each other, and they give the strongman a lot of hell; they think he should release me, but he doesn't want to release me. He wants to make a slave of me and control me. They have a dummy they made of me and he's got it wired to me and they're going to 'f' me in effigy, but I protect myself. My body will not respond to them, but they do make me lubricate by golly, I get that wet feeling. I don't know how they do it. They say they do it with their computer."

I said, "They don't have a computer!"

Mary said, "Well Lexie, I don't know what they've got, but that's what they say. And you know my hands, they can make my hand hurt instantly, even when I've got my wrist brace on. I know they can harm. I don't know how it's done, but I know one thing—that hisser. I knocked it out of existence in one spot, but they replaced it a different way. The one that makes me laugh sometimes, he tells me where it is."

"Is he right?"

"Yes, I found it last night. I found it! It glows in the dark and looks like it's going down the hall. You see, I'm out of bed sometimes two or three times during the night, and I remember the first time I noticed this hissing thing. I noticed a streak of red light, just like the light on my speaker phone, and it goes down the hallway and into rooms. They say they can see me with it. He doesn't have good vision, but he can see me with that. He doesn't have to put the noise on with it; he does that for irritation. He hears me telling you this. Lexie, I have no privacy. Every word I say, they repeat to me afterwards. That's why I tell you not to say some things to me sometimes."

"Well, let me know when I can tell you the things I want to tell you, okay."

"They even listen to the way I pray to God. They tell me I will never make it with God."

We talked about Wommack's book. Mary said, "I told God I wasn't accustomed to prayer in my youth. Our prayers were the Our Fathers and the Hail Marys. The Catholics pray to the Virgin Mary, and they pray to the saints. Well, I never prayed to a saint. Whenever I prayed, it was always to God."

"But at that time you didn't know Jesus."

"I said a lot of Hail Marys when they prepared me for communion. You have to go to confession because you take communion the next day. I think that's the way it worked. And gee, I never knew what to confess when I went into that little box. Oh, I think I told them about stealing the raisins from that little store. I leaned down when he wasn't waiting on me, put my hand in the bin, it had a cover on it, and I got some raisins and put them in my coat pocket. I ate those on my way home. I guess I had some wickedness in me.

"We all do."

"My poor sister, she wouldn't even think of doing anything like that. And when we left home ... I instigated that. I shouldn't have done it either."

Returning her attention to the conversations of the demons, Mary said,

"I don't know if I told you, but they say they're homosexuals, but they're bisexuals. They talk about doing this to me and that. They talk about getting one in front of me and one in back, and this leader is supposed to be a genius. He says he takes photographs of me in the bathtub. They say they have a prostitution house and people come in and 'f' it. But one of his things is that he gets into my rectum. And when anything touches my body, I go nuts!" she said angrily.

"But anyhow, he says he wants to make my front into a penis."

"Mom, that's stupid."

"Yeah, but that's what I hear. So maybe that'll give you an idea of this spirit, what kind of spirit it is."

She wants me to use the information she gives me to identify the demon strongman by his "fruit," his manifestations, by what he does and how he acts, as explained by Garrison.

I stopped her from speaking, and in Jesus' name bound and cast out Satan, as I was hearing a lot of static on the telephone, and Mary said she wasn't doing anything to cause the extraneous noise. It sounded like scraping something along the counter and crumpling up papers. I still hear a lot of static on the phone line, and Mary says it's them.

She continued, "You know what? It just dawned on me, the noise you hear on this phone. They don't want you to hear what I'm telling you. He's telling me now they're not responsible for what will happen to me when they leave. Well, let's keep that in reserve. I feel this has got to come to an end. Yes, it will. It has to."

I said, "Yes, it will. God will use this for good, somehow."

Monday, September 3

Mary has no energy and is anxious for her blood test results. She said she slept fairly well, and stayed in bed until 9:30 a.m., but could have slept longer.

She said, "I have a funny weak feeling that's not me. I didn't eat much dinner last night, just cream of wheat, because I didn't want to chance throwing up. I need to go out today and get some things."

Tuesday, September 4

Another bad night. Mary didn't call before bed last night because it was late. I talked about praising the Lord out loud, telling her He inhabits our praise. She responded that her tired body doesn't always remember.

Her dishwasher is not cleaning properly. She had a repairman out three times. He told her she was not loading it properly, but she wants a new one. I discouraged her from buying a new one; the one she has is only a few years old. Perhaps it's out of rinse agent.

Wednesday, September 5

Mary called. "Hot or not hot, I'm making soup today. I bought some of that Safeway meat. Then I think I'll go down to that Alpine Hearing Aids."

I asked, "How did you sleep last night?"

"Well, when I got to sleep I slept good. It could have been around 2:00 o'clock. But when I woke up on my own, I had some action."

"At what time did you wake up on your own?"

"I didn't look at my watch. It's kind of funny; I had the window open and the fan on in the office, and it pushes that smoke they make back at them. He said he's gonna defrock me. It's a pack of lies. I am so sick of it. I didn't get out of bed until 9:30, and then the hisser was on me, and he said he was going to throw s-h-i-t on me; he gets so nasty. He told me to turn my fan off. So I turned my fan off, but he didn't turn off the hisser, so I turned my fan on again."

I talked again with Mary about not interacting with them, but filling her mind with godly things, putting on praise music, and singing along in her mind. This gets me so down. I feel so bad for her, I can hardly stand it. And I probably appear critical to her. I don't mean to; I want to be supportive. But how do we deal with supernatural interference? We need to cast them out. That's what Jesus taught his disciples to do. We can't expect Mary to release herself, although I have read that renewing one's mind, and being filled with light, can cause them to leave.

Monday, September 10

Last night at bedtime, Mary called so we could pray together. She confirmed it was the spirit of fear that has been harassing her. I wonder why she said that. At the time I accepted it, but now I question it. As demons are liars, I wonder if it was the Holy Spirit who told her, or if the demon said it to her. The demon may try to throw us off track.

Mary called at 9:33 a.m.

"You know," she began, "when I went to that service station, he charged me a lot of money. He charged me $1500 last time. I have another appointment this morning, but I will not keep it. Fans or fan belts. I can't read his writing. He fills my car up with gas, but he charges me. I asked him to check the oil because I had trouble that time. That's when he told me I needed this kind of belt."

I said, "Take Sally with you when you go back; bargaining is one of her strong points."

Mary said, "When she picks me up to go to the doctor, I'll ask her. I weighed myself after my bath yesterday, and I was eighty-one pounds, so I need to eat, although I'm not hungry."

I wanted to ask her what she said to me last night, about being able to discern truth or lie, but she said it wasn't a good time, which meant *they* were listening.

September 30

I have been doing warfare on Mary's behalf. She said today they had left her alone. However, when I talked with her yesterday, she told me she didn't do too well Friday night. They told her they were punishing her. She called Friday night, but I was already in bed, half asleep, and I didn't pray as intently with her. Going back to Thursday, I prayed most intently with her, again using what I'm learning from Garrison, and Mary did well. She told me Friday, during the day, they were furious. She said they told her I hurt them.

Mary and I long for this trial to end. I continue to wait for Christian prayer partners, unafraid to cast out demons. Yes, we are battling with supernatural power greater than the power of man, but the power of evil is not greater than the power of Jesus Christ, nor is it greater than the power of the Lord within man.

We need to get together with Mary and get the demons totally and forever out. Although both Mary and I are thankful for any relief and sleep she gets. Surely the Lord has strengthened her to withstand this trial, and we are so thankful we have a Lord we can trust.

CHAPTER 17

DO CHRISTIANS BELIEVE DEMONS EXIST?

But don't rejoice because evil spirits obey you; rejoice
because your names are registered in heaven.
Luke 10:20 NLT

AFTER 11:00 A.M. Mary called and said, "I've had my coffee
and talked to the Lord in prayer. It was lengthy."

She told me about the new hearing aids she picked up yesterday.
"They're small, and you have to get it into the ear canal right. And if it
should fall out ... you know, it can slip out easy. They should hang on your
ear. It wasn't designed right."

Her adversaries kept her awake all night, so she stayed in bed later
this morning. I encouraged her to go to bed earlier, but understandably
she procrastinates, attempting to avoid the harassment that plagues her
each night. She was disappointed about not being up in time to go to a
women's meeting affiliated with her church. I'm glad she's making friendships, and I'm disappointed she didn't get the sleep she needed last night.

It seems difficult to get a few Christians together. When two or three
gather in His name, He is there with us [Matthew 18:20]. When we are
together in His presence, and in His name we cast demons out, demons
have no choice but to go. The problem is finding born-again Christians
washed in the blood of the Lamb, who believe demons still exist. We read
about them in the Bible. God created us and the angels for eternity. He
prepared a lake of fire for the devil and his fallen angels, or demons. Why
would someone believe something that existed two thousand years ago no
longer exists today? [Revelation 20:10] God's creation is for eternity. We
must put our fears aside; remember, God did not give us a spirit of fear
[2 Timothy 1:7]. But because demons do have powers, and because they

hate us, most people would rather serve the Lord by bringing you a casserole to eat than join you in prayer and in binding and casting out demons.

I saw Barbara yesterday at church. Although she is willing to help us, and has another friend to join us in prayer, her own personal life requires her time now. Her husband is having a critical surgery today. I sympathize and I do understand, and yet I also want help for my mom. I mentioned to Barbara that I might go to our prayer ministry director and ask again for people to pray with me. She said he would only point me back to her. Mary is such a trooper. She said she has withstood this for so long she can wait.

October 10

Mary said, "I'm okay, but it was gruesome this morning. He took hold of my left hand, and he really hurt me ... "

"Mom!" I cut in, "Tell him, 'pain cannot successfully come against my body, because Jesus bore all my pain.' [Isaiah 53:3-4] You have those scriptures. If you've been reading them aloud each day, you would have them memorized by now, and you could use them against him. That's the warfare! That's how Jesus responded to the devil" [Matthew 4:3-10].

She answered, "Yes, but I don't think about Scriptures at the time. Edwin asked me how I was doing. I just said 'okay.' He mentioned some woman once, but she didn't want to bother with me. She just said you pray and pray and pray. She wasn't too interested in coming to see me and really work on it. You know it's no good if someone isn't interested. You need someone that knows something about it."

I said, "Well, tell Edwin I'm willing to come up and lead the prayer; I just need believers to agree with me."

Mary said, "The churches are failing us. It's in the Bible; do they go over it like it's a myth? You can see her attitude and know she isn't into anything like this."

I said, "Yes, the churches are failing us in this area. People don't believe these things unless they have experienced them. Where's their faith in the truth of God's word? Even Christians believe more in our own understanding than in the Word of God. Solomon wrote in Proverbs that we shouldn't do that [Proverbs 3:5-6], but we do. We place more faith in science and doctors than we place in God. These people who gloss over your problem probably think something's wrong with your brain because you're old. And that's untrue!"

Mary said, "Demonic oppression has got to be out in the open, because I'm sure there're many people with this problem keeping it to themselves. How people are picked by these devils, I have no idea. No one knows how it happened to them."

Although Mary doesn't know how she became the unhappy recipient of such unwanted company, sometimes we can know. For example, participating in occult activities can bring demonic problems.

I said, "Unconfessed sin can open doors to the devil and his demons."

Mary said, "Why doesn't it effect people?"

I said, "Mom, the devil has some people by default. Why would he bother unbelievers already destined to spend eternity apart from God? He hates God, and he hates believers. I've heard many times that believers are targeted."

Mary said, "It's a hard thing to believe. And if people who are believers don't believe, they can't really help you. And these ministers [pastors, clergy], they help people with a lot of problems, and they keep busy. But I guess this type of problem doesn't come up often, or if it does, they put it aside, like they do to me. But by golly, it's true; the Bible shows you and talks about these demons. They were pretty prevalent in Jesus' time, so why wouldn't they be today? Well anyhow, I'll endure. I know the Lord will come through for me."

I said, "You have a good grasp on it. You've learned a lot. You should speak up to people."

"Well, I know. But when they're politely pushing away ... it's not a pleasant idea. Some people are afraid of being afflicted themselves. Well, I'll continue on."

"We have to keep in mind that there is a good purpose for this trial [Romans 8:28-29]. We know the Lord is in control of this and all things. And we must serve Him. We must tell others; some haven't yet heard that these things are true.

"And hopefully, when we tell others the truth about the existence of the spirit world, the heavenly realm of things unseen that are eternal, they *will* believe. And when they do, many people suffering from demonic oppression will be understood, helped, and released. By turning to Jesus, who came to set captives free [Luke 4:18], they will be set free by God's power."

October 16

It depresses me that I could not get a group of born-again believers together who will agree with me and cast out those evil demons. The people I know, both friends and family, either have unconfessed sin in their lives, or don't believe in demons, or are afraid of demons. Most churches focus on things other than deliverance ministries. Isn't it reasonable to go to one's own church? Meanwhile, Mary continues to exist under horrific oppression, living solely by the grace of God, with little sleep and without much desire to eat.

She called this morning.

"I was chasing spirits last night," she said, "and I almost got one. As I think about it now, it was kind of funny. They were coming at me; I heard what they were saying, and I decided I would sleep on the porch. They don't like that because they can't get to me as easily. When I analyze it, they just try to scare me. I showed them I'm not fearful. They towered above me, and I ignored them because I was making up my bed. I looked up and saw them in the living room. One at a time comes out onto the porch. They just irritate me. I went into the living room and I just wanted to crack him one! They were taller than my sliding doors, and they can just deflate and inflate. Finally there was one that I think is the leader. He's the shrimp. I wanted to crack his head open! They look like a football with a head, no hands, but stilts for feet. You can't see the stilts, but they tell me what they've got. I almost got one Lexie! Now it's funny! I almost got one, the shrimp!

"I said to the Lord, 'I don't know if it's right or wrong, but I know he got scared for a change.' That's my story, which certainly wouldn't be believable to most people. Anyhow, I feel fine. I'm going to the audiologist. I had the hearing aids in my ears the other day and one fell out, so I'm going over to their office to put them in. And I want them to be a little louder. I heard, but they could raise the sound a bit. I have an eleven o'clock appointment."

I asked, "How much sleep did you get?"

"Well, not too much; it was after 2:00. But for dinner I ate that leftover beef. I put ketchup on it before putting it in the microwave, and it tasted like some pretty good boiled beef. I could get it down. And I had cauliflower and some asparagus. I should have been sleeping because I didn't get much sleep the two nights before. But I couldn't sleep right away. They gave me a little activity, but not much. I added something new to my protective paraphernalia. They wanted to know what it was, but I put it on in the dark, although they can see in the dark. They didn't like it. I want to get rid of them! It's time for them to go! And from what I read in my books, you know, you can use some of these tactics, so we shall see. He hasn't won a round yet. There's nothing to win. There is no prize. But he doesn't want to lose face."

October 22

I spoke with Edwin on the phone and briefed him on our history through this trial. I told him Mary and I have learned something from each book we read, and from each step we took in our efforts to help her find freedom. And it seems simple. We need to gather together and cast them out, as prescribed in the Garrison books.

Edwin said the discussion leaders for his weekly Bible study—which Mary attends—will meet tomorrow afternoon. He will talk with a few of them and see if they are willing to help us. He said he has been to a lot of third world countries and has seen evidence of demons. I told him several ways the demons have manifested themselves in Mary's life, with talking and other sounds, with touching, and with visions. I randomly selected from my journal a conversation I had with Mary and read a paragraph or two to him. "Wow," he said, "she really is oppressed."

October 24

Mary called in the morning and talked about the fires in southern California. She said she prayed for those affected, she knows the Lord will look after them, and she lamented that "animals always suffer."

I asked her how she slept.

Mary said, "I slept good on the porch again. They didn't harass me; they left me alone."

"So you just fell asleep like normal and woke up by yourself?"

"Yes, sometimes this happens. I'm optimistic."

Why did Mary have a good night's sleep last night, and not the previous nights? The Bible tells us if we resist the devil, he will flee from us. The previous two nights I was pretty tired. When Mary called before bed, we offered a simple "thank you for the day" prayer, and a simple, "please protect Mom through the night" request to God. Last night I put more effort into praying with her. Filled with earnestness, hard to muster when one is tired, I prayed with Garrison's book, *The Keys to the Kingdom,* in my hands so I could refer to it. I talked with the Lord about the promise in His word that whatever we bind on earth, He will bind in heaven, and so on. At the end of the prayer, I addressed the evil ones who, according to Mary, are always listening in to our conversations. Binding the spirit of fear, the spirit of bondage, and all the demons with them, I told them they could not speak, nor work. I quoted Scriptures Garrison printed from Isaiah, Revelation, and Hebrews, and I spoke these things with authority and addressed the demons in the name of Jesus Christ of Nazareth.

We have done this before, and like last night, were effective in pushing them back. Demons living in the unseen realm know who Jesus is. They know He is Lord of all, and He sits at the right hand of God. They know Jesus conquered Satan by his work on the cross. And they know the day will come when they must go into the bottomless pit [Revelation 20:1] and the lake of fire burning with sulfur. I have commanded them to go to the pit before, and they responded to Mary, who told me what they said, that it is not yet the time.

I hope to get together with Edwin and friends, and by the power of Jesus Christ flowing through us, finally cast the demons out of Mary's house, her body, and her mind.

October 27

I talked with Edwin again this afternoon.

He said, "I'm not in that ballpark. Here's what I think you can do .... If you really believe these people have those abilities they say they have, take

Mary there or bring them out here. The other thing you can do is—this is one of the hallmarks of the Pentecostal churches; talk to one of their pastors and find out if they have any experience with this kind of thing.

"I think you should find someone in your own area. It looks interesting, and I don't have time to get into that. It's not that I don't care for your mother, I do. It's just not in my area of giftedness. We can pray for your mother. We'll do that. And I'll send the books back to you."

"That's okay," I said. "Just give the books to Mary, and I'll pick them up."

About 6:00 p.m. I called Mary, as I should tell her Edwin will not help us. I understand he says this is not his area of knowledge or interest, but I feel disappointed anyway. I hoped she would take the news better than I had.

She was preparing her dinner. "I decided I'd have some frittata tonight," she said.

I asked her about the church Board meeting she attended this morning. When it was over, there was to be a pancake breakfast.

Mary said, "The meeting went on and on, and when it was over, I drove over to the pancake breakfast with one lady, but it was almost 12:30, and they were finished."

"Good thing you had that yogurt this morning before you left," I interjected.

"Yes, it was!" She continued, "I said to the lady who had been with me at the meeting, 'I'll go home and make my own pancakes,' but I put too much wheat germ in them; they were so thick. I'll thin down the rest of the batter tomorrow.

"I think I'll get the zucchini and onion ready for the frittata," Mary continued, "and get the eggs in later. My sister and I used to make it. That was our main dish when we were at the ranch. We loved it. That will be my main dish. And I bought some kiwis. Well, how did your day go?"

I told her about my conversation with Edwin.

November 1

Mary called after returning home from her Bible study. She recounted the early morning, telling me the demons awakened her several times to tell her the time, "so she wouldn't be late to her class." But they always lie about the time.

"I finally got up," she said, "I looked at my watch, and it was before 6:00 o'clock.

"I saw Edwin, but I didn't have a chance to talk to him. He's always at the front door—but I park overlooking the golf course and come in the other door. His wife came up and hugged me and gave me a little peck on the cheek. I told her one day I would ask them over and we'd have a talk.

"I enjoyed my Bible class, but I did something foolish. When you live the way I live, you know, I worked on the wrong lesson. I didn't do the whole thing, but I did a lot. We're on the eighth lesson and I did the seventh lesson. I hadn't written those questions in the book last time; I wrote them on the tablet you gave me. We all like Genesis a lot. It's too bad Annie can't get interested in the Bible.

November 15

Before I finished breakfast, Sally called.

"Do you watch *The 700 Club*?" she asked. "Turn on channel 13," she urged. "There's a story coming up about a man who demons caused to have a heart attack."

I tuned in the television set and saw Pat Robertson, whose program I often watch in the evenings on another channel.

A video played showing a man helping neighbors move boxes. After carrying the boxes, and now back in his home, he felt a crushing sensation deep in his chest. He knew he was in trouble; he believed he was dying. When the video finished, Robertson introduced us to his guest, Joe Stallard, who told us his story.

Robertson asked, "You began to hear voices; what did you hear?"

Stallard said when his wife left the room, he began to hear a voice, an impression. It told him, "Bind the spirits." He responded, "What?" It became insistent and told him to "bind the spirits." He didn't know what that was and didn't have energy to speak the words. But as he spoke the thought, "I bind the spirits in the name ... " the most hideous sound of laughter he had ever heard interrupted him. It shocked him, and as he stood there, he began to realize what was going on. He became hopeless as there was an overwhelming sense of power involved.

Stallard said, "My knees began to buckle; I was going down, and the thought came into my mind, call on Jesus. As soon as that thought came into my mind, I really began to hear voices. 'How stupid are you? Are you crazy? You know that won't do any good.'

"With literally no strength left, all I could do was just mouth the words in a silent whisper, 'My Lord Jesus ...' As soon as I did that, instantly, I felt an arm around my shoulders. This was not a voice; this was a physical thing. Something grabbed me and lifted me, and my mind went clear. At that point, I was almost in a kneeling position. There was no thought, no emotion, just a voice, a single voice saying, 'I'm here.'"

He said he turned his head to the left and saw a hand on his shoulder, draped in a white robe. And he felt another hand being put on his chest, and strength returned to him, and the crushing sensation began to leave.

Robertson said, "You literally saw the hand?"

Stallard said, "Yes, I saw the hand; I saw a sleeve. I felt if I'm having a heart attack, how can this have anything to do with anything spiritual?"

Robertson asked, "Did you ever see this demonic spirit?"

Stallard said, "No, I didn't see anything, but as I heard the voice, 'I'm here ...' the crushing sensation left me and I began to breathe."

He said he began to have, "an incredible sense of calm, and I knew everything was going to be okay."

Stallard said, "The presence with me stayed for several days, and I couldn't talk about it for several days. That was two years ago."

While talking with Robertson, Stallard said he wondered about his experience, "Why did you come to me? And the Lord really convicted me. He said, 'Of course I came to you; I died for you.'"

†

Late morning Mary called and said she slept poorly, as the adversaries had given her a bad time. About 2:00 a.m. she moved from her bed onto a chair to try to sleep with less physical interference. This is not a recliner, it's a green leather upholstered chair with an ottoman—not at all comfortable for sleeping.

I told her Sally had called to tell me about the interview on *The 700*

Club, and I wished she could see it. She suggested it might be on channel 25 in the evening. It did come on, I telephoned Mary, and she got to see it. When people neither understand nor believe her story, it's helpful for her to see others also going through supernatural spiritual attacks. As the apostle Peter writes,

> "Be careful! Watch out for attacks from the Devil, your great enemy. He prowls around like a roaring lion, looking for some victim to devour. Take a firm stand against him, and be strong in your faith. Remember that your Christian brothers and sisters all over the world are going through the same kind of suffering you are." 1 Peter 5:8-9

Some people don't believe demons (often referred to as devils) are real. Who do they think harasses and torments people, bringing illness, addiction, and myriad ailments? There are several instances in the Bible where Jesus casts out demons. Are they afraid? It could be the spirit of fear clutching them. Cast it out! God did not give us a spirit of fear, but of power, love and a sound mind [2 Timothy 1:7 KJV].

November 18

In a brief conversation with Mary, I learned that despite our efforts in prayer last night, she had an awful night, sleeping less than an hour the entire time. I told her to skip church today, something I generally would not say, as she needs to learn as much as possible and worship together with other believers.

But speaking with her again later, she sounded vibrant. She told me she was exhausted, but she did go to church, and she shopped for groceries. When she got home she discovered the milk carton was leaking. She had lost a lot of milk already, so she took the carton back to the store. Mary does what she wants to do; she always has. I thank the Lord for giving her strength and keeping her safe during this difficult time in her life. I called to tell her I had seen Barbara at church, who asked about her, and prayed with me. We bound the devil, loosed warrior angels, and she told me she still didn't know when Karen would be available to join us. I was happy to learn her husband was recuperating and was not in pain.

By phone to Walnut Creek after Thanksgiving

I said, "I'm glad you slept well last night."

Mary said, "I did fine until 3:00 o'clock, when they tried to give me the works. I heard voices like a man's voice, and then they did the rosary."

"The rosary?"

"According to them, they're Catholics in real life."

"Mom, they've never been in 'real life,'" I said, meaning they have never lived in a body in the natural realm as we do.

"Everything they say I have to discount. Well, that was my morning. Now I'm going to do desk work."

Thursday, November 29

As I hadn't talked with Mary for 25 hours, I called her.

Mary said, "Ever since I came home from Milpitas, I've not had much sleep. I just got up. I had to change beds in the night and went from the office out onto the porch. I wanted to sleep so bad. They want to make you itch, so you scratch and you don't sleep. And they suck your breath, so you gasp. I really let go. 'Why dear Lord? I can't take this!' At daybreak I thought, 'I've got to get out of here, and go someplace else.' I went into my room and closed the door. And that did it. They didn't come into my room, and I went to sleep."

I said, "Mom, can you see how ridiculous that is? Spirits can go through walls and windows."

"Yes, but no matter how ridiculous it is, I'm feeling all this cruelty. They even poke around my behind, and they say it's so they can 'f' me like a little boy. It's so disgusting. I pile so much stuff around me so they can't do it, but I can feel something. Anyhow, I was a mess, but I'm sort of rested.

"I think the woman who sold me this house had this problem. I thought about her, and, oh my gosh. Anyhow, I'm a mess, and I don't like it, and I don't think I can go to that thing on Sunday. If I could only run away from them and hide. Those spirits come right through the window. There was one in the mirror. Their images don't worry me so much, but I don't like it. I want to destroy them. He's so evil!"

I said, "We have to get rid of them."

Mary said, "This morning they're teaching the spirits how to suck my breath, so I gasp, and then I'm awake. It makes me jerk; it's very hard on the nervous system."

"What does Jesus say when you talk to him?"

"He doesn't say anything, but I read that suffering is good. It seems to me it should be finished by now. I've had enough pain and loss of sleep, which is very bad for the body. I can hear them now telling somebody to put it on automatic. All I know is I'm trying to get to sleep before anything happens, and then bingo, I jump. I know this morning I had a few jerking motions. One of them just about knocked me for a loop. I don't know if it was them or not. My nervous system is about destroyed. And they tell me I don't know the magic word, and all that kind of stuff. They say they will stay and torment me until I die."

I said, "I don't think that's right, or true, or will happen."

She continued, "They are people of the darkness. They've got them all over, and there's no way I can fight them. I get so frustrated. I have no place to hide.

"I think I'm about as bad as I've ever been. This kind of living is catching up with me, both emotionally and mentally. Oh, and they give me orders!"

"Tell them you're a slave of Jesus, and only Jesus can tell you what to do."

"They can read my mind. Sometimes when I think of something, they say it, and say it's their idea. I'm so tired. I've got to eat; I don't want to stop eating because I'm so skinny. I hear their voices all the time. I hate them. It's very hard to keep my mouth shut."

Mary knows she needs to respond to them verbally with Scripture. She tells me often they tell her the Scriptures don't phase them, which we both know is a lie. She needs help. We need believers to gather in the name of Jesus, then call upon Him to use His power to force them out of her mind and her life.

Like most nights, we prayed together over the telephone before Mary went to bed. We focused on God, not on the demons—which I often admonish her to do. I know it's difficult for her, as she responds that she's living with a group of people constantly talking to her, lying to her, and harassing her. Remembering Joyce Meyer's phrase, "Praise and be raised;

complain and remain," we try to get our priorities right, incorporating quiet warfare into our prayer.

November 30

I was happy when the telephone rang early this morning. Mary sounded good and had a good night's sleep! Hallelujah! She was so tired after seven nights of torment.

I thought about yesterday's conversation, about her going into her bedroom around 5:00 a.m. and closing her bedroom door. As we talked this morning, I said my comment that closing her door didn't make sense, because we know demons are not limited by physical walls. But as I considered her action, I realized that closing the door on them was an act of resistance. Her next comment came as a surprise to me. She said, "They told me to close the door." I had no comment.

December 2007

The demons have repeatedly told Mary they have wired her home. At first she believed them, as it sounded logical to her, but now, after two years, she knows they lie about everything. She asked me to bring her a broom, which I thought she wanted for the floors, so I brought her a nice new broom.

When she called she said, "I didn't get to sleep until 5:00 o'clock in the morning. I went around once with the broom you brought me. I went around the edge of the ceiling where they have connections. It's irritating to some of the demons. Oh yeah, some of them don't like it. But because the pipsqueak rules the roost, he dictates what they will do. They even said they had my keys, and they would throw me out of the house. And when I say prayers, they quiet down and listen. They say the prayers are for me, not for them. Of course they're not for them. And then it starts in again. I go to bed, and they get their images or "fabricated spirits" to bend over me. I have my cane, and I struck a couple of them. How can you sleep with those ugly things coming at you? Some of them are at the foot of the bed and they get tall."

I asked, "Do you say, I cast down imaginations ... I take every thought captive?"

Mary answered, "Oh yes. And then they say, 'We're just rotten.' They fixed the hisser. I didn't break it, but I've lessened it. I wish I could get it all. They say they want to kill me and throw me out in the street, naked. Oh, they've got the stories.

"What I wanted to say is, I've been battling those other things for quite a while. But when they stand over me, I use my cane, and I got a couple of them. But this morning *she* said, 'He's in bed with you.' No one is allowed in my bed! I did not turn to look. Anyhow, when she tells me there's a body in my bed, I know it's a lie so I didn't look. Then she repeated, 'It's Walter and he's dressed like a woman.' They say they'll use her as an alibi when they kill me. She goes on and on. Finally I said, 'Shut your rotten mouth. I don't want to hear from you.' I called her a witch. I don't like being tormented all night long! I told the Lord, I can't *not* get angry. They're listening now. They say I'm a liar. I say I'm not a liar; I'm telling it like it is."

Finally she said, "I don't know about Joanna. I'd love to listen to that music, but if I'm not rested, and if I have to wait for her ... she may want to socialize. If I depend on someone to drive me, I don't think I should take that chance. I hate to miss it, but I've missed a lot."

Mary sounded sad. She wanted to hear Joanna, the pastor at Mary's Methodist church, play. She invited Mary to a concert where she will perform.

"It would be great to go with Joanna tomorrow: Italian music, an eight-piece band. She's quite musical; she partakes in the singing of the hymns. But I don't get it. How can they go through Bible school and not know about demons when they're throughout the Bible?"

Thursday, December 6, at Milpitas

Awakened at 8:00 a.m. by the office telephone ringing, I got up and saw Mary sleeping with her fan oscillating, moving the air in the room. I closed her door. I heard her read Scripture aloud in the night, and I wondered whether to get up and go into her room. But she stopped speaking, and I wasn't really awake anyway. It seemed to me I had just gone to sleep when I heard her doing battle. Later she told me it was about 4:00 a.m., and after the battle she went back to sleep.

Yesterday at church Mary and I met with Barbara and Karen in a small prayer room. The only window was a small one in the door. There were two wicker chairs with cushions, a love seat, and a straight-backed chair, the seat upholstered in the same fabric as our pew seats, a pleasant light turquoise color. The walls were decorated with a cross and posters of well-known prayers.

Mary had not met Barbara, although she knew about her current labors. Karen had been to my home two years ago, when she came with David to pray for Mary. The women asked Mary what was going on, and she told them some lies the demons say.

Attempting to ascertain if the demons had "rights," Karen asked who lived in Mary's place before she moved in. We explained briefly, telling her what little was known about the previous occupants.

We talked about Russell's involvement with Masons and told them we prayed the prayer of release for Freemasons and their descendants, to renounce all activity and curses. We told them we collected and disposed of everything Masonic that had been in Mary's home, including Russell's apron, his Masonic Bible, even his baby cup. The four of us prayed against everything Masonic, rituals, etc.

We continued praying and asked the Holy Spirit to guide us and to disclose to us whatever we need to know to accomplish our purpose. Karen wondered if there was a remaining cause, and if it could be voodoo, as Mary had told her the demons said they have a doll of her, and they inflict pain on her hand. We discussed having already prayed, confessed, and renounced sins of deceased ancestors, without knowing what their activities were.

Based on what I read in Garrison's writings, I recognized manifestations, or works, of the spirit of fear, the spirit of bondage, and even a perverse spirit. We addressed those issues and bound and cast out all the strongmen and all their demons. During the session, there was a point where even the demons, with Mary telling us what they were saying, confessed they had no right.

As we wrapped up our session together, Karen prompted Mary to confess, that is to say out loud, positive things: "I am free because of you, Lord Jesus! I am forgiven because of you, Lord Jesus! I am washed white as snow because of you, Lord Jesus! I am your child." I told Karen and Barbara both of us have been saying these things from the Scripture list in the Anderson book, *The Bondage Breaker*. Karen told Mary that whatever the demons might say to her, she should declare *to Jesus* that she is the opposite. She should not speak to demons.

The Lord Jesus was with us in that room. We called upon Him, and invited Him to join us, and whenever two or more are gathered in His name, He is there [Matthew 18:20]. With His power, His authority, and His name, we bound the demons, cast them out, loosed Mary's human spirit, and we loosed the Lord's warrior angels to take the demons away in chains and send them where He wants them to go. We thank you, Lord Jesus, and we praise your name forevermore! Amen.

December 7

I don't understand. Why are the demons not gone? Haven't we done everything we can? Haven't we called upon the Lord, as He taught us to do [Matthew 18:19]?

Mary wants to go home today. We both have 1:30 hair appointments at different salons, so I told her yesterday we must leave by 11:00 a.m. I could not get to sleep last night until about 5:00 a.m., so I didn't get up until 8:30. I peeked into Mary's room. The fan was still going—on high, and she appeared to be sleeping. Her head was on one pillow with a second one on top of her head, which was wrapped in two scarves. When I went by her room yesterday morning, she had turned off the fan. She said the demons blow icky odors toward her, and she uses the fan to blow those odors away as it's uncomfortable to breathe that air. She said it sometimes smells like stale coffee.

†

We haven't been active in warfare since Wednesday, when we met with Karen and Barbara. We have been believing in the Lord, and waiting for His warrior angels to take the demons away. Neither have we discussed what's been going on with her. Now she's home alone, and I'd like to know about the past two nights. At 5:47 p.m. I dialed Mary's number. The phone rang and rang, and I could not leave a message. When I dropped her off at home earlier today, I neglected to stop call forwarding. Now I must wait for her to call me.

It's two weeks before Christmas, and I haven't even purchased cards yet. While preparing to do errands, including finding cards, I thought of a particular Scripture. Proverbs 26:2 teaches," ... an undeserved curse will not land on its intended victim." "That's it!" I thought. "That's one Mom can say to the creeps when they threaten her. Surely this will drive them away." I called right away, but had to leave a message.

December 12

Mary called to tell me about Ann. "Well, now we know why she's complaining about the eye—she doesn't put the drops in."

Ann is in early stages of dementia and doesn't reason like she once did. Her short-term memory also has been affected.

I asked, "So how are *you* doing?"

Mary said, "Oh, he gave me such a pain in my hand last night. I lose sleep, but I'm dealing with it. I keep praying there will be a way. I maintain my optimism."

"Mom, use Scripture! Say, "It is written. Pain cannot come against my body because Jesus bore all my pain! By His stripes, I am healed!"

"Yes, that's good."

"Mom, you have them written down. You only need to learn a few. That's the sword of the Spirit! Go through all those typed sheets, cut out the ones you feel are most relevant, tape them onto a clean sheet of paper, and use them. When they do or say something to you, respond with an appropriate Scripture! Doesn't that make sense?"

"Yes, it does."

December 19

Yesterday was Mary's 95 TH birthday. I forgot the table decorations, and I still can't find the birthday card I bought for her, but we had an enjoyable time. I hosted a birthday lunch for her and some of her friends and a few of our relatives at one of Mary's favorite restaurants in Jack London Square. Mary likes parties.

December 21

Mary called to say she was up by 9:30 a.m., but didn't sleep before 2:00 a.m. when she changed rooms and beds. I'm absolutely amazed by her God-given strength. Just knowing what she has gone through for so long wearies me, depresses me, and sickens me. I pray for her throughout the day. Whenever I get an idea that may help, I talk to the Lord about it. Today I asked Him to strengthen *her* angel—so that angel would have power against the enemy and be able to protect Mary from their interference. Don't we all have guardian angels?

Mary used her vacuum cleaner on the walls yesterday, and the demons told her she sucked up their lines; she destroyed their hisser lines. She slept on the sofa, with her head at the south end, facing the kitchen, and they couldn't reach her. But later they said they put their lines back up, and they got to her again.

"It's a funny deal, Lexie. Sickening," she said.

I said, "It sure is."

"The demons are always blabbing; they say I can go into any room, and they're liars. They see me protecting myself, and they say you don't need all that stuff, and I don't talk to them. It takes too long to get ready to fight. I just pile myself up with protection. I sleep in my robe, in case I have to get up. And I keep my raincoat over my bed all the time because they have a hard time penetrating that. You learn these things. They say, 'How do you sleep?' and I don't say anything."

Mary said her church asked members to bring a poinsettia, and she wondered if she should bring it early or bring it on Sunday. She also told me JoAnn had sent her a prayer book.

December 31

I picked Mary up and brought her here for Christmas. I went to my neighbors' house for cioppino on Sunday, the 23RD. Mary was invited, but preferred to stay home. On Christmas morning I baked pies, and then we drove to Ann's to pick her up. We drove to Ann's cousin's home in Livermore for a lovely Christmas Day and dinner.

Mary has been sleeping poorly because the creeps have been messing with her hand. Each night she was here over Christmas, she kept icepacks in the freezer in her room so she could use them at night when needed for pain. Time flies, and although we pray each night before bed, we haven't spent a lot of time in prayer, or in warfare.

I came upon the Scripture in Luke 18, where Jesus told his disciples the parable about the unjust judge who didn't fear God or care about what people thought. He talked about the widow in town who continued to come to the judge to ask for justice from her adversary. "Because she keeps bothering me, I'll see that she gets justice," the evil judge finally decided. And then Jesus said, "Won't God bring about justice for His chosen ones, who cry to him day and night?" I reminded Mary about this Scripture, and we resolved to pray day and night for her release.

The Wommack devotional surprised me yesterday morning. His entry for December 30TH says to "Use Your Delegated Authority." He writes,

> "There is no place in the New Testament that tells us to ask
> God to do something about the devil. Rather, we, (the church)
> are told to do something about the devil. This is because we
> have been given delegated authority over the works of the
> enemy. God desires that the church be enlightened to this, and
> walk in victory."

When Mary called last night, very tired from lack of sleep, I told her we must fight. I got my Garrison books, and again we prayed and fought. We used Scripture to bind and cast them out and loosed Mary. When we hung up the phone, Mary said they were mumbling among themselves.

This morning she sounded chipper. She slept better. I need to compile another set of Scriptures for her to use against them, but time slips away, and I have been spending more time with Ann. It's already 2:00 p.m. I haven't had lunch—or accomplished what I need to accomplish—and yet I must get on the road, pick up Mary, and get to Ann's place.

CHAPTER 18
GETTING CLOSE ... OR NOT

When the unclean spirit is gone out of a man, he
walketh through dry places, seeking rest, and findeth
none. Then he saith, I will return into my house from
whence I came out; and when he is come, he findeth it
empty, swept, and garnished. Then goeth he, and
taketh with himself seven other spirits more wicked than
himself, and they enter in and dwell there: and the last
state of that man is worse than the first.
Matthew 12:43-45 KJV

MARY SLEPT WELL last night! We are so close! Garrison talks
about our part and His part. I confirmed to Mary that one
manifestation of the spirit of fear is to attack nerves, causing pain and
damage. We bound the strongman and all his demons, and asked the Lord
to do the same from heaven. We spoke destruction to the works of the
devil in Mary's house.

January 8

After a quick shower yesterday, I drove to San Ramon to pick up Ann;
then with Ann in the car we drove to Mary's. I loaded Mary's suitcase into
the back of the car, and the three of us drove into Walnut Creek. As we
approached the address of our planned destination, we saw Ann's cousin,
Sheryl, standing on the sidewalk.

"It's closed! The restaurant has closed!" Sheryl said as she piled into the
car. "We're around the corner," she directed, and we parked in a conve-
nient metered lot across from a Mexican restaurant. Ann was happy to see
more of her cousins inside. After lunch we said our goodbyes and headed

for Whole Foods. Mary had eaten only a few bites of the enchilada she ordered and said she wanted something more to eat. She bought a banana. As soon as we were back in the car Ann wanted Tylenol, so I stopped at the drugstore near her home. Ann waited in the car while Mary came in with me looking for more to eat. I aimed her toward the nuts.

After dropping Annie off in her lobby, I brought Mary home with me. We had only a few minutes before heading into San Jose for Mary's optometrist appointment. They helped her select low vision devices, showing her quite a few magnifiers. She purchased a hand held model, 4x power, with a light.

At breakfast the following morning we talked about the night. Mary and I both slept, but we each said it was a couple hours at a time. Mary was awakened several times with pain in her hand. "But it's different now," she said. I have noticed an improvement in Mary's battle with the evil side. Either they bother her less in daylight hours, or she has learned to cope, and when to fight or ignore them. She is learning to fight through renewing her mind by reading the Bible and using the authority she has in Jesus.

6:00 p.m.

Returning to my home, Mary got out of the car in the garage. She looked toward the side door and pointed toward the floor. "See that little face?"

"No, Mom," I said, as I looked toward the door.

"They put that there to scare me," she said.

"There's nothing there," I said, and told her that's why we say, "cast down imaginations." She knows she's the only one who sees their images.

January 29

Mary had a bad night.

"This gets to me, Lexie, but I'm ever hopeful. I couldn't sleep. It annoyed me. If it isn't in one way, it's in another way. All the racket they make! So when I got up this morning I thought I'd be a wreck, and I don't know why, but I haven't gotten sleepy. Of course I do make strong coffee. What do you know that's bright and cheery?

"He's [Walter] getting very rotten. I'm too tired to talk about it, but it's nothing but vulgarity. That's how they keep you awake. They said they were at a party. I don't want to hear them; they do it on purpose. They call them dancing zombies and say they're druggies. They say they want to make me one of those. It's so ridiculous, Lexie. Oh yes, they say they will shoot me with drugs when I'm asleep; they'll make money off me. Then the kingpin said he wouldn't do that to me. They're always talking about 'f-ing' me; it's disgusting! They're good story tellers, but they're awful stories. I can't believe there are such creeps! Who made them like that? Well, that's my punishment, they tell me. I have to hear them so I won't sleep. I've learned to kind of steel myself against that condition, but you know what, it does something to my system. It puts my heart into a very nervous state. I try to think other things, but I can't block them out. And then they tell me what they'll do. You wouldn't believe it. I don't know how anyone can talk like that. I've been putting up with this crap every waking hour.

"They say they'll do surgery on me and give me a penis. And they listen to everything that goes on. It's constant from the time I'm awake until I'm knocked out by sleep. Not a good night. Today they're driving me nuts. I don't want to wear all that stuff. They make me feel like something is there, in my way, so I have to block everything. And they've informed me I better buy more Kotex because I've used them up. Well anyhow, I've prayed to the Lord that I can soon go to bed without all that paraphernalia. And I will. Well, the good news is, since I've been having that brandy my appetite has increased. I'm eating a little more."

February 1

Mary slept about four hours after moving into her bathroom. She stayed "in bed" late—on the bathroom floor. She knew by their conversation that other "people" were fooling around with her hand and made it hurt.

"In one breath they tell me there are only three of them making voices. They said this the other day. They tell me they're actors. Sometimes I can distinguish who's doing it. He feels he's got something to torture me with. My hand was good, and they'll be talking, and I know it's them; they make my hand hurt. And he makes my furnace sound like it's on, and then he blows cold air.

"The result is your mother is a tired old lady. I slept, but the pain lasts a while, and I'm kind of bunched up on that little pad I made for myself. I fixed it so my back doesn't hurt so much, but there isn't much room for turning. I dozed, and it felt good. Then I talked to the Lord. And then I looked around; I've got to straighten up this office/bedroom, so Tony and Enzo will have space to put their things when they come to visit."

February 2

Another poor night, but Mary didn't complain about it. She told me she was cleaning up her apartment for "the boys," and by putting away her "bathroom bed" she got some exercise. She sounded all right; she had some energy in her voice.

We decided I would drive to Walnut Creek, after stopping in San Ramon to help Ann with her medications. I told Mary I would bring my cushioned exercise mat to her, to put on the floor in her bathroom, should she need it. We'll eat dinner together, combining what we each have on hand. I'll bring what's left of the roasted vegetables I made last night, and she has some chicken wings. We'll make a salad too.

I reminded her to read Wommack's devotional for today. He talks about fighting and hating evil, which he calls a righteous anger.

February 8

I'm desperate to help Mary get rid of those pigs invading her mind, and I recalled Sheryl suggesting I contact Neil Anderson. I searched the web and called a Tennessee phone number. The recorded voice told me Anderson does not do personal counseling, but I could find a link on their website listing Christian counselors. I found several names in California, the two closest being Connie, whom we know, and a woman named Deanna [not her real name]. I called her.

It's wonderful to talk with someone who understands this subject! I outlined the facts of the problem and told her what we've done and what Mary has learned. Although I have been binding the demons and the strongman, I haven't bound the demons *to* the strongman, which she told me to do.

"Then have them leave," Deanna said.

"I did cast them out," I said. "They say they won't go!"

"They have to go," she responded in an even, matter-of-fact voice. "You are a believer, and they have to obey."

She said Mary should bind them too, and after casting them out, pray a sealing prayer. Ask the Lord to seal the work that was done so the demonic spirits cannot come back.

"Ask the Lord to put a protection around Mary's head. Say something like, 'Father, we seal the work that was done by the power of Jesus, and ask that in His will, you confirm that [work]. We thank you that you have broken the bondage, and seal that in to Mary.' And then, give her communion."

"Give her communion?" I asked, surprised.

"Oh yes, you can do that. Give her bread and grape juice. Do you have anointing oil?"

"No," I responded, still surprised, although I guess I shouldn't be.

"Well," she said, "get some from a Christian bookstore, and put it on her forehead."

During our conversation I mentioned several authors I had read, and asked her if she was familiar with Mary Garrison. She said she was not. She asked me if I had read *Pigs in the Parlor*, "a little thin book."

"No," I said, "I haven't heard of it." Afterward I found it online and ordered two copies, one for me and one for Mary.

While in discussion with Deanna I disclosed that the spirits bothering Mary were sexual spirits. She brought up names I had not addressed, as I didn't understand much about them and didn't recall Garrison naming those spirits. Deanna said they are *incubui* and *succubui,* names of the male and female sexual spirits. She said I could look them up.

(If one thinks seeking demons would be fun, you are dangerously misguided. Do *not* attract demons. They are not fun, but vulgar, God-hating, people-hating beings that want only to steal, kill and destroy [John 10:10].)

Mary has told me that the voices of most of the demons bothering her sound like a human male voice, but one of them sounds like a female. She tells Mary she's a lesbian. Mary hates her because somehow this demon causes Mary's body to lubricate. I told her I would talk with Deanna again, to find out when we could meet her. I told Mary that Deanna's concern was that Mary would have to keep them out once we cast them out.

February 22

As I haven't heard from Mary I dialed her number, but found the line busy. After trying several times I called both the operator and repair, both of whom confirmed the phone was off the hook.

I called the neighbors living below Mary, and Jim answered the phone. I refreshed his memory about who I was, explained to him that Mary is to call me each morning, and I have not yet heard from her. He said her car was in its carport and told me he would put on his shoes and go upstairs and tell her to call me. That was at 1:20 p.m.

While waiting for Mary to call, Sally called. When she dropped off the Hammond book last night at Mary's front door, the lights and the television were on. She knocked lightly, but Mary didn't come to the door. Sally said maybe she had fallen asleep and she didn't want to bother her, so she left the book on the porch.

It's 2:00 p.m. now, and I have heard from neither Mary nor Jim. In biblical days upset people fasted. We eat. I ate my lunch, leftover Chinese fast food. It wasn't great the first time, and today it wasn't better, but I told myself I should eat something. At 2:40 p.m. I decided again to call Mary. This time the phone rang, but no one answered. I got the answering machine and left a message, "This is Lexie. Call me."

I dialed the neighbor again, "Hi Jim, I still haven't talked with Mary. The phone rings now, but she hasn't answered it. Is she okay?"

Jim said, "She was fine. I'm surprised she hasn't called you. I told her to go back inside and make sure all three phones were back on the hook. She blames all this business on spirits."

I said, "Oh, has she told you about her problem?"

Jim said, "Yes, and all she has to do to make them go away is tell them she loves them."

He told me he used to be Christian, but now he follows Meher Baba. He said Jesus or Mohammad or Buddha, and he named a couple others, come back every 700 to 1400 years in human form.

"They're all the same guy," he said. "We all reincarnate."

He said Mary was on her way to an appointment when he went up to her apartment.

I called again, and this time she answered the phone. She had been to the hairdresser. "Of course!" I thought to myself. "How could I have forgotten that? She goes every Friday."

I warned her not to do as Jim had said. "Do not, under any circumstances," I said, "tell the demons you love them. We hate them!"

She agreed. I said love can be like worship, and we only worship the Lord. I talked with her briefly about the beliefs Jim had shared with me.

"Oh yes," she said, "They're the ones who sent that guy here, the one that cost me a lot of money." When she said that, I remembered. A counselor with an office in Walnut Creek came to Mary's house, and brought her a framed picture of Meher Baba, saying to Mary, "he was like Jesus." We both knew at the time the man didn't get it, but today it makes more sense, as Jim (erroneously) believes Jesus and the false gods are all "the same guy."

Mary thanked me for the book, which she found outside her door. She took it with her to the hairdresser, began reading it, and liked it. When the demons saw the book, she said it frightened them. They are probably familiar with the book and its truth. Hallelujah!

She asked when Sally left the book for her, and I said it had been last night on her way home from her brother Bob's birthday dinner.

"I heard the knock," she said, "but I thought it was *them*. I was in the kitchen, it was dark, and I didn't budge. But if Sally had called out to me, I would have let her in. One little knock. I ignored it. They want to scare me all the time, like someone is coming in. I can't begin to tell you Lexie, but all the evil comes out in the dark, not in the daytime. In the daytime they're entirely different, but at night they're all evil. I must call Sally."

March 13

Mary said, "I got kind of used to them, but I don't like them. One came over and he has fake hands, but you can't tell because they're dressed up awful, I can't tell you. He's holding a big white bag in front like he's going to come over and suffocate me. The kingpin knows I will keep fighting this until I die. I will not give in. And he said something to this guy that shrinks up and gets big and everything. They're not supposed to touch me at all, but they lean over you, and sometimes when they do that I'll sling at them, and they back away. One night I almost got one; the ones controlling them pulled him away. I told them I'll kill them, but I can't kill them, because they're nothing at all.

"They even control my fan; I don't know how, but they got it so it won't go very fast. I have to get it close to me."

I asked, "Do you understand this is a mental battle?"

"Yeah, but they can make you see things. Believe me, they can do other things too. And some things they can't do. But my fan, that makes me mad!"

I asked, "How do you know they're doing anything with your fan? You have several speeds to control."

But Mary continued telling me what the demons do.

"They know when I have a disapproving look on my face. Even though this is nothing to some people, when you're in this, it's real. And they even do it when I'm praying. Even when I'm visualizing Jesus Christ, they've got these figures all over. How do they put that into my mind, so I see it? I just turn away. I can stop it that way, but I'll be praying and oh ... it's just sickening. And you know, I'll be watching the television, and I'll see something ridiculous, like wings on people. They spoil my picture. It's disheartening.

"I said to the Lord tonight, 'Oh dear Lord, I know you hear me, and you know my body can't take much of this. It upsets me, my stomach and all.' I'm like somebody over a barrel, I feel helpless, and there's not a single place I can hide. My mind isn't affected, but they can plant something in my mind. And I hear their voices. I don't like hearing their voices, and yet that's what I've got. I keep asking God, how can they do it? Anyhow, that spoils my nights. My nights are awful. You can be sound asleep and they want your attention, they want to know you're awake and you're hearing them. They can look at you and know you're awake, even though I don't talk. Tonight he's angry about something; I don't know what."

I said, "He's always angry about something."

"I know. He's supposed to go. He wears me out. It would be much easier if the Lord would tell me what I'm doing wrong. It would be much easier if I could talk to someone who's gone through this. They don't print everything they've been through in these books. You've got to take it. No matter how many Scriptures I've given them. They're so used to them. Some of them bother them though."

I asked, "Are you putting on the armor every day?"

"Oh yeah, that makes them feel bad. But then they forget about it. I think sometimes ... "

"We *will* get rid of them."

"Oh, we've got to, we've got to, we've got to ... "

Then she said, "They say they've learned a lot from me they approve of. They don't want to leave me. They've said they like me better than others. They like the way I do things better than some people do. They're watching everything I do. I tell you I'm going mad; every hour I have somebody blabbing away. They're right there in your ear. You can't knock them out."

I agreed, "It's a horrible thing."

"Oh, it is! It's a terrible thing! I don't know how some people can go through this. I know that mentally they're not going to crack me up, or I'd be cracked up by now. But some people would be cracked up by now. I don't know how God allows it. I don't get a lot of things."

"What can I do for you tonight."

"Nothing. Well, say a prayer that sends them away. What a story I heard in the morning hours. I knew it was too good to be true. They're great actors, Lexie. How they put on an act! You think, oh, this time they mean it. Oh yeah, but as the hours wear on—it goes on so long, Lexie—they don't want you to sleep! They knew I was praying, and they put on such a performance. They knew how bad they had been ... I won't go on with the big story.

"Finally I said to myself, I don't think this is true, and it wasn't. They're lying all the time. So I say under my breath, "liar, liar, liar" and they know what I'm thinking. I don't want to be bothered with them tonight. He's always trying to rape me. Well, he hasn't. And I tell him, "If anyone comes near me I'll have Jesus do something to them, because I'm committed to Jesus Christ. I'm saying to God, protect me. I've also said, put a freeze on them, and he told me it happens. Deflate them and freeze them. I have to do something so I try it and it works."

I praised Mary for this, telling her this was fighting, resisting, a good thing to do.

She continued, "I don't think the Lord will let anything happen to me. But that's the battle. This is such a stupid battle. He knows I hate his guts."

Monday, March 17, 2008

Mary called and said, "I take a beating every night. The kingpin [strongman] is out to destroy me. I'm weakened."

I asked, "You said something about one that acts like a female?"

"Yeah, he acts like he wants to help, but it's just talk. He doesn't practice the mean things; the kingpin provides all the abuse. They say they can't help it, he's their boss. So Little Mary has to take it. Whatever I say in Scripture doesn't mean a thing to them anymore. But I know if we get a group of people to pray against them, it will get to them. I'm lying there talking to the Lord, and the Lord protects me. But it angers me, and I'm trying to control the anger because that doesn't help. I will use a new tactic."

"Yeah, it's called praise."

I told her to play praise music all day. Connie also told her to do this.

March 18

Mary called about 11:00 a.m. She sounded cheerful, but said,

"I had a bad night with the same old pattern, and I had a long talk with the Lord this morning. Something came to me; I took it from there. So far it seems to be the answer; it's a good one."

Mary stammered a little, and said, "I asked the Lord a lot of questions today."

She didn't tell me what they talked about; she changed the subject to Ann. I asked what her ideas were. She said, "Just to say my Scriptures out loud." But I think something may be going on that she is not ready to tell me about.

Two days later Mary called and said, "Your mother isn't doing too great. I don't know how long I can go on like this. I sure need some help because I sure have some devils. They have the audacity to say I'm doing all this misery to myself. I keep reading different passages to them, which doesn't seem to do any good. I finally went from my bed to the couch last night. They were giving me a beating that I couldn't stop."

I asked, "What were they doing?"

"Ooh, tormenting me! They don't let you sleep! They had a couple fans blowing on me. I had my fan on too. They just torment you. They pick a way, and they're so proud because they can keep me awake all night. This morning they say I look ugly, and they think they're doing a good job of tormenting me. This is hard to believe. Just visualize if you constantly had people you don't like in your house. It's hard to concentrate on Jesus Christ even. There are so many of them. You can't get to sleep. I pray to the Lord. He's hearing it all. And I must control the way I say things to them. My heart starts to race. I don't have a chance. I call them beatings, and I'm being beat up all the time. And then in the morning I want to sleep. I don't know if it was 5:00 o'clock or not. I've told the Lord I don't enjoy turning night into day. Look at the time I'm up. I need my sleep; I don't get enough sleep. It's terrible for me, and affects my vision. There are other things they do. They suck my breath, making me gasp. That's not comfortable. That's not good. Oh gee, I can't go into details. Such rotten things. They feel good about it, and they lie and lie and lie. They've got acts going on, like people want to help me. You don't want to hear it, but it's in your ear; you just hear it. And you can't turn it off. I say to God, 'I have no place to hide; I need my freedom. I have no place to hide.' Well enough of that, but I want you to know I will not be fit for much."

(She was planning to come to Milpitas.)

I said, "I think they know they'll be cast out, so they're stepping up their efforts."

March 27

My alarm went off at 6:30 this morning, and I noticed the fan in Mary's room was turned off and she was still in bed. So far, so good. I picked her up last Friday to bring her to Milpitas for Easter. I planned to bring her home yesterday, but my ESL class was last night, so we decided to leave early this morning. She wants to be her home in time for her Bible class.

In the car she told me she had a restless night, tossing and turning. She rarely moves at all, in an effort to remain in all her gear and be protected from the enemy. I asked her if it felt like a battle might be going on, but she said no. I was thinking of the battle between good and evil that I felt was being waged when the Lord fought for me and released me from the demon group tormenting me. Perhaps she has a different perception than I had years ago when the Lord released me from the tormenters.

✝

I met with Paul at church, and gave him a synopsis of what has been happening for the past couple years, and how we dealt with each issue as we learned about it. He agreed to get some people together to be on our team to cast out the demons. I had heard nothing by the following Tuesday, so I sent him an email. He replied that he and Barbara would come to my house on Wednesday at 1:00 p.m.

As promised, Paul and Barbara arrived at the house, and we prayed for Mary. When the demons spoke to Mary, she told us what they said. Knowing they were listening to everything, Paul engaged them in spiritual warfare, quoting effective passages from the book of Colossians, and other Scriptures, to the agitated demons.

However, when Paul glanced at his watch and discovered it was four o'clock, he said he and Barbara had to leave. Mary told me later the demons' reactions amazed her; they were extremely uncomfortable, in a way she had not experienced previously. She said Walter was suffering greatly and said repeatedly he "can't take this." She and I both believe that if Paul had been able to stay longer, the demons would have left Mary.

I have since learned from others successful in casting out demons that it can take some time, in one recorded instance, twelve hours. Some may leave right away, but certainly not all of them.

CHAPTER 19

A TRIP TO THE HOSPITAL

Continue to work out your salvation with fear and trembling, for it is God who works in you to will and to act according to his good purpose. Philippians 2:12-13

"**I**'M GOING TO bed; don't call me," Mary said last night, so I was glad to hear from her this morning. When asked, she responded that she slept in her bed all night, as she has done for the past several nights. She reminded me this trial was going into a fourth year and told me about the time—in the beginning—when she thought she heard an animal in the house and had put flour on the kitchen floor to see its tracks. She had told her neighbors about it. And she told me how much the hisser had scared her when she first heard it.

I finished reading *Soul Ties* this morning, before taking care of property management activities. By the time I had picked oranges and picked and washed the lettuce, it was after 3:00 p.m. Winding through the serene green hills of Sunol, I made my way to Mary's house. She delighted in showing me her "garden," which has grown to be quite a few containers full of green and blooming things. Two brightly blooming pots each had a crowd of cyclamen, which Sally had given her two years ago. They have not been repotted, yet they thrive. I hadn't realized how many orchids she has accumulated. Several large pots of cymbidiums were praising their creator, showing off their dazzling good looks. Inside the house, two Phalaenopsis were doing likewise.

Mary and I sat down to pray together. We talked to the Lord and I read aloud portions of the book, *Ridding your Home of Spiritual Darkness*. As demons began bothering Mary shortly after moving into her home, we prayed for forgiveness and repentance of any past sins that may have been committed in Mary's condo by prior occupants.

I flipped through the pages in the book where I had noted certain passages and read aloud underlined portions that could have relevance to her case. When I got to the chapter titled, "A Demonic Foothold in the Land," I sensed an evil presence. I could feel the hair on my body rise, along with an oppressive feeling and headache. We continued with prayers regarding the land and broken covenant. The two of us agreed [Matthew 18:20] and cast out demons by name. Mary listened to the strongman's excuses for not leaving. We were thankful when Mary felt the Holy Spirit had loosed her human spirit and we perceived His presence, bringing to mind that we should break demonic soul ties. We continued in prayer, pleading the blood of Jesus, again commanding the evil ones to leave Mary. Then in faith we turned the situation over to the Lord.

April 18

Mary and I already read *Pigs in the Parlor*, an enlightening and most helpful book for any similar situation, and now she is reading *Soul Ties*. She read a lot of it while at her hair appointment today. I told her I've been reading Hammond's book about breaking curses. I expect the next time we get together to pray about these things, the Lord will lift any curses, and we can command the demons to leave.

April 20

Mary called on Wednesday to tell me she had a good night's sleep and was looking forward to shopping with Sally on Friday. I took her home yesterday, after having brought her to Milpitas Sunday. We studied curses together and prayed to the Lord to lift all curses that may have come upon her life through personal or generational sin. We prayed warfare prayers and commanded the demon of curse to leave her in Jesus' name. The demon told Mary he was not a demon of curse. I asked the Lord to give Mary the best night's sleep she has had in three years that night. She slept well in Milpitas Sunday night; she told me Monday morning it was the best sleep she has had. How we praise the name of the Lord! I wanted to cook for her Monday night, but she insisted we go out for Chinese. She drank a lot of tea, even though I reminded her there was caffeine in it. Yesterday morning she said she didn't sleep, and that it must have been the caffeine, as she was not disturbed by evil. Again, we praise you, Lord.

April 27

I called Mary as she was finishing her lunch. She stayed after church for fellowship and met a couple more people. We talked about the gospels. Yesterday I directed her to the passage in John [18:6] where Judas, along with Roman soldiers and Temple guards, came to arrest Jesus. When He spoke to them, they all fell backward to the ground. I wanted to illustrate to her the mighty power of Jesus and the authority believers have been given to use His name to do His will.

June 6

Mary called from Walnut Creek and told me her night was brutal. She stayed in bed on the porch, battling until 2:00 a.m., and then went to the couch. I said I would personalize Psalm 91 for her, so she could easily say it aloud. We concluded our conversation so she could go down to the Farmers Market before they pack up and leave.

Saturday, June 7, 2008

While rereading *Ridding Your Home of Spiritual Darkness* and going through notes I had made, I realized that in past years I have had boarders in this house who committed sexual sin, even though house rules prohibit circumstances that allow this to happen. I prayed about that sin and asked His forgiveness. As I continued reading and thinking about the house I live in, I realized prior owners also may have opened doors to evil. I recalled our escrow period during which the seller, Mr. S, was a difficult man. I went into my room, got down on my knees, and talked to the Lord about this house, asking forgiveness for all of us, including me, who committed sins here.

July 11

Not hearing from Mary, I called to ask how she was doing. She sounded sad, almost to tears.

Mary said, "I can only say, not good. I just got up. I cannot go on like this."

I asked, "What's the problem, did they wake you up too early, or did you not get to sleep?"

"They won't let me sleep. I just get to sleep, and they wake me up."

I suggested we pray together, but not wait until bedtime, as we usually do, when we're both tired.

"We need more than prayer," she said.

July 14

Mary had slept on the couch, all wrapped up, and she did get some sleep. She said she is coming to terms with this. She is talking to the Lord.

"It's not what He said; it's what I asked him. There's only one way to fight this ... all the noises in the night and in the morning. Just put myself in a groove, I decided. Luckily for me, God does it for me; I put myself in a kind of stupor and I just think 'Jesus Christ' all the time and I know it will work and He will lead me out of this mire."

She said she wished she had music to combat all the noise, so I reminded her to put her CD player on "rep all." She couldn't find the button to do that. When she does find the correct button, the letters shown on the menu are tiny and difficult to see.

The next day Mary called.

"I had a terrible night; I can't sleep. You know how sleepy I was when I talked to you. I get myself in bed, and I'm getting ready to get settled, and here comes that noise, here comes that hiss. I have such a racket that I cannot sleep. Noise does something to my nerves. I just can't go on. I got out of that bed and into my own room. Well, it followed me, but I stayed there and endured. I did the hallelujah to the Lord, and I did prayers. I stayed in bed until after they wore themselves out. There was still noise, not as furious, but I still couldn't sleep. So I thought I better get up and get going. I'm going out to get some food I need into the house. I was so jittery, and they go on and on—you can't turn them off. I say to God, 'Where can I go to hide?' I can't go to the car and hide. I said to the Lord, I didn't think it was right.

"I've been burping all night. I don't even know if the gastroenterologist can help me, or if it's just stress from this situation."

July 18

Sally took Mary to an eye specialist today. He told her to go back to her regular eye doctor and get reading glasses so she can read without bothering with bifocals. She felt encouraged regarding the macular degeneration, as he said he didn't think her eyes were too bad.

"He thinks those vitamins I'm taking for my eyes are good," she told me.

August 5

Again Mary had not slept. She recounted her night saying, "Well, after the parade of images, I got the hisser and all those smells, but I determined to sleep through it. So I turned on the fan to blow away those smells. They also have a fan they turn on. So I put a pillow on my head and then I put my fan on to push stuff up to them, or so they say. That's what keeps you from sleeping! I must have fallen asleep, and I don't know when I woke up, but he [the demon] has a habit of waking me up at 2:00.

"At 5:00 o'clock in the morning they give me this story. They make it sound like they're all fighting to free me, and all the others are too ... and I know it's all lies, all done to deceive me. I keep praying to the Lord. I'm waiting for him to restore my privacy. So anyhow, that's how they keep me awake. Oh Lexie, what stories! You'd be amazed. He can hurt you, and he even hurts them, they say. It's over and over, and in the end it's always the same thing, until they exhaust themselves. Then I'm allowed to sleep. Well, it could have been worse. I got a few hours before they woke me up, and then I got a few hours after 5:00 o'clock. I don't need to open my eyes to see the clock because I hear the shower downstairs. The downstairs neighbors go to bed early, and she gets up around 8:00 o'clock. I got up after 9:00."

August 18

Mary called about 10:00 a.m. and she sounded chipper. She had slept well. We prayed a Psalm last night before bed, and she took two Advil tablets. She said maybe she should take only one, as she was still sleepy. We didn't talk much, as I'm swamped today with work, with Ann, and with Susan (Russell's niece) coming down from her home in the mountains.

September 5 (fasting)

I brought Mary home yesterday. I had picked her up on Monday—Labor Day—and on the way down to Milpitas we stopped in to visit with Ann. Mary had not seen Ann's new apartment in the assisted living section. She liked it better than Ann's first apartment because the living room is larger, but there is no balcony.

The first night Mary was here, I heard her in the predawn hours, fighting verbally. She is getting bolder in resisting the devil, and she is becoming more familiar with Scripture. I am confident it won't be long.

I have read quite a few books on spiritual warfare, and now I'm reading Cymbala's, *Fresh Wind Fresh Fire*, focusing on prayer. He emphasizes that Jesus taught us His Father's house is a house of prayer, not "a house of sermons," or other ministry projects. He mentioned spiritual warfare and related an account of a young woman troubled by a demon which he successfully cast out. I also am focusing more on prayer now than warfare. While it is vastly important for her to resist the devil, Jesus teaches us that some demons "come out only by prayer and fasting" [Matthew 17:21 and Mark 9:29].

In the Bible we read about sackcloth and ashes and fasting. We all have troubles in this life, and many of us turn to God for answers. But what kind of fasting should we do? Jesus fasted forty days—and then was tempted by the devil. Did he go completely without food for that period of time? Did he pick a few berries? He must have drank water from streams. We are told angels tended to him afterward [Matthew 4:11]. And what about Elijah when running from King Ahab and Jezebel? After his fast, ravens brought bread and meat to strengthen him [1 Kings 17:4-6].

I've done twenty-four-hour fasts, eating lunch and not eating again until lunchtime the following day. I've read about three day fasts. Queen Esther had the Jewish people fast from food *and* water for three days, which averted disaster for her people and rescued them from annihilation [Esther 4:16]. That would be a challenge for me, and probably for most of us. Isaiah's discourse in Chapter 58 gives us the Lord's view on fasting.

Some of our family members observe lent. "What are you giving up for lent?" someone might ask. Few people I know continue with that tradition, but it's a fast, isn't it? It's sacrificially resisting carnal cravings. I love desserts and sweet things. I love homemade cakes, pies, cookies, dark chocolate candies, lots of those things. I love ice cream, jam on toast, and honey. I decided to attempt a fast from sweets and gave up all those things. After a week into my fast—which seemed liked two weeks at least—I committed to continue for forty days. I had leftover homemade chocolate cake (from scratch, never from a mix) in the freezer, neatly packaged in serving-sized pieces. I had made the cake for guests who came for dinner and began my fast from sweets the following day.

As I entertain, and always serve a homemade dessert, what would I do when I had friends or family over, I wondered? Days passed, and I noticed that although I would have loved to eat a "goodie," I didn't have to. I had the strength to say no to myself. I didn't pray about my fast from sweets. I thought, "This is such a small thing, a feeble effort." But one evening, when some cousins I hadn't seen in a couple years were coming for lunch the next day, I mentioned it to the Lord. I simply asked if I should eat dessert with them or not. A little surprised, and so pleased, I heard an impression from the Holy Spirit tell me it would please the Father if I continued my fast. I felt encouraged to continue. He was aware of this small effort! After that I simply told guests I wasn't eating sweets for a while, and they all just went ahead and enjoyed their desserts. Sometimes I ate a piece of fruit while they ate dessert.

September 8

Mary's voice sounded tired. "I've even had notions of going away, far away, for a while." Then she continued with her current agenda, "I picked up my tickets for the Will Rogers show. They have the bus, but we have to be ready by 1:20 p.m. The show starts at 2:00."

Mary had purchased tickets for herself, for me, and for Ann. I wanted to drive to the theater in Walnut Creek, but Mary wanted us to take the bus that left from her community. She thought it would be easier than finding parking. I drove from Milpitas to San Ramon, where I picked up Ann, along with her "limousine," a folding red walker, and we piled into the car. We drove to Walnut Creek, picked up Mary, and drove back down the hill to the staging area for the buses.

Once the ladies were seated in the auditorium, an usher asked me to remove Ann's walker to an area outside the auditorium which I did. We all enjoyed the performance, and when it finished, I quickly hopped out of my seat to fetch the walker for Ann. No problem. Until I tried to get back to our seats, and saw a sea of patrons vacating their seats, coming toward me, each with companions, each engaged in conversation. I could not get through. Once I got back to Ann's seat, where Mary was happily keeping her company, we inched our way out of the auditorium.

Ann had to go to the restroom. If you've ever been to a theater, you know there is always a line at the ladies room. Long story short, we missed the return bus, and had to call a taxi to take us back to Mary's place.

October 4

When I called Mary around 7:00 p.m. she said she felt dizzy. I asked her about lunch, as she hadn't eaten much yesterday. Perhaps she had low blood sugar; I suggested she have some orange juice—she didn't have any—or apple juice. I held on while she struggled to open the jar. When she came back to the phone with the juice, she said she wanted to lie down. I told her I would call back in an hour.

I set the timer on my stove, as I wanted to be sure she ate some dinner and didn't just crash for the night. The buzzer went off, and as I walked toward the phone, it rang. Mary said, "Oh Lexie, I feel awful ... " She had thrown up multiple times, she was dizzy, and I asked her if I could call 911. She didn't object.

Dialing 911, I was transferred to the Contra Costa Fire Department emergency number, who sent people to help her. They took her to the nearest hospital. I called and asked about her apartment. "Yes," I was told, they "had secured the apartment." Apparently Mary was alert and talking with them.

At Kaiser Hospital a CT scan of her head was done, and other tests. I called the hospital several times, inquiring whether they would admit her. At about 12:45 a.m. I was told, "They're still doing tests." The phone rang at 2:00 a.m. I was in bed, but not yet asleep. "We're keeping her overnight," they said.

The following morning Mary was still in emergency. Hospital staff were waiting for the admitting doctor to assess her. Call again in two hours, they said. At 1:15 the doctor was with her; did I want him to call me? "Yes," I said, "I would like him to call me."

When Dr. Ortiz called, he said the CT scan showed no evidence of a stroke. He wanted her to stay in the hospital one more day, but as she was not a Kaiser patient, he asked if we should move her to John Muir Hospital. My suggestion was not to stress her further, and for just one day, keep her there.

He mentioned giving her medications for nausea and to help her inner ears. He said, "The stress she is under [demonic] and not sleeping increases her chance of vomiting." He prescribed a drug for her and told me Mary had spoken with him confidentially about the stress she has suffered with hallucinations and voices. He said she was a very intelligent woman, and of sound mind. I sure appreciated hearing that. In a sentence or two, I told him she suffered from demonic oppression, which is real, and which one can read about in the Bible. He said he would call me again the next morning, and that she would probably be ready to go home about 9:00 or 10:00 a.m.

October 9

It was after 11:00 a.m. when I arrived at Mary's room at Kaiser Hospital on Sunday, the 5th. She was sleeping, so I sat down and began reading the book I had brought with me. As the afternoon wore on, they gave Mary lunch, instructions on how to use a walker, an evaluation from a physical therapist, and finally at 4:00 p.m., the okay to go home.

Kaiser insisted she use a walker as she still suffered from dizziness. But as they would neither give her one nor sell her one, we stopped by two drugstores on the way to her house, to see if I could buy one. No deal. At Mary's house, we packed up a few things and I took out the garbage, as some food had been left out when she was whisked away to the hospital.

Our next stop was a grocery store at Milpitas, where I purchased steaks and frozen peas. I got Mary into the house and began fixing dinner. Jack had driven down to Milpitas. I cooked quickly, we ate quickly, and I drove Jack to the BART station where he would catch a train to the San Francisco airport to fly out to Thailand.

I spent much of Monday finding a walker for Mary and ended up with just the right one—a "junior adult" walker from a medical supply store in San Jose. Mary has been sleeping pretty well, not talking much about demonic forces. It's 10:47 a.m. now, and she's asleep on the couch in the family room. I have found her there twice before.

October 21

I dropped Mary off at the hair salon Friday, then drove up the hill to the house to water her plants. I sorted the mail, discarding a few requests she receives for charitable donations—about 90% of her incoming mail—and I checked her fridge for any rotting food. With perfect timing, I walked back into the shop as she was writing her check for the wash and set.

Three o'clock was approaching, we hadn't had lunch, and Mary wanted a chocolate milkshake. She recalled a previous Friday when I brought her lunch from the nearby diner while she was under the dryer. Today we drove to the diner where we each ordered a burger and a milkshake. They still make their shakes the old fashioned way, just ice cream, milk, and chocolate syrup. Delicious!

Back at Milpitas, we received a visit from a physical therapist named Paolo. His assessment of Mary's strength and condition was that she should not be living on her own at this point in time. She was still experiencing dizziness and was continuing with the prescribed drug. Paolo advised her not to go outside without the walker. The next time he came he said she could put the walker away and use a cane. Inside the house, she doesn't use any assistance walking, and she's no longer holding onto the walls.

Earlier this week he had given her exercises to do. I asked about upper body strengthening, and he added two more exercises. His current assessment was that she should stay with me another week, but she balked and said she wanted to go home on Friday. She'll probably win, but I have two concerns: she may not continue with the exercises, or she may not do them as directed. I have been doing them with her and counting for her. My second concern is that she may not eat as well. At my home, I can be sure she gets three meals a day. And she gets more sleep here. She looks better now than she has in a while, younger and more vibrant.

She slept a lot in the hospital even though it was only overnight, and thankfully she wasn't bothered much by evil. But here, there have been attempts at harassment, and I too have been bothered by these unseen invaders, while sleeping or going to sleep. Monday night as I was falling asleep, evil invaded my thoughts and dreams. I recognized it, awakened, and rebuked it. I recited appropriate Scripture, and finally, "laid down and slept in peace, knowing that the Lord alone, makes me dwell in safety." [Psalm 4:8]

October 31

Another week has gone by. Mary reminded me today she has stayed with me for almost four weeks since being released from the hospital. Paolo, the physical therapist, came by twice this week, and released her to be on her own inside her home, but not to go outside alone. She is still unsteady; she wobbles and veers a little to the left when I walk with her. He said she could fall. Previously she told me she would get someone to take her where she needed to go, but this afternoon she told me she would be careful. "I'll hold on to the cars on my way to the garbage," she said.

We pulled into the parking lot about 11:30 a.m. The farmers' market was still doing business, and we hurried to the chicken man. All morning I heard how anxious Mary was to get a chicken.

"I haven't had one in weeks," she lamented.

"I'm all sold out!" he said. "I had a big order."

He said, "They bought my chickens to give to all the vendors, because today is the last day of the season."

We both told him how disappointed we were, and he said that if they give him a chicken, he would give it to Mary.

"It will take time though ... do you have more shopping to do?" he asked.

I took Mary's arm, and we walked over to a strawberry booth, where she bought a basket of berries. Next we went to a vegetable vendor with a good variety, and everything looked nice. Mary bought artichokes, green beans, zucchini, and a cauliflower. I longed for the gorgeous red lettuce, but decided it would be too many hours before I could get it to a refrigerator. And unfortunately, the chicken vendor was not given a chicken to sell to Mary.

Upon arrival at Mary's house, we saw that Sally came during the week to pick up last week's chicken, the one we had forgotten in the fridge. We didn't want it to go to waste, so we called and told her we left it. After Mary put her things away, she looked through some mail, and I drove her to the hair salon. From there I went to grocery stores, where I got everything on Mary's list. When I drove back to the salon, she was waiting for me outside on a bench.

Overall, Mary slept pretty well while she was with me in Milpitas. She didn't ask for the fan, and although she put a scarf on her head each night, she commented that it also keeps her hair in place. She still has the big spoon—the end of the handle stuck out from under her pillow—and she kept her bag of "protective items" nearby. Last night, however, was not as good. She hadn't called me, saying she didn't want to keep waking me up, but she spent most of the night on the sofa. Lord, when will this end?

November 19

Mary called just before noon. She didn't get much sleep, and she told me about the images she had seen.

"It looked like a football with a big head, bigger than a normal man's head. He's down near the floor, staring at me. He hurt my ankle, and I kicked at it, and he said I kicked him in the face. Well, I won't go into details, but I don't like it. Now there's another one! They're dummies, but he controls them. Their eyes and mouths move. He's the one who posts those pictures up on the wall. See? Right now that one appears. Some of them look like Arabs."

I had talked with her last night before bed, and she was doing warfare before going to sleep. This is good; she needs to assert her authority in Christ.

CHAPTER 20
DEMONS CHANGE MARY'S CLOCKS

We know that we are children of God and that the world around us is under the power and control of the evil one. 1John5:19 NLT

A ROUND 4:00 O'CLOCK Mary called for a telephone visit. She had no sleep last night as the demons blew disgusting odors at her and jolted her awake whenever she began to fall asleep. This morning's Bible study was excellent, and Judy [not her real name], the pastor's wife, greeted her and asked how she was. Mary responded that she didn't get any sleep, "you know, with my problem." She said Judy got a look of fear on her face, so she didn't say anymore. We talked about how many people—even Bible-reading Christians—just don't believe in, or greatly fear, demonic intrusion. They can't even talk about it.

The evil ones are now manifesting visions in front of Mary while she's driving. She sees something, slows down, and when she gets closer, she realizes it's just one of their images. We talked about the danger of driving with this occurring, and she said she's driving very little now.

We pray constantly about this situation, and I wonder if we're doing something wrong. Mary holds on to the Scripture about the woman who repeatedly came before the judge until he got so tired of her he granted her appeal [Luke 18:2-5].

January 21

Mary has an eye doctor appointment, so I got up early and drove to Walnut Creek. Thankfully, her eye exam showed no progression of macular degeneration. Her vision remains stable, the same as six months ago.

After the appointment we picked up a couple things for lunch, then drove across the parking lot to the diner where we ordered two chocolate milkshakes to go. At Mary's place we each made our own tuna sandwich, our way, to go with our shakes.

When we finished eating, I brought out the envelope I had prepared, addressed to Russell's niece. I asked her to get Russell's ring. I had explained a few days ago that as Russell had been involved in Freemasonry, his ring might be an item to which demons could attach. Although she didn't wear it, she didn't want to give it up. We both have given up quite a few things during this trial. Again she lamented destroying her quan yin figurine, which she enjoyed for its lovely appearance. I again pointed out that in some cultures it's considered a god, and as such is undeniably displeasing to God. We prayed about the ring, lit a few matches over the sink, and ran the flame over the ring. We put it in the envelope, and I mailed it on my way home. It was out of Mary's place. Is there anything else?

The next evening Mary called about 10:00 o'clock and talked about the little football-shaped things the demons cause her to see. As she continued her story, I began typing her conversation.

Mary said, "They're around my bed all the time, every night. I'm not exaggerating. And tonight I had on Channel 25, which was interesting, and they made it all snow. He put his figures on it. I turned it off and on again, but the snow was still there. They messed with my phone, but I kept trying until I got through. Spirits, you can't tell what they might do. They're doing things that some of the spirits say are illegal for them to do. And I'm the goat. I've just got to take it. They don't want me to tell you; they seem to be afraid of you."

She was tired and said she had already prayed, so I said a brief prayer with her, and we hung up.

January 24

Mary called to say she had slept, "Very badly. Something has to be done. I didn't sleep, but I dozed, and they annoyed me with their antics. It's really getting to be a terrible problem. I can't go on like this; this wrecks me."

I said that Paul, from my church, and Mike, formerly with our church, both had experience in spiritual warfare.

Mary continued talking about the demons.

"They do all that talking; they say they're going to set me free. But they make that *heat*, so I turned on my fan, and they put on a fan, so I've got it coming from both sides. Your mom is an optimist, 'as it came so it shall go,' but I'm awake and tormented all night. Well, this was too much this morning. I've been having a rough week. They changed my clocks. But they put them back again. They do it real quick.

I said, "You've got to refuse to believe it. It may be your eyes."

Mary said, "This all started weeks ago, when I got up at 3:00 o'clock [a.m.]. When I sleep I keep the curtains pulled open, but it was very dark, and they said they put a curtain up. All I know is I see darkness. I keep a light on in the darkness to keep the spirits from wandering around. They don't like light. I jumped up; I was going to be late for something, and it's all dark. And then I see that my clocks were different, and my watch was different, and later they put them back and the time was correct again."

January 26

We prayed together before she went to bed, and Mary slept a little better last night. She told me that some nights ago she had an unpleasant dream about me. I told her when I have a bad thought or dream I say out loud, "I reject that thought!"

She said, "I don't have to say it out loud; I know how to resist it." I explained that it is important to say some things out loud, and I reminded her we "have the power of life and death in our tongue" [Proverbs 18:21], and that God created the world by *saying* things. God said, "Let there be light," and there was light [Genesis 1:3].

When she told me she often talks out loud to herself, I reminded her we are not to speak idle words, that we are accountable for them [Matthew 12:36]. I'm still working on this myself.

March 2

Mary said, "It was just that quick! I'm sitting on the couch watching the telly [television], and suddenly I feel like something's coming toward me, like a moving shadow, so fast I can't picture it.

"Another time, I was lying down. I had just gotten in bed, and something went by me. It was a slim body. And then this one says it was him. It startled me tonight; it created a little wind that made me look up. Well, thank God it's only a shadow that evaporates. I don't even think about that because I've got live images here that are supposed to be spirits. And they change in front of me. They'll come through the porch, get tall— above the doors, a big monster, but I'm familiar with them. And they can shrink themselves so small I can step on them. They're under my feet. And they get mad! How would you like to be taking a shower, and there's a head there, no body, and it's trying to look in the tub while I'm taking a shower. Oh gee, I've seen it all now.

"They surround my bed. I caught one *in* my bed. I don't want them in my bed! They're fakes. They're like marionettes. The other spirits make them do things. They mouth words to me that are evil. They mouth that they want to 'f' me, because that's all they talk about—sex. I could write a book on this, but it wouldn't be interesting. It's dumb and useless.

"He's quite an artist. He's got pictures on the wall. The pictures move around. Isn't that something? It's disgusting!"

March 17

A couple weeks later Mary called and said, "I'll wonder what the time is, and they tell me, and it's a lie, the incorrect time. I'm looking forward to a normal life when I get rid of them."

Mary has been saying for several weeks that the demons change her clocks. Today I changed all my clocks to daylight savings time.

April 25

I took the day off to have lunch with a friend, and afterward I drove to Mary's. I talked with her Thursday to let her know I'd be coming, and offered to stop by the grocery store for her. But she said she'd stop on her way home from her Friday hair appointment.

We spent a few hours together, and I turned her heat up, as it was only about seventy degrees in her apartment, and that's cold for her. We need to get another thermostat, as this forty-five-year-old one is difficult for me to read, and practically impossible for Mary to read. She had it turned to "cool" rather than "heat." I don't like her blaming the demons for turning off her heat, when it's possible the problem is not understanding how to control the thermostat. We shared a lovely New York steak, along with baked yams, an artichoke, and baked apples.

Recently the clocks in Mary's home have been more troubling to her than the thermostat. "The demons change my clocks," she has complained to me. For several months, sometimes in the middle of the night, they lie to her about the time. They say it's 7:00 o'clock (in the morning), for example, when it's only 5:00 a.m. Two mornings a week it's important to Mary to get up at the right time so she will be on time for her Thursday morning Bible study and also for her Sunday church service. She has called and awakened me before dawn on several occasions to ask me the time. "It's 5:00 o'clock Mom, go back to sleep," I tell her. "If it's still dark out, go back to sleep—it's too early," I have said.

Last Thursday my phone rang at 5:10 a.m., again at 6:29 a.m., and again at 7:15 a.m. Each time Mary called, she asked me the time. When I talked with her in the evening, she said she arrived 45 minutes prior to her class and sat in the car for a while. When she went inside, she set up chairs for the group. She had been up since about 2:00 a.m. because she didn't want to miss her class. (My poor little mom. This breaks my heart.)

Demons know very well who Jesus is [Luke 4:34], and they hate God. Their mission is to destroy people, especially those destined for salvation. It's understandable they would be particularly active on nights prior to Mary's planned meetings for worship and Christian fellowship.

Today my neighbor Donna called and asked if I wanted to go for a walk with her. Yes, I always want to go for a walk! And along the way I recounted to her the story of how Mary cannot see her clocks correctly. As we walked along, I realized suddenly the watch Mary wears is a larger man's watch, and it may have belonged to Russell! Connie thinks the reason the demons remain is they still have a "right" to stay, which may be in a piece of property belonging to Russell. Was this revealing? Donna thought so. How can I get Mary to give up that watch?

April 29

Mary called and asked, "What time is it?"

"It's 9:45."

"They *like* to change my clocks; it's fun for them. He does it because it pleases him. They're sadistic. I didn't have a good night. They rejoice when I don't get sleep. Well, I won't be making cookies today."

Although Mary has told me many times over the past several months the demons change her clocks, I thought maybe they caused her to see the time incorrectly. But the other day she said, "He [Walter] changes it; I watch it moving."

May 7

Early this morning the ring of the telephone awakened me. Of course it was Mary.

"It's 6:45," I said into the phone. At least it was daylight.

"I've been up since 2:00," Mary said.

"Mom, go back to sleep. I'll call you at 8:30," I told her. "Okay," she said, and hung up.

Her Bible study is so important to her. She spends hours each week preparing the lesson. Visually difficult for her, she uses a strong magnifier with a light that illuminates the magnified portion of the page. She moves it along each line. Writing her answers is also difficult. She prints with large letters, but still has difficulty reading her own notes, although they are quite legible. She asks someone to read her answers when it's her turn to respond in the group.

I was up by 8:00 o'clock, but waited until 8:15 to call her. When I called, I got the answering machine. I tried again to reach her, every five minutes or so, until I decided she must have left early for class.

Mary and I pray individually, and we pray together about delivering her from this torment. Day and night she lives with prying eyes, intrusive, often vulgar words, ugly frightening images, and lies. She says they change her clocks, turn her heater on and off, and tell her what to do. She bathes in the dark because they watch and comment. When she turns on her television set to learn from biblical teaching or other Christian programming, she sees their faces in front of the screen. She sees demonic appari-tions rather than Charles Stanley or whomever she wishes to watch. Thankfully she knows they are lying, she knows these things are "imagina-tions," she knows she is saved and loved by Jesus, and she knows He knows what she's enduring. So we wait (somewhat patiently) for the Lord. I con-tinue to hope to find a group of people, a handful really, who believe and don't doubt, who know Scripture—the Word of the Lord—the sword of the Spirit, and who are not afraid. I know we can cast these devils out!

May 8

Mary called midmorning. "They wait for me to call you, and when you give me the time, they change it back on my clocks. What you don't understand is that they can change the clock instantly; I see the hands move! I caught them at it! No clock will be alike unless he makes them all right. It's aggravating. What're you gonna do?"

I suggested she try not to let it bother her, and they would probably stop doing it. She agreed, but worries when she has an appointment. Sometimes I feel she perceives me as being critical of her when I offer sug-gestions or tell her what to do or not do. I certainly don't mean to be, and I tell her that a lot.

A woman who rents a room in my house gave me a slip of paper with the name Dr. Norvel Hayes on it. She had written, "Demonology confer-ence, Tennessee." She said she had seen this man on God TV when she was in Europe last weekend. I googled him and watched a YouTube video where he told of casting out devils from a male teenager unable to speak or function normally.

"A kid streaked [naked] across a Christian campus and becomes demon-possessed and completely won't speak to anyone. *Norvel* casts it out and the kid ... [*returns to normal*]." He said you have to stick with it. He stayed alone with the young man, and it took about twelve hours to get the demons to leave.

I looked over Hayes' website and discovered he has written books regarding deliverance ministry. I called to place an order and spoke with a young man who listened to a synopsis of Mary's story. When I mentioned demons, he responded with Luke 9:1, "When Jesus had called the Twelve together, he gave them power and authority to drive out all demons and to cure diseases." He said, "Make sure all unbelief is out of the room during deliverance." More good advice.

June 2

Mary called late in the evening to tell me Barbara, her downstairs neighbor, had come upstairs to look at Mary's orchids. Although Barbara doesn't know specifics regarding Mary's problem, she knows Mary "has trouble with spirits." Mary asked Barbara about the woman who had lived in her unit before Mary bought it. Her name also was Barbara. Mary asked where she's living now, but none of the neighbors seem to know.

One day (before Mary lived there), people were looking for upstairs Barbara, but no one could find her. Downstairs Barbara decided to look around outside, and as she was walking past the carports, she found her sleeping in her car.

Mary has considered going to her car to sleep also, but has resisted and stayed in the house. What do you think? Were the demons in the unit before Mary moved in? At Gateway Church, we talked about the possibility that demonic spirits were there before Mary. The land the senior community was built upon was once Native American territory, and blood may have been shed there. It's also possible sinful activity occurred in Mary's unit prior to her moving there.

August 13

Mary said, "There's another demon now. He hurts me. He says, 'your clock is going backward, and you can't do anything about it.'"

When she called me to learn the correct time, he told her he changed my clocks too. "That's another lie," I said.

The demons are pretty shook up. They tell her they can't go on this way. They have been saying that quite a bit. We are getting tough with them now with Eckhardt's book of prayers that defeat demons. Walter says he has called others in, and Mary confirms, "they're all over."

August 23

Mary called and said, "I got up at 1:00 a.m. and was up until 2:30. When I found out the clock changed, I did go back to bed, my feet went out from under me, and I hit the side of my head and my nose. It happened fast ... like something tripped me, although I felt nothing. All I felt was when I banged my head on the foot of the bed. Something had to trip me sideways ... well, it's something unusual for me."

After a pause she added, "You don't know all the things that go on around here."

August 24

Mary and I think about and talk about what can be done to solve this problem, and who might be able to help us. I mentioned to her a pastor named Mike, a former associate pastor at our church who understands spiritual warfare.

Mary called around 10:00 p.m. and asked me, "Does Mike know about the manifestations? That they're in my cupboard? That there's a head in the oven? I am thoroughly infested with them. They are on the floor, and then I get in trouble if I step on them. I hurt them, and he gets mad at me.

"They want to see me bathing. I bathe practically in the dark. He told them to make me fall. They want to control me. I was almost through, and he was mad, so he threw something at me in the tub, and you know what it was? It was a plastic bottle. I still have it here. It's not my bottle, and I'm in the bathtub. There are a lot of things I can't figure out when they do them to me. That bottle is not mine! It made a racket on the floor behind me!"

Mary has inside demons, and outside demons that don't talk. She told me sometimes the things going on are so unbearable she wants to cry, but can't. Again tonight she told me she can't cry ... that she hasn't cried from youth ... that something has been repressed. She wonders if Mike has read *Pigs in the Parlor*.

August 25

Mary said, "I got up late; I had an awful night. This morning they tell me they will not let me have *any* sleep. The noises they make ... they say I can't win. I'm only one and they are many."

I reminded her we have more support than they do, per Elisha to his servant [2Kings 6:16-17].

We talked about Mary's early years, after her mother died, and her preliminary training in the doctrine of the Catholic Church.

"What made you turn away?" I asked.

Mary replied, "The stories my stepmother told about the priests. They were fooling around sexually with women, young girls, getting them pregnant. When they came to a village [in Italy] they would need someone to clean for them. Those poor girls. I didn't like that. Also, I didn't like that they had to eat fish on Fridays. And they didn't give the gospel; I didn't get that until I started Protestant churches. What else? Praying to the Virgin Mary, praying to the saints." (Her last reasons, no gospel and praying to saints, may be recently acquired, because as an adult Mary did not attend any church before this trouble began.)

She continued, "I didn't go to church often. I went to first communion and confirmation, and I had to go to catechism. I learned a lot of things through my stepmother's knowledge, and I wrote it down in Italian, so I could read it and remember it. But I didn't have much catechism either. I did what I needed to do to pass. But there was no fanfare; we didn't come home to any party or anything. It was a nothing. She [her stepmother] spent money on those dresses, and we had to wear them the following year for confirmation. By then those socks were too short for me; I don't know how I held them up to my knees. You know, we had to wear those white socks. She was just doing her duty. We had to do communion, and we had to be confirmed. That was the end of that.

"She was interesting in that way; I used to like her stories. She imbued me with a desire to go to Italy. She was not that holy, but she knew the rules. Well, there isn't much to learning the rosary; they repeat it. She did that once in a while, not often, but occasionally I'd catch her with those beads in her hand."

We all need God.

Mary finished her story, and as she said earlier she hadn't slept well, I asked her about it.

"Oh, Lexie, that deafening noise. Then they take a rest. They are quiet for an hour or so, and then they're at it again. So today I'm kind of a rag.

"Their images are everywhere—under my feet, on my windows, on my pictures [on the walls]. I'm looking at my pictures, and I see one of their faces. I'm sinning; I'm saying bad things sometime. Of course *they* use foul language all the time!"

August 28

Mary said, "Now he's irritating me with a fake blowfly ... around my food. Even when you know it's fake, it's annoying. It's that Porgi. He plays little boy games. He's got a trumpet, and he's going to irritate me with that thing."

September 1

I spoke with Mike and we set up an appointment for September 8TH. I said I'd bring Mary to his home.

Later Mary explained to me, "They're all mad because I'm kicking them out. They know I'm going to have a minister talk to them. The demons awakened me during the night, and they're going on and they're lauding me ... it's a goofy story of course, but it went on at length. That spoils my sleep. I finally got to sleep while it was still dark, but my lack of sleep goes on. I get up tired; it's very nerve wracking. I have a bunch of them attacking me. Sometimes I come out and say things. I can't help it."

September 14

On Tuesday, the 8th, Mary and I drove over to Mike's place, where he talked with her and we prayed for her against the demons. Mike and Mary talked about issues from her past, and Mike assured her that was finished now. He said she moved into a place where something had happened. Something went on in that home.

Mike explained, "Sometimes they [demons] mix lies with some truth to confuse you. It sounds like some very bad things happened in that place, and those things gave them some power at that location. Your mother's place needs to be prayed through again. What happened there, before, has to be prayed over and covered with the blood of Jesus."

He added, "Barbara sleeping in the car *is* a sign."

Mike believes the cause of Mary's demon problem was already in her home when she moved there. He thinks the previous owner seeking refuge in her car was an indication that she too may have suffered from demonic intrusion. I agree with him.

He illustrated his point by telling us a story. He told us about the home of a family who used to attend our church. One of their children was disturbed continually, had trouble sleeping, and kept saying, "There are flies in here."

"Previously," Mike said, "When others owned that home, a girl had been abused there. When we prayed over that [child's] room, they [demons] had to leave because there was nothing for them to hang on to. They have to have a reason to be there, and that was their reason—the girl being abused there gave them a spiritual right to be there. When we prayed over that, they had to leave. When their little boy came back that evening, he said, 'Oh, Mommy, no more flies.'"

Mike continued, "Sinful events open the door for the enemy to come in and hold on to that location. The most powerful things in this world are sex and blood, so the enemy works through sex and blood a lot. They get power from it. Tormenting you about it gives them power."

Mary told Mike she gets so mad at the demons tormenting her, that she feels she has to apologize to God. Mike told her, as I also have told her, "They don't deserve any respect or dignity."

"Here's the thing," he said. "I know that God can set you free. I wish there was someone in Walnut Creek you could call on. I can pray for you today and let's see what happens, but I do think it will take praying through your home, based on what you said."

Mike taught us to make what he called a "devil sandwich" (submit to God, resist the devil, and then thank God). He said the first step was, "When those thoughts come, submit to God. Whatever the demons tell you, you pray the opposite. Don't talk to them. Say, 'Lord Jesus, I praise you that you love me and that ... ' Just talk to God; don't talk to them.

When you argue with the enemy, you will lose. Start with God, talk to God. That's *submit*.

"Then the second step is to *resist*. When you feel they're starting to go away, say 'I resist you in the name of Jesus Christ.' Focus on God, not on arguing with them. That's how Eve lost. Say, 'In Jesus' name I command you to go.' If they get you to focus on the enemy, turn to God and focus on Him.

"Then when you feel peace, the third step is to *thank* God."

Mike told us he has been helping people by using spiritual warfare for twenty years. And as Connie also had suggested, Mike recommended that Mary play spiritual songs and Scriptures continuously on CD in her home.

Mike spoke some Scriptures for Mary to follow, including Hebrews 10:17-18; James 4:7-8; 1 Corinthians 6:19-20; Ephesians 4:28.

We left Mike's home with fresh thoughts and hoped for the best.

September 20

Mary called late Sunday evening to tell me, "He didn't want me to sleep; he wanted me up so he could talk to me. And I don't want to talk to him. And that heater—or whatever I'm feeling—makes me sweat. Well, I was annoyed with him. He's got a temper!

"You know what, this is what he says. I hear some of these stories over and over. He says a Portuguese step mother raised him. There were some dry leaves, and he put them up on the roof, kind of a cracker-box house, and he ignited them and they couldn't get out, so they burned. And you don't know what he can do.

"He messed with my eye. It has a film over it. I don't know why I'm getting a film in that eye, suddenly overnight. I got an eye wash. This is my bad eye, but I need it. I can't afford to have anything wrong with my vision. Well, anyhow, those were the stories I hear. He keeps harping on it. I have no way out in case of a fire. There is only one door. But the HOA put more smoke detectors in, so there's two in the hallway, one near each bedroom.

"Oh boy, is he mad! Oh, I pray to the Lord, please let this trial be over."

The next day when Mary and I talked on the phone, she said, "My situation is not very good. There are two new spirits now. They're twins, and they speak Italian. And it's all about sex. I don't like the way they're talking. It's awful; they seem to think I owe them something." To me it seems Mary continues to be absorbed with the stories the demons tell her, rather than try to implement Mike's suggestions.

November 14

Mary called before getting ready for her bath. She said their images were everywhere, and she always has two of them in the bathtub. When she gets soap on them, they just stay there. Now that it's November she's getting cold, and they mess with her heater. She said they make it sound like it's on, but it isn't.

While we were on the phone Mary said, "Here comes one little thing. He's coming in to see me. Now he's going to rise. They rise up, and they get bigger and taller and taller. They can get down to about twelve inches, then they look kind of cute—but it's not cute! When they rise up, they have these old man faces. I have one here now ... oh golly ... I stared him down and he disappeared."

November 21

Mary called at 11:08 a.m. "I'm tired. I only had one good night of sleep, Wednesday, when I took a nap and didn't wake up until the following morning. But I wasted time, not knowing what time it was. Of course when I talk to you they make it like your clock. I went to the hairdresser, an hour ahead of time. I looked at the clock at Safeway, and I had to hurry because it was almost time for my appointment. When I got there, she said I was an hour early, and I said, 'Oh dear, they did it again.' It's not fair to mess with people's time. I don't like it—and that's why they do it."

"The newest one [demon] that's here says he wants to make me like a little boy. Can you believe that? He can make me sick. I felt sick when I went to bed, but thank God I did not get sick. Oh yes, they can hurt you. I've been praying about it to the Lord. They're miserable; they live the wrong life. I'm preaching that all the time—the truth. There's a straight path and a crooked path, and if they stay on the crooked path, they'll ....

"They agree with me, but the evil one, he just believes in doing harm. He doesn't see that he's a miserable cuss. Well, I have the right time now, but it can change any time.

"My furnace is not operating properly; it's running, but there's no heat. I'm cold. I don't use the switch; I just turn the dial. I have to get the little stool to stand on."

December 5

I drove to Walnut Creek with Mike, David, and a friend of Mike's named Crystal. Mike prayed for us, and we walked through each room in Mary's house, anointing doors, windows, and mirrors with oil. I had prayed with Mary before bed last night, and she told us they didn't bother her last night. She explained to us all how they keep her awake: "The hisser, circus noises, noises like the heater is on when it isn't on. And that's just to keep you awake," she said. "And then the images," she continued, "they tell me that once they're gone, the TV will be okay. I've stopped watching the TV." (Because she can't see what's being broadcast; she sees images they put on the screen.) "There's also a big tall dark thing—they said they were guarding me. The images don't talk."

Mike asked Mary, "Do you hear anything right now?"

Mary said, "I hear Walter [head demon] whispering."

She told us about seeing images while driving. "I want to be sure the image is theirs. When I get close I run over them. But one day it was an actual person, and I didn't run into him. It was someone on a motorcycle with a white cap. He [Walter] wants to kill me."

Mary continued, "He's talking soft. I don't know if he's lying or not. He said he's alone, and he doesn't like to be alone, so he's leaving here. But he's speaking softly."

She doesn't think he's alone, but she doesn't hear Porgi or He-She.

Mike said, "Some may have left when I told them at the beginning that they could leave without a battle or they could stay and battle."

Mary told Mike they have a dummy of her, and she feels what they do to the dummy's body. They have hurt her hand, but Porgi said it would be okay when they leave. Each of us walked around the apartment and prayed through the house. Mike addressed various elements that came to our minds as we prayed ... a façade; a man destroying a woman; blood crying out for judgment; justice; Masons.

Mike told Mary it might be helpful to pray these or similar prayers:

> "If there is a part of me still in darkness, ask the Lord to bring that part into the safe place that you have created in me."
>
> "Keep expanding the light and pushing back the darkness."
>
> "Lord, bring me to your safe place; bring me to your light."
>
> "Lord let me sit in the center of your light, your truth, and your peace."

Mike suggested she learn Philippians 4:8:

> And now, dear brothers and sisters, one final thing. Fix your thoughts on what is true, and honorable, and right, and pure, and lovely, and admirable. Think about things that are excellent and worthy of praise.

We left Mary's place hopeful the work we did would be successful and at long last Mary would be free. However, about 9:00 p.m. that same evening Mary called and said, "So far, nothing new. First Walter kept talking like he was glad to be leaving me. He said he was going on a trip, and then I got all those images, and then he said he changed his mind. He said he didn't like my attitude, and he will beat me up like before. I wonder if there is something wrong with *me*? I don't think so, but I'm not doing so good with my prayers."

December 6

The following morning Mary told me about the activities she had endured since we left yesterday.

She said, "I didn't take a bath last night because they wanted to freeze me. They were nasty. They seem to think they can control me. Now I don't know if my heater will come on. I was lying here thinking about Hammond [author], and wondering, what is my destiny? They have been bugging me for hours."

She said she didn't touch the television set, which was on when we left, and after we left, it was fuzzy, so she turned it off. The set in her bedroom worked. "But he is determined," she said. "He has a sadistic nature; he wants to do all sorts of dirty things. When I went to bed, Porgi said he's not going to do all the things he wants to do to me. I think they get tired when they're doing all those things to me. I didn't talk to them."

December 7

Mary called to tell me about her night.

"They had an awful screeching sound going on. No one could stand it, not even the other demons. Then they had alarm clocks going off, a bunch of them, going all over. I knew no alarm was under my pillow, so I pulled my comforter up around me, and put my pillow over my head, and prayed to the Lord. I asked for wisdom and courage and patience. When the screeching finally subsided, I didn't want to get up.

"It was still dark when a loud shriek started ... and his workers didn't like it. He says he locks himself up in a room so he hears nothing. He said he was paying someone to bring this over. The guy making that loud business said, 'You'll drive her out; no one can stand this.'"

Mary lamented, "They want to make a fool of me. People won't believe me. Well, I know I'm still in my right mind, but I'm sure worn out. I don't do as much as I should. These things wear you out. They get mad when I tell you. They don't want me to tell anyone. In case they kill me, I want you to know. Well, anyway, the time is near. This cannot go on forever. But that kingpin is a sadistic thing. He wants to hurt me."

I will pick up Mary on Friday after her haircut and bring her to Milpitas.

December 8

Mary said, "He knows I can hear everything he says, and he doesn't like it. They can be lies, but they say they're working on my house. He put more hissers in my house, one at the head and one at the foot of the bed.

He said, 'You sleep through it anyhow.' Well, I have adjusted, I've had it so long, but I want them out of here!

"Now they're doing something else, but they're fighting over it. One wants to do something, but another says, 'No, you can't do that; we'll get in trouble.'"

December 23

Mary said, "They want to order me around. They had the hisser going around my neck and head. I can sleep through it after a while, but it takes me a while to get to sleep when it's on. They wanted me to get up at 8:00 o'clock; I don't know why they want me to get up so early."

Actually, she does know why; she knows it's harassment.

Mary said, "You [Lexie] only know a little bit of it. It's hard to put up with the things they do. No matter what you say to them, they ignore it. When I read the warfare, they're good for maybe 5 minutes, but that doesn't last long. They want to bother me over and over. You have to be in the situation. If I could just scream at them! You can just be pushed so far, and I'm pushed so much."

Mary knows screaming at them wouldn't get them out, and she doesn't scream at them out of consideration for the neighbors; the walls in her old building are poorly insulated.

Mary said she slept pretty well last night in her own bed.

"I got the treatment, but finally moved to the right side of the bed where it didn't reach me, and I had the fan on so the heat didn't reach me so much either. But you also have the hisser on, and it's like someone picks on you all the time. And they're vulgar. They say they will rape me so they can photograph me, and he can get his jollies. I can't escape, and it's affecting me. I have to start thinking of other things, but it goes on in the background. I tell you, I feel that I could really kill them. I get that rotten talk so much. And they put on an act, like a performance, and you can't help but hear it; it's in every room in my house. He gave me a song and dance early this morning saying, 'We can't live with you, and you can't live with us. We bought this place.'"

CHAPTER 21
MARY'S VICTORY

Now there is in store for me the crown of righteousness, which the Lord, the righteous Judge, will award to me on that day—and not only to me, but also to all who have longed for his appearing. 2 Timothy 4:8

W E'RE BEGINNING ANOTHER year. Surely this year will bring Mary freedom. Although she called this morning to tell me she spent a second night on the couch.

"I didn't sleep a wink," she said. "They were horrible! They know the right thing to do, but they don't do it!"

"It's not their nature," I replied, sadly tired of hearing her same story retold morning after morning, and tired of responding in a way I know is of no help to her.

She planned to sleep on the couch last night, saying they didn't reach her as easily there.

"I roll up like a cocoon; I don't move around a lot. I curl up with a pillow on top of my head. Sometimes I can get where they can't reach me."

Apparently not last night. Weeks have gone by without significant change in Mary's battle. Today is the 19TH, and she has a 10:00 o'clock appointment with a podiatrist for a painful ingrown toenail. I asked her to take a cane with her, and after our conversation I prayed the Lord would keep her on her feet. She's taking a taxi today, and although it's a short distance to the doctor, it's pouring down rain, forecast for several days. It's difficult for me to accept that this frail ninety-seven-year-old is out in stormy weather—especially following a gloomy sleepless night.

†

On February 22ND, I took Mary to see her cardiologist. She told him of her concern over her diminishing energy level. He took her off one blood pressure medicine, prescribed another, and asked us to come back in two weeks. When we met with him again on March 4TH, she reported she felt no better. She still weighed 85 pounds—she hadn't lost weight—and her blood pressure remained normal. The doctor said, "Let's do a stress test," and although that sounded neither helpful nor appropriate to me, we scheduled it for a few weeks later.

When I talked with Mary the next day, she told me she didn't feel well enough to go to the hairdresser, and on Saturday she was no better. I told her I couldn't come up to see her that day because months earlier I had planned a social function at my home for volunteers active in our ESL ministry. She said she understood. She hadn't asked me to come up.

The following day, I called her at 8:30 a.m. and she said, "I'm not going to church; I've been going to the bathroom a lot, and I think I need to go to the hospital." Immediately I said I also would skip church; I would dress and come up. I said I would call her when I left my house.

When I called a few minutes later, she didn't answer the phone. After two more calls, I called 911. After asking them to take my mom to John Muir Hospital, I began my drive to the hospital. While driving past Danville, the emergency room doctor at John Muir called my cell phone. He said Mary was very critical. Her body temperature was very low (91.4° Fahrenheit), her kidneys weren't functioning as they should, and her liver wasn't clotting blood.

Mary looked quite pale as I entered emergency room station 5. We greeted each other. She said she was very cold. The attendants were trying to warm her, with thin blankets and a machine called a Bair Hugger that blows warm air into a disposable plastic air blanket. One problem was the constant removal of her blankets to pick and prod at her. They asked myriad questions, each one causing her to lift her tired head from the pillow in an effort to hear them. She left her hearing aids at home. Who would think of that at a time like this?

When the doctor came in, I asked why her body temperature was so low, and he said they had done a lot of testing already, and discovered she had lost a lot of blood. They had ordered two units for her. He said the blood would infuse slowly, as they didn't want it to lower her body temperature. He mentioned that sometimes the body doesn't like the transfusion. I calculated mentally that two units would finish dripping by about 11:00 p.m.

This was great news. She had simply lost blood. I wasn't concerned about the cause; we would figure that out later. I remembered a few years ago when Mary also felt a loss of energy, and we discovered she had lost blood due to internal bleeding. The cause had been an ulcer bleeding in her stomach, which was cauterized. She was hospitalized for a couple days, took three units of blood, and recovered beautifully.

"Whew," I thought; "she will be okay." I told her she would be okay. Another doctor came in and said to me, "Your mother is very ill; one factor determining whether she lives or not is her own will." Her comment went over my head. Mary had a zest for life; of course she wanted to live. Sometime later Mary was taken to the second floor, to the cardiac care unit, to a pleasant room with a large window.

I stayed with her all afternoon, and as it became dark I kissed her cheek and she kissed me back. I said I would see her tomorrow, that I was going to her apartment to lock up. Mary's neighbor told me EMTs (emergency medical technicians) didn't lock doors when they came for people in emergency situations, and they had to jimmy a window to get inside.

When I arrived, Mary's door was closed, but unlocked. I made sure the heater was off. I pulled out a few plugs and checked the fridge. The meat we purchased on Thursday, after her doctor appointment, was unopened. I wrapped it and put it in the freezer. I went home.

About 1:15 a.m. the phone rang, awakening me, and a sick feeling came over me as I answered. The nurse calling said my mom was very sick. I knew that. She said she would probably pass away soon. I didn't know that. She asked if I had picked out a mortuary. It upset me—shocked me—to hear this question. She was calling from the nurse's station, and from there could see the monitor in Mary's room. She told me the nurses with her now were having trouble getting a pulse. She paused for a moment, and then said, "The screen on your mom's monitor has just gone blank." Just like that. It was over. Mom was gone.

†

I had told Mary several times yesterday she would be okay. I really believed that. Had I known her body would not respond I would have stayed with her, but while I was there her body temperature climbed from 91.4° to 95.36° Fahrenheit. I thought she was getting better.

Over the next week I wondered why her cardiologist hadn't done a blood test when we went into his office, and why they didn't take her temperature. Ann's cardiologist always draws blood. We can learn so much from a simple, inexpensive blood test. We could easily have known the volume of her blood was dangerously low. The Bible tells us, "The life of the flesh is in the blood" [Leviticus 17:11]. I wondered why I had not remembered that when Mary lost energy a few years back, they revived her with three pints of blood. I wondered if getting her to a hospital twenty-four hours earlier would have saved her life. Why didn't I call 911 for her on the Saturday morning of the Volunteer Social? They would have taken her to a hospital. I didn't think of that until after her death. She didn't express deep concern to me. And yet, maybe if I had called paramedics, and her life had been saved, I wonder if that would have upset the plans she may have had with the Lord.

I remembered the day she told me she had a long talk with the Lord, asking Him many questions, but without disclosing to me the subject of the conversation. She had been reading Lutzer's book, *One Minute after You Die*. I recalled some things she said to me in recent months. She told me about another book she read, that she found so enchanting. Her eyes sparkled when she talked about it. Had Mary prayed for death as an escape from demonic torture? I believe so. She had mentioned to me several times she would rather be dead and be with the Lord than continue with the torments she suffered. She wasn't afraid to die as she knew she was saved. A few years ago she grinned and told me proudly she had "been born again." As she progressed through the last book she read, *Heaven: Better by Far* by Sanders, she talked with me about it. I believe that book helped her decide.

†

When I stopped thinking about what I wanted, I thought about what Mary wanted. She wanted peace and sleep. She wanted freedom from demonic torment, and she wanted her privacy. She was so tired of unwelcome evil spirit beings responding to her thoughts, watching her shower, manipulating her vision.

Demons tormented her since November 2004—over five years. It was too much. They were inside her mind continually, trying to scare her, taunting her, blowing hot or cold air on her, lying, being angry, threatening punishment, jolting her, mocking her, keeping her from sleep with their touch, their noises, their hissers, and hindering her vision with images—on the TV screen, on the windows, on the floor, on the bed, in the bath, in front of her car, everywhere. Shortly before she died, I took her for a routine eye exam. When she was asked to read the eye chart, she told the examiner she couldn't see the eye chart—*they* had put an image in front of it.

Occasionally she spoke to me while I sat beside her in the hospital room on the last day of her life on this earth in her mortal body. Each time she told me *they* were still present. *They* still had their hisser on. "How evil is evil? You have no idea," she had said to me many times. Mary died on March 8th. She fought a good fight. With the Lord's help and guidance, she battled for five years. She learned endurance.

I'm thankful for the Scripture, "We are confident, yes, well pleased rather to be absent from the body and to be present with the Lord." [2 Corinthians 5:8 NKJV]. Each one of us who puts our trust in Christ will be with Him instantly in death [Luke 23:39-43], and will live with Him for eternity. Mary's in heaven with our Lord. I feel blessed she came to know the Lord, and that I will see her again. No longer is she harassed by evil, and she knows one day the Lord will avenge her suffering. The devil and his demons will spend eternity in the lake of fire [Revelation 20:10]. That's Mary's victory.

†

Did Mary want to die? No, she loved life, and we both believed she would be delivered, that the demons would be cast out. Was she afraid to experience new things? No. Did she volunteer to die? Yes, I believe she prayed to the Lord and asked Him to bring her home, as she became so very weary coping with her situation. She was tired and discouraged. Tired of fighting demons. Tired of being too exhausted to enjoy her days, to get outside to enjoy the beauty of spring, her favorite season. She was tired of not having energy to play golf, one of her joys. And it discouraged her that the church had let her down.

Why do people skip parts of the Word of God they don't understand, or don't believe, or choose to disagree with? Either it's the inerrant word of God or it isn't. Each of us has to decide. Mary chose to believe the Bible, and to believe the promises she read throughout its pages. She chose to believe a better life is ahead for those who know Jesus is the son the God, and that he died for our sins and rose to life again [John 3:16-18].

For five years Mary and I read the Word together, seeking truth and seeking to understand this intrusion from the unseen world. We studied, learned, and prayed together. We wondered why and how this happened. We wondered why it didn't stop. She learned God's rules for life—love God, obey, pray, confess, repent of past sins, and love your neighbor as yourself. We understood that unconfessed sin opens doors to evil, and we know we all sin, even when we may not realize it is sin.

Demons are spirit beings without a body you and I can see, but they are as intelligent and real as you and I are. They have personalities, just as we have personalities. Peter writes that we are to cast our care upon the Lord. We are to be vigilant and sober because our adversary the devil, as a roaring lion, walks about seeking whom he may devour. He follows that by saying that after we have suffered a while, God will make us perfect, establish and strengthen us [1 Peter 5:7-8, 10].

Some people believe one can tell a demon once he must go, and he goes. Unfortunately, it doesn't always work that way. Hayes, in his book *How to Cast Out Devils,* tells of a case that took twelve continuous hours before the demon left a young man. Why did Mary's troubles continue for so long? One reason may be that she didn't remember all the instructions she received from people who came to help. I made notes and wrote their instructions for Mary, but in the middle of a night, for example, she had difficulty finding an appropriate Scripture to say aloud to her adversaries. She had many helpful notes, but she had difficulty with memorization. And suffering with macular degeneration, she required not only her glasses but a magnifying glass to read her Scripture notes to the tormenters. I don't think it helped, either, that she was curious about what the demons were talking about.

Mary didn't know Jesus as her Savior, shepherd, and protector when this trial began. Demons had already invaded her mind when she asked Jesus into her heart and to be her Savior. Her only church experiences had been taking first communion and confirmation through the Catholic Church around age seven—eighty-five years prior to the start of this trial.

I have heard believers in Christ say Christians are protected from demonic influence and intrusion. Quite the converse; Christians are targeted. Doesn't the devil already have the rest of the world by default? We are protected when we draw close to and obey the Lord, who is holy and doesn't tolerate darkness. But if our lifestyle causes Him who is holy to move away from us, the sinner, where is that protection? We must quickly confess our sin, and at the slightest attempt at interference from evil immediately rebuke it using the sword of the Spirit. It's very important to know the Word of God, the Bible.

I have also heard demons can't come in unless they are invited. This may apply to Mary's circumstance. Do you remember when she heard singing at night? When I realized the probable cause was demonic, I told her she must not allow it, but she responded to me she "liked it."

A question both Mary and I had is, why didn't the church respond? When she tried to share her experience, many Christians recoiled from her, as if she might not be mentally capable, or they might "catch it." In these last days before the Lord returns, we need to be cognizant of the unseen world, and we must arm ourselves, as Paul taught in his letter to the Ephesians.

Suffering people often ask, "If there is a God in heaven, why did this happen? Why do bad things happen to good people?" God is aware when bad things happen in our corrupted world, and He cares. The Bible offers many comforting Scriptures. These come to mind.

"The Lord's loved ones are precious to him; it grieves him when they die." Psalm 116:15 NLT

"Fear not, for I am with you; be not dismayed, for I am your God; I will strengthen you, I will help you, I will uphold you with my righteous right hand." Isaiah 41:10

"The Lord also will be a refuge for the oppressed, a refuge in times of trouble." Psalm 9:9 KJV

"Surely goodness and mercy shall follow me all the days of my life; and I will dwell in the house of the LORD forever." Psalm 23:6 NKJV

So what's going on? Let's start with the fact that God is holy. When he spoke to Moses from the burning bush, he told Moses to remove his sandals, that he was standing on holy ground [Exodus 3:2-5]. God commands obedience. For over four thousand years, God has been overseeing the growth of His children. Actions have consequences. By remaining close to God and obedient to Him, we are under his protection, like being under an umbrella. But when we think, say, or do things not pleasing to Him, we step away from that umbrella of protection. If it's storming, we get wet; we can become open targets for the devil and his demonic forces. We may not see them, but they are a relentless storm.

"Nothing like that will happen to me," one may think, but stepping away from God can open a door to evil. We don't have to sin to be attacked. Chronically ill people may find the spirit of infirmity at work. Evil can attack us before we are born, possibly resulting in congenital abnormalities.

There is hope for afflicted people. Jesus healed people when he lived on earth in human form, and He still heals today. He uses us, his servants, to say healing words (Scriptures) over people, and He pours down His power to heal [John 14:12, Mark 16:17]. Christian television channels broadcast testimonies of healed people. We don't know all the answers, but we can learn enough truth from God's Word not only to get through—but to enjoy—this gift, and this test, we call life.

Why isn't everyone healed? While we know the mind of God only to the extent that He reveals it to us in His Word, a couple possibilities come to mind, unconfessed sin and unbelief. Faith is a theme we see throughout the Bible. Faith is believing without seeing. God wants us to believe He will do what He says He will do, even though we may not yet see it manifested. Jesus taught that with even a little faith—as little as a tiny mustard seed—we can speak to a mountain, tell it to move, and it will move [Matthew 17:20; 21:21]. One's mountain may be an illness.

Unbelief pulls in the opposite direction of faith. Remember Wommack's example of the two horses hooked up to different ends of the same cart? One horse is Faith. The second horse is Unbelief.

How Did this Happen?

I looked back at Mary's and my interactions and experiences over the last five years. We listened to stories from Mary's neighbors and talked with friends who helped us, both from our own and other churches. We read various books about spiritual warfare. I believe the demons were in place at the house Mary bought in Walnut Creek. They were there when she moved in. Although we know they lie, they told her she was in *their* house. People we worked with, familiar with spiritual warfare, believe sinful activities may have taken place in Mary's unit prior to Mary purchasing it, giving demons a right to be there. She purchased the unit from the trust of a widow who was no longer capable, according to what we were told, and who was moved to another home where she would have care. Was Mary in the wrong place at the wrong time?

Why Wasn't Mary Delivered?

There may be several explanations why Mary wasn't delivered from demonic torment. Could one be her age? She suffered through this affliction from age ninety-two to ninety-seven. For many people we might consider this old, but Mary wasn't as old as the chronological record shows. She had an enthusiasm for life and a positive attitude. She enjoyed people and many activities, including her love for golf and for gardening. She cooked, entertained, read, and enjoyed knitting and crochet. After retiring, she learned to play the organ. Using easy-to-play music, she enjoyed playing the tunes of her youth. She bought a computer and learned to use it. Like Moses, who began his ministry at age eighty, Mary was a live wire at that age.

But by ninety-two trying to memorize Scripture was difficult for her. Throughout this trial I guided her to use the sword of the Spirit and combat the evil ones with appropriate Scriptures. That sword, the Word of God, is the Christian's only offensive weapon in a spiritual battle. (See Ephesians Chapter 6.) She wanted to memorize Scriptures useful in spiritual warfare, but as we continued to add Scriptures to her repertoire, and with chronic sleep deprivation, she was unsuccessful. Instead, she read Scriptures from pieces of paper I typed for her, using a large font. If she needed to take a scriptural shot at demons harassing her in the night, she would have to turn on the light, put on her glasses, find the appropriate Scripture, and grab her magnifying glass. She was also limited by not recalling instructions received. Mary received suggestions, and I wrote down a lot of them for her, but this too became burdensome.

Paul, from my church, came closest to success in casting the demons out. Mary and I believed we would have succeeded if he had more time the day he and Barbara came to the house. Of those people who were not afraid to command the demons to leave, Paul's efforts were most effective. Mary said the demons became most agitated and argued with each other about leaving. And remember Hayes said it can sometimes take twelve hours or more before demons leave.

Besides casting the devils out ourselves, we prayed that the Lord would release her. We knew Jesus told his disciples, "This kind can come out only by prayer" [Mark 9:29]. And as Daniel experienced [Daniel 10:12-13], answers to our prayers also can be intercepted by evil forces.

I remain convinced that had we been able to gather a group of believers together, those who do not doubt, and if we continued to fight them with Scriptures—individuals taking breaks as necessary—we would have succeeded in causing the demons to leave.

I feel like I failed her. She told me a couple times the demons seemed to be afraid of me. They admonished her not to tell me what they were doing. There were several evenings at Walnut Creek when I began warfare with them and ordered them to leave. I used appropriate Scriptures, but like Paul, I didn't stay with it long enough. I too was tired and would have an hour drive to get home, so I quit harassing them before they had so much they could no longer stand it. Scripture wounds demons.

Why *Mary's Story* Was Written

Mary wanted her story shared and asked me to write this book. She wanted others who suffered with similar problems to be understood and to receive help. As our cousin responded to me, after listening to Mary tell him about the problem, "It must be in her head; we're so sorry," many people are unaware of demons and how they can influence a person's thoughts and actions, let alone get into one's mind. Among my own friends and family, only a few read the Bible, and that's where we learn truth.

How very lonely it must be for an oppressed person who has no one to talk with about the problem and whose family or friends don't believe what the victim is communicating. If someone in your family is hearing voices, please don't give up. Encourage them and teach them with the Word of God. Only Jesus can cast out demons, and although some can be cast out by prayer, generally he uses us, His body of believers, to do it.

Mary wanted people to read the Bible and come to know the Lord. During her struggle, as she began reading the Bible, she became more content and peaceful. She often said to me she wished she had read the Bible earlier, that her life would have been different. I agree. I too wish I had read the Bible earlier in my own life. I would have made better choices. As Charles Stanley has often said, "We reap what we sow, later than we sow, and more than we sow." The Lord forgives us of confessed sin, but we still suffer consequences of poor life choices.

This experience, horrific as it was, made a tremendous and positive change in Mary's life. She came to know and love our Savior, Jesus Christ. Only the Lord can change people. Only He can soften hard hearts. Mary learned truth about the Kingdom of God through His Word. She learned she has an eternal home with Him.

Thank you for reading Mary's story. May God bless each one of you.

ACKNOWLEDGEMENT

Many thanks to each of you, mentioned and not mentioned in this book.
You helped Mary and me along this journey.
Thank you for your time, your recommendations, and your prayers.

A special Thank You to the members of the
Bay Area Writers' Critique Group, faithfully led by
Carol Lee Hall

APPENDIX A
JESUS' (OR DISCIPLES) INTERACTIONS WITH OR REFERENCES TO DEMONS OR DEVILS

Matthew 4:24

Matthew 8:16, 28

Matthew 9:31-33

Matthew 10:8

Matthew 12:22

Matthew 15:22

Matthew 17:18

Mark 1:24-26, 32, 34, 39

Mark 3:14-15

Mark 5:15

Mark 6:12, 13

Mark 7:26, 29-30

Mark 9:38-40

Mark 16:9, 17

Luke 4:2-3, 5-6, 13, 33-35, 41

Luke 8:1-2

Luke 9:1, 42, 49-50

Luke 10:17

Luke 11:14

Luke 13:32

Acts 10:38

Acts 13:9-10

1 Corinthians 10:20-21

1 Timothy 4:1

James 2:19

1 Peter 5:8

1 John 3:8-10

SUGGESTIONS FOR AVOIDING SPIRITUAL DECEPTION

Occult

Learn which practices are of the occult and stay away from them. Look up "occult terms" as there are many. To name a few: astrology; automatic writing; black magic; divination; fortune-telling; Ouija; psychics; sorcery; tarot divination; witchcraft, etc.

Prayer of Release for Freemasons and their Descendants

As you have read on previous pages, this Prayer of Release was a significant help. If applicable, you may read it (and pray it) for yourself online at https://jubileeresources.org/pages/freemasonry. It is from the book by Dr. Selwyn Stevens, *Unmasking Freemasonry -Removing the Hoodwink,* published by Jubilee Resource International, Inc.

BIBLIOGRAPHY

Anderson, Neil T., THE BONDAGE BREAKER, Eugene, OR, Harvest House Publishers, 2000.

Anderson, Neil T., VICTORY OVER THE DARKNESS, Ventura, CA, Regal Books, 2000.

Anderson, Neil T., THE STEPS TO FREEDOM IN CHRIST, Colorado Springs, CO, Gospel Light, 2004.

Bubeck, Mark I., PREPARING FOR BATTLE, a Spiritual Warfare Workbook, Chicago, IL, Moody Press, 1999.

Bubeck, Mark I., THE ADVERSARY; the Christian Versus Demon Activity, Chicago, IL, Moody Press, 1975.

Bubeck, Mark I., OVERCOMING THE ADVERSARY, Chicago, IL, Moody Press, 1984.

Garrison, Mary, HOW TO TRY A SPIRIT; by their fruits you will know them, Mary Garrison, Chelsea, AL, 1976.

Garrison, Mary, THE KEYS TO THE KINGDOM ARE BINDING LOOSING AND KNOWLEDGE, Mary Garrison, 1982.

Garrison, Mary, HOW TO CONDUCT SPIRITUAL WARFARE; as I see it!, Mary Garrison, 1980.

Gothard, Bill, RESEARCH IN PRINCIPLES OF LIFE BASIC SEMINAR TEXTBOOK, Institute in Basic Life Principles, Inc. 1981

Hammond, Frank and Ida Mae, PIGS IN THE PARLOR; the practical guide to deliverance, Kirkwood, MO, Impact Christian Books, Inc., 1973, 2006.

Hammond, Frank D., SOUL TIES, Plainview, TX, The Children's Bread Ministry, 1988, 1995.

Hayes, Norvel, KNOW YOUR ENEMY; How to Combat and Overcome Demonic Forces, Tulsa, OK, Harrison House, 1990.

Hayes, Norvel, HOW TO CAST OUT DEVILS, Cleveland, TN, Norvel Hayes, 1982.

Ingram, Chip, THE INVISIBLE WAR; what every believer needs to know about Satan, Demons, and Spiritual Warfare, Grand Rapids, MI, Baker Books, 2006.

Logan, Jim, RECLAIMING SURRENDERED GROUND, Chicago, IL Moody Press, 1995.

Meyer, Joyce, BATTLEFIELD OF THE MIND, Warner Books Edition, Warner Faith, New York, NY, 1995.

Meyer, Joyce, ME AND MY BIG MOUTH, Warner Books Edition, Warner Faith, New York, NY, 1997.

Pierce, Chuck D. and Rebecca Wagner Sytsema, PROTECTING YOUR HOME FROM SPIRITUAL DARKNESS, Ventura, CA, Regal Books, 2000, 2004.

Prince, Derek, BLESSING OR CURSE, Chosen Books, Baker Book House Company, Grand Rapids, MI, 1990.

Prince, Derek, WAR IN HEAVEN, Chosen Books, Baker Book House Company, Grand Rapids, MI, 2003.

RBC Ministries, OUR DAILY BREAD, Grand Rapids, MI. www.odb.org

Regier, John, President (from 1996-2006) BIBLICAL CONCEPTS IN COUNSELING, http://www.biblical-concepts.com/aboutus.html

Regier, John, CARING FOR THE HEART MINISTRIES, http://www.caringfortheheart.com/index.html

Stevens, Selwyn, UNMASKING FREEMASONRY - removing the hoodwink, Wellington, New Zealand, Jubilee Resources, 2004

Warren, Rick, THE PURPOSE DRIVEN LIFE; what on earth am I here for? Grand Rapids, MI, Zondervan, 2002.

Merriam-Webster Inc., WEBSTER'S NINTH NEW COLLEGIATE DICTIONARY, USA, 1989.

Wigglesworth, Smith, SMITH WIGGLESWORTH ON HEALING, New Kensington, PA, Whitaker House, 1999.

Wilkinson, Bruce H., Editor, et al., THE DAILY WALK BIBLE, Wheaton, IL, Tyndale House Publishers, Inc., 1997

Wommack, Andrew, A BETTER WAY TO PRAY, Tulsa, OK, Harrison House Publishers, 2007

Wommack, Andrew, ONE YEAR WITH JESUS IN THE GOSPELS; Yearly Devotional, Colorado Springs, CO, Andrew Wommack Ministries, Inc. 1999.

Wommack, Andrew, YOU'VE ALREADY GOT IT! So Quit Trying to Get It, Tulsa, OK, Harrison House, 2006

MY NOTES

MY NOTES

CPSIA information can be obtained
at www.ICGtesting.com
Printed in the USA
FSHW020310190521
81571FS

9 781735 242507